A man
who is not afraid of the sea
will soon be drowned, he said,
for he will be going out
on a day he shouldn't.
But we do be afraid of the sea,
and we do only be drowned
now and again.

John Millington Synge
The Aran Islands

To Hélène...

The Complete Book of
Sea Kayaking

Fifth edition

Derek C. Hutchinson

With illustrations by the author

Approved by the British Canoe Union

A & C Black • London

First published 1976
Second edition 1979
Third edition 1984
Reprinted in paperback 1985
Fourth edition 1994
This edition published in 2003 by
A & C Black Publishers Limited
38 Soho Square, London W1D 3HB
www.acblack.com

Reprinted 2006

ISBN 0 7136 6675 7

A CIP catalogue record for this book is available from the British Library

Illustrations by the author
Design by James Watson
Printed and bound in Belgium by Proost International Book Production

A & C Black uses paper produced with elemental chlorine-free pulp, harvested from managed sustainable forests.

Note: All units of measurement in the following text are imperial. A conversion table may be found on page 202.
Individual paddlers are referred to as 'he'; this should, of course, be taken to mean 'he' or 'she' where appropriate.

Contents

Foreword to the previous edition

When I read the original *Sea Canoeing* in order to assess the amount of revision that would be needed for a new edition, I felt like someone wandering through ancient ruins. Was 1974 such a long time ago?

Sea Canoeing was the first book written about kayaking on the open sea, and back in 1974 when I wrote it a certain paddling ability and a certain amount of experience on the part of the reader could be assumed. At that time, almost all 'paddlers' had some previous paddling experience before venturing on to the sea. Today, many people choose sea kayaking as their first attempt at the sport. So it has proved necessary to include, or to expand in greater detail, the elementary skills and basic strokes. The rewritten and enlarged relevant chapter (Chapter 2), based on the clinics and classes which I hold for novices as well as for the more experienced, could now probably stand as a book in its own right.

Reading through the introduction to the third edition I came across a reference I made to the North American Continent. It almost made me laugh out loud. I had bemoaned the fact that '...only a handful of Americans paddle a kayak on the sea with any kind of dedication', and I went on to say '...this is your heritage. Don't neglect it'. And that really was how it was!

It is difficult to believe that now, because things have turned a full circle. The United States and Canada jointly now have more ocean paddlers than any other country in the world – and the numbers are increasing.

Over the years, *The Complete Book of Sea Kayaking* (formerly *Sea Canoeing*) has become, internationally, an indispensable reference book for those who kayak on the sea. I hope that this completely updated and expanded edition will continue to delight and enlighten my readers.

In keeping with current accepted terminology, and to save confusion with open canoe paddling, I have discarded the generic term *canoe* for the more specific word *kayak*. However, there are no rewards for spotting any slips in this.

I could have wiped the slate clean and the introduction to the earlier editions could have gone forever. That would have been sad and merely destruction for destruction's sake. So the old introduction and conclusion stand. Like an old ruin, they remain for you to wander through and enjoy.

Welcome to *The Complete Book of Sea Kayaking*...

Foreword to the 5th edition

It was August 2, 1975 – and about 8 p.m. in England. For me it was lunchtime in Eugene, Oregon where I was taking summer school classes at the University of Oregon. I had just completed my first Master's Degree and I was now working toward my Ph.D. The weather was nice and I was enjoying a relaxing break between classes. It would be seven years before I would get into a kayak, and little did I know that on the other side of the globe it had started to rain and the North Sea was getting rough. Derek Hutchinson turned to Tom Caskey to discuss the possibility of tying their kayaks together if they hoped to survive another night at sea, when a smokestack appeared on the horizon. On the third attempt, the parachute flare finally launched to the sky. The Ostend ferry picked up the exhausted pair, and the attempted crossing of the North Sea in single kayaks ended eight miles off Dunkirk. They had paddled at least 100 miles during a 34 hour period. Within a year Derek and Tom decided to try the North Sea Crossing again. Dave Hellawell joined the pair because, as Derek has often reminded me during the early years, the rule was 'less than three there should never be' when venturing onto the open waters in sea kayaks. This time, 31 hours after launching and paddling 100 nautical miles, Derek Hutchinson stepped out of his single kayak onto a beach in Belgium as the first man to officially cross the North Sea in a single kayak.

I began my sea kayaking career in Santa Barbara, California, by taking a whitewater kayak onto the ocean and paddling close to shore. I stayed on the shore side of the kelp beds because a capsize meant swimming to shore dragging my swamped kayak and paddle with me. Launching and landing through the surf zone while remaining upright was as unpredictable as the throw of a dice. I often describe myself as a self-taught sea kayaker – I am one of those folks who enjoy the challenge of figuring things out for themselves. Unfortunately, I have spent a lot of time re-inventing the wheel.

For the last 22 years I have directed Adventure Programs at the University of California, Santa Barbara. Aside from my love of the ocean and adventure, one of my motivations for taking to the ocean in a kayak was the possible development of a sea kayaking program. As our campus sits right on the cliffs overlooking the Pacific Ocean, a sea kayaking program seemed like a good idea.

Looking back at my precarious introduction to the sport, I laugh at my 'self taught' concepts. In the mid 1980's I came across a 122 page book entitled *Derek C. Hutchinson's Guide to Sea Kayaking*, and I read it cover to cover. Searching to see if this new guru of mine had written anything else, I found a copy of *Sea Canoeing*, which enlightened me even more. I realized my feeble beginning in the sport was not sea kayaking at all – I was an accident waiting to happen. Derek Hutchinson taught me to sea kayak, even though it was seven years before I would meet my kayaking hero. Over the years, I have lost count of the number of expert kayakers who have shared similar stories with me; 'if it weren't for Derek's books I would probably not be here today,' as well as 'he is the reason I started sea kayaking.'

Derek began writing his first book on sea kayaking a couple of years before his successful crossing of the North Sea. In 1976 the book was published and the world had its first instructional book on the subject of sea kayaking. As an educator, kayak designer and adventurer, Derek has been on the forefront of the sport of sea kayaking. By being the first he has set the standard.

In the past the six years I have had the pleasure of regularly teaching with Derek, and more importantly, have come to regard him as a close friend. Derek's keen mind and his constant desire for improvement became apparent to me as a result of our endless talks where we would analyze techniques, discuss philosophies, share teaching methods and critique equipment designs. During the last couple of years, Derek has told me he needed to update *The Complete Book of Sea Kayaking* because he needed to make some changes, and add sections that are missing from the sport. Having seen the additions and changes to the newest edition I can say that Derek is true to his word.

This new edition of *The Complete Book of Sea Kayaking* has a wonderful section on the forward racing stroke and the use of the wing paddle, as it is becoming part of the sport of sea kayaking. If you are interested in the history of kayak design, Derek takes you on a delightful trip down memory lane in his workshop. This latest edition also contains new and updated information on choosing a kayak; kayak design and features; paddles; rescues; carrying kayaks and launchings. Derek has added some tricks from his pool classes to help you prepare for the open water. His experiences in Alaska have prompted him to include a section on crossing mudflats and quicksand with your kayak without getting stuck. As you would expect, Derek has not only kept up with the kayaking times, but has remained a leader in the field.

There are a lot of imitators out there, but only one Derek Hutchinson – for this reason Derek is considered by many to be the 'father of modern day sea kayaking.' If you consider the information contained in many of the sea kayaking books available, you will realize that it is Derek's knowledge, experience and passion for sea kayaking that keeps his books at the forefront of the market. I guess when you do something well, it's difficult to improve upon.

If you are going to buy a book on sea kayaking, why not choose one by the man who had the nerve, foresight, skill and practical experience to be the first – and who still leads the pack. This latest edition of *The Complete Book on Sea Kayaking* is a must have for your sea kayaking library.

I want to thank Derek for opening the world of sea kayaking to myself and many others. Also, thank you for keeping me alive!

Wayne Horodowich
Director of Adventure Programs at U.C. Santa Barbara
Founder of the University of Sea Kayaking
Producer of the "In Depth" instructional video series for sea kayaking
www.useakayak.org

Acknowledgements

For a book of this nature, it is inevitable that the material will have been acquired over many years and from many sources. Much of this particular book has grown from experience shared with paddlers whose skill, courage and opinions I value highly.

It would therefore be impossible to mention all those to whom I owe my gratitude. However, I feel I owe special thanks to the following:

The late Brian Barton, of the B.C.U. Life Guards; Duncan Winning, for his generous information about Scottish kayaking; Mike Clark of Canoeing Magazine, for his ready help in tracing specific photographs and other research; Mr. Graham, Curator of Whitby Museum; Mr. Tynan, Curator of the Hancock Museum, Newcastle; the Chief Librarian, Public Library and Museum, South Shields, for permission to draw and study their kayak; Chris Hare and Chris Jowsey for their help in some of the historical research; Frank Goodman, who knows about plastic kayaks; Stewart Cameron and the staff of Metromedia; Bill Gardner who is an expert on talk balloons; Kevin Danforth of the British Canoe Union; Alistair and Marianne Wilson of Lendal Paddles; Chris Cunningham of Sea Kayaker Magazine; John Nixon of H.M. Coastguard; Denis Ball of the B.C.U. Surf Committee. A special thanks must go to my daughter, Fiona, for her tireless modelling of hand positions; my wife, Hélène, for her unfailing encouragement and help in a thousand different ways – and to Mike Hanson, who said, "Why don't you write a book?"

For their help with the Racing Stroke, I am indebted to Barney Wainwright, the Sports Science Officer of the British Canoe Union, Imre Kemecsey, racing coach and Silver Medallist at the Rome Olympics, and Greg Barton, four times Olympic Gold Medallist, Debra Moore, Archivist – Hudson's Bay Company Archives.

Introduction

Contrary to first impressions, this book is not simply a textbook on how to progress in a particular sport. Rather it is a record of one man's discovery of a very special kind of freedom. Through the ages, man has always pursued his quest for personal freedom and has always sought to satisfy his tremendous longing to explore the unfamiliar and the unknown.

Many of the more popular rock climbs are now worn smooth by countless grasping fingers and chafing boots. Hill walks which were once a real adventure are now well-trodden scars on the grass and heather. The kayak, however, cuts no groove and leaves no scar. The same stretch of water can be paddled every day but the surface may never be the same twice.

The sea provides the unfamiliar, the unworn and the unexpected. Sea kayaking gives a person the opportunity to venture on to a wild, unpredictable expanse in a craft that moves solely by the strength of their arm, directed by their experience and knowledge. Facing the challenge of the sea in this way causes a paddler to journey into the genuine unknown – the unknown and untried areas of his own soul. The sea kayaker depends on neither wind nor engine; he shares his craft and responsibility with no one. The kayak man challenges the sea in what appears to be the most diminutive and delicate of crafts, even more fragile in appearance than the smallest sailing dinghy. Nevertheless, the man who paddles the kayak well is the master of one of the finest, most seaworthy crafts in the world. It can lay beam on to a breaking sea many times its own height. The fastest and most dangerous of waters which are treacherous terrors for even the largest sailing boat or motor craft can be conquered by the shallow-draughted kayak. It can hop from bay to bay seeking shelter and passages where no other boat can or dare go, and it can avoid the roughest water by hugging the shore. It can capsize and be righted by a dexterous paddler without him ever having to leave the security of the kayak.

For the paddler on the sea there are still challenges. One part of the British Isles where kayakers can find the satisfaction of discovery and the excitement of mastering wild waters is off the west coast of Scotland. Here the islands are intersected east to west, and the flood tide rushes between them creating many dangerous passages. Here, off the northern shore of Scarba, when the tide is flooding, is the Grey Dog whirlpool. The first time I saw this I was about 300 yds. in front of a large group of kayakers. The sea was flat calm, the sun blazing down. Between the islands I could see the surface of the water jumping and pluming in cascades of spray surf. It wasn't until I glanced sideways at the islands that I realised I was being swept along at a phenomenal rate. The speed with which I executed the 180° turn would have to be seen to be believed, and only by paddling with every ounce of a strength born of desperation could I make headway at all against the fast-moving water. At last I managed to manoeuvre the boat to the nearest shore, where we all landed. A short walk brought us to a view of a terrifying whirlpool, with its surrounding violent swirls completely filling the narrow strait between the islands. What would have happened to us had I not stopped when I did hardly bore thinking about.

Even more frightening is the 'Hag', the great whirlpool in the Gulf of Corryvreckan, between the islands of Scarba and Jura. The flood tide rushes through at about 8–9 knots at a depth of more than 500 ft. Where it hits an underwater rock pyramid, the top of which is about 90 ft. below the surface, the enormous surge is forced upwards to meet the mass of the upper layer of water, 90 ft. deep, forming the 'Great Race'. This rushes out into the shore of Scarba and round into the Gulf again, only to collide with itself, forming the whirlpool of so many legends. When a westerly or south-westerly gale blows against the spring flood, it creates such turbulence that the roar can be heard 10 miles away. The first waves of the 'Great Race' can be 30 ft. high and the vortex 30 ft. deep.

Paddling in areas such as this, one is dwarfed by the tremendous power of the water; yet the advanced paddler can feel confident and secure in what must be the only small boat capable of coping with it.

The strength of the wind and the height of the waves and swell are sometimes such that a rescue, other than an Eskimo roll, would be impossible. You are then aware of the presence of others only when they appear on a wave crest coinciding with your own upward rise. Communication is therefore non-existent: each man paddles his own lonely trip with his own thoughts, hopes and fears. He pushes himself to his limit, facing a personal test far beyond anything that could be devised on paper. That is why, when people say that sea kayaking is non-competitive, I feel obliged to point out that it is competitive in the broadest sense of the word. The dedicated paddler aims not so much to win prizes and cups as to improve his last performance or, taking up the challenge of some difficult crossing or trip, to seek new ways to prove his own capabilities, skills, endurance and courage.

Before discussing planned kayak training, it is perhaps well to point out that it is not necessarily a difficult or even a slow task to master paddling techniques to quite advanced standards. I once found that I was short of a man for a display of canoe polo at a gala a month away. My younger son Graham was 17 years old. He was willing and I was desperate. He was given the crashest of crash courses, and by the night of the gala he could Eskimo roll every time and perform quite advanced white-water strokes so competently that no one could have guessed that he had only had one month's experience.

It is generally accepted that there are three broad levels of competence in kayaking: the novice, the proficient paddler, and the advanced paddler. The novice is someone who should go on to open water only when it is calm and only under the strictest supervision. He is feeling his way in the sport, and the least change of wind or sea condition can put him in danger and place a great responsibility on the leader of his party. Every kayaker should be able to swim. The proficient paddler has been guided and instructed to handle his kayak on the sea under reasonable conditions. His boat is seaworthy for he now knows what basic equipment is needed for his boat, his safety and his comfort. He knows the minimum

number of paddlers on the sea together is three and he is able, with the assistance of his two companions of the same standard, to rescue himself should he accidentally capsize. He will be able to negotiate small waves, taking them on the beam, as well as coming into shore both backwards and forwards. Any ambitious trips should be under the supervision of a competent leader.

The advanced kayak paddler has a high degree of skill in surf; he can plan and lead long open-water expeditions under adverse conditions of wind and tide. He can Eskimo roll successfully on the first try by a number of methods in rough water. In keeping with his knowledge and love of the sea, he has a knowledge of weather and coastal navigation, and his stamina will enable him to paddle many miles without effort. The minimum number of paddlers of this standard on the sea together is two.

It might be relevant at this point to discuss just what a sea 'canoe' is. A canoe has been defined as 'a boat pointed at both ends, which is suitable for being propelled by one or more forward facing paddlers, using paddles without any rowlock or other fulcrum, and is light enough to be carried overland by its crew'. In North America, 'canoe' is the name given to the traditional Canadian canoe, usually paddled with a single-bladed paddle, where 'kayak' is used only when referring to the decked-in type of craft originally used by the Eskimo and paddled with a double-bladed paddle. I usually mean a Canadian canoe only when I use that exact phrase. To me, a canoe can mean a slalom, a sprint or white-water kayak. The word 'kayak' in my vocabulary is reserved to mean any sea boat which has obvious origins in the skin boats of the Arctic. Having said this, if the reader finds a seemingly indiscriminate use of the words 'kayak' and 'canoe', I would plead the necessity of making the text less repetitious as well as the fact that many sea paddlers paddle slalom 'canoes' fitted with skegs. This book deals only with the single canoe or kayak, a craft in which sleep is almost impossible, unlike the double kayak in which one of the occupants can rest, sleep or even cook food while the other paddles' on.

Since I completed the first edition of *Sea Canoeing*, sea kayaking has undergone something of a transformation. Extended expeditions have become an ever-increasing challenge. They appear to fall into two categories: the unprotected, open sea crossing; and the prolonged coastal paddle along lonely, inaccessible and, in a number of cases, virtually unexplored coastlines.

In 1976, after an unsuccessful attempt in 1975, I led a kayak expedition of the North Sea from Felixstowe to Ostend. After paddling for 31 hours and being out of sight of land for 30 of those hours, we landed at our planned destination – due more to a piece of wet-finger navigation than to the days of chart planning that had gone on beforehand. Incidentally, this has, to my knowledge, never been repeated.

My next venture was an expedition to the Aleutian Islands, the wild home of the Aleuts who had once been the finest kayak hunters in the world. 1978 turned out to be the worst summer many of the Aleuts could remember. We paddled a distance of 250 miles, from Dutch Harbour on Unalaska Island to the even more remote tiny village of Nikolski on the western tip of the island of Umnak. I returned to Alaska in 1980 and with four others I spent a month exploring the islands of Prince William Sound and filming the Killer Whales that abound in the area.

What caused this sudden surge of exploratory zeal among kayakers? Perhaps the greatest revolution has been the advent of watertight hatches, bulkheads and the fitting of small hand-operated bilge pumps. Prior to this the weight of a fully laden expedition kayak made it almost impossible to empty by normal deep-water rescue methods in anything but a calm sea. However, the addition of these 'amenities' now made it possible for kayaks carrying in excess of 200 lb. of equipment to go to sea in the knowledge that long drawn-out struggles in icy water can be dispensed with during rescue manoeuvres. They have given the kayak a seaworthiness never before dreamed of.

As the level of skill and experience amongst paddlers increases, more of them are feeling the urge to go it alone. This is not to be condemned, but applauded as a feat of utter commitment. It is on a par with solo free-climbing. Solo kayaking in rough seas is the ultimate in challenge and risk, and it is also the ultimate in that special kind of freedom.

My greatest pleasure has been the wonderful reception my book has received in the United States and Canada. It is amazing to think that Britain, which at present leads the world in the sport of sea kayaking, has only the Celtic coracle as its indigenous skin boat, whilst the North American continent has the full range of Eskimo kayaks to call its own – yet only a handful of Americans paddle the kayak on the sea with any kind of dedication. I would say to may friends in the US – this is your heritage, don't neglect it. Lecturing and coaching in North America over the last few years has given me the opportunity to meet many of the new breed of ocean kayakers. Although their numbers are still relatively small, the sport is gaining in popularity. A number of British kayak designs are becoming prominent, but a good deal of the water used by North Americans is protected from the open ocean. For this reason the West Coast designs differ markedly, in most cases, from those in Europe. For purposes of comparison, therefore, I have included in this new edition some of the more popular 'new world' designs.

It is sad to end this introduction on an unhappy historical note. The graceful and unique Greenland kayak owned by the South Shields Museum is no longer in existence. Due to an administrative error, this fragile 100-year-old boat was given away to a local beach club, where it was used as a plaything and subsequently disintegrated.

If you would like specific advice on any aspect of sea kayaking, please write to me through the publishers, and enclose a large SAE (the stamps must be British). Address your enquiries to:

Derek C. Hutchinson,
c/o A & C Black Publishers Ltd.,
37 Soho Square, London W1D 3QZ,
Great Britain

The Gulf of Corryvreckan – the Great Whirlpool – 'The Hag' can be clearly seen, near the centre, with its accompanying tide race and overfall. The main flood stream is moving from left to right, but the water at the bottom of the picture is moving from right to left. The distance from coast to coast is one sea mile

(Photograph: John Dewar Studios)

Plate 1 *Alistair Wilson resting, Icy Bay, Prince William Sound Alaska*

THE KAYAK

All equipment must be seaworthy in that it must be either watertight or able to withstand the action of saltwater, wind and rain. The kayak should be long enough to bridge the smaller wave troughs and should have a straight keel to enable the craft to maintain a course in a head, beam, following or quartering sea. The rocker (Figure 1), or the curve of the keel upwards fore and aft, enables the kayak to manoeuvre. In sea kayaks the rocker must be limited, or else the boat becomes difficult to manage in a quartering sea.

Since relaxation is important when the time spent in the cockpit may be prolonged for many hours, stability is absolutely vital. This is mainly governed by the kayak's width and hull shape. Generally speaking, wide boats are stable; narrow ones are unstable.

Hull

The V-shaped or *chine* hull (Figure 2), the traditional shape of many Eskimo kayaks, gives directional stability as long as the amount of rocker is not excessive. However, with such a hull it is unfortunately almost impossible to maintain fast forward speeds because as

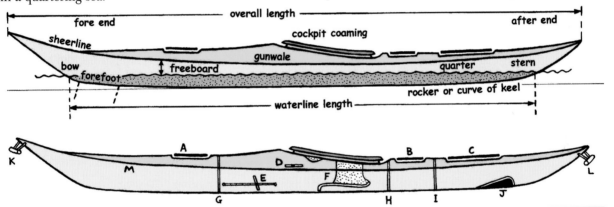

| Figure 1 | Names given to parts of a sea kayak |

A, the front hatch; B, the 'day hatch', leading into the smallest compartment; this is the only hatch that is safe to remove out on open water; C, this rear hatch gives access to the widest of the storage compartments. Some room is taken up by the skeg box but this is only really important when one is packing with supplies for more than a couple of weeks; D, the sliding control which raises and lowers the skeg. It is usually positioned on the right side; E, the adjustable footrest. The tracks should be rinsed and kept clear of sand; F, the seat and cockpit coaming are usually all in one piece, enabling the seat to be 'slung' from the coaming without touching the bottom of the hull. Sometimes the seat is cushioned underneath by a small block of foam fitted between it and the hull; G, the front bulkhead separating the cockpit area from the front watertight compartment. For tall people, many manufacturers will alter the position of the bulkhead and in some cases a specially strengthened front bulkhead can be fitted and utilised as a footrest; H, the bulkhead immediately behind the seat. This allows the kayak to drain almost completely when the boat is lifted bow first and held upside down; I, this bulkhead separates the day compartment from the main rear storage space. This is accessed by a much larger hatch than the other compartments; J, the skeg box is the sleeve into which the skeg is retracted. It should be rinsed and kept clear of small stones; K & L, are the carrying or towing toggles. They should not be able to trap the fingers and they should allow the kayak to rotate in the hand of anyone swimming and pulling the boat; K, this is the seam line where the two halves of a composite boat are joined together. On the inside, the joint should be finished smooth with no jagged edges. This line also forms the gunwale.

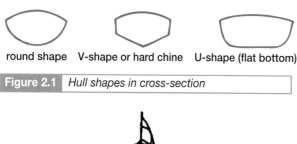

round shape   V-shape or hard chine   U-shape (flat bottom)

| Figure 2.1 | *Hull shapes in cross-section* |

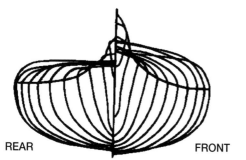

REAR   FRONT

| Figure 2.2 | *This modern compromise incorporates the best qualities of the basic cross sections in Figure 2.1. what you see are the 'lines' of a Gulfstream Sea Kayak. This line drawing, is simply the various cross sections of the hull and deck taken at fixed intervals from the bow to the stern and then depicted in sequence superimposed one upon the other. The gunwale line or join line, can be seen separating the deck from the hull. The bilge (side of the hull as it leaves the gunwale) is gently rounded. It is the careful configuration of these soft chine curves which gives the hull its stability and speed. NB Designers lines are always covered by copyright.* |

the speed increases the boat tends to plane on the flat chines. The kayak thus retards itself on its own bow wave. Despite this, as long as the bottom V is not too acute these boats can be extremely stable and comfortable. In rough steep seas their movements are predictable, increasing confidence and allowing more relaxation than some other boats.

The round hull is the traditional shape of the Aleutian Islands kayaks. It is a faster shape than the chine hull because it offers less harsh resistance in the water and it gives a softer ride in beam seas. The true round hull is basically very unstable and requires skill in handling. Modern sea kayaks have a modified round hull which gives speed without the unsteadiness.

Many recreational boats have been bought with flat bottoms and wide beams under the mistaken

idea that this type of stability is also seaworthy. In a flat sea the kayak does sit flat on the water, but because the hull shape also follows the wave slope (Figure 3A) it is unsuitable for anything but a flat, calm sea. The round and V-shaped hulls, on the other hand, can compensate for the wave slope, the shaped bottom enabling the occupant to lean into the wave (Figure 3B) for the necessary bracing stroke.

A sea kayak needs a high bow, the hull approach to which should be an acute V to slice through oncoming waves. Some fullness in width, however, should be retained near the bow if possible. Extremely fine and narrow bows, although elegant in appearance, cause the kayak to plunge into the waves and thus submerge the fore end and throw spray over the paddler.

The amount of freeboard (Figure 1) should be small so as to provide little to be caught by beam winds, although the after end may have to be raised to compensate for the high bow.

Rocker

Rocker is the term applied to the curve of a hull fore and aft. This rockering tends to govern directional stability, making the kayak easier to turn. The amount of rocker in sea kayaks has to be limited, as it causes stern drag, hence a reduction in forward speed. The

A

Flat bottomed boat thrown over by wave

B

Rounded hull can be leant into wave

| Figure 3 | *Behaviour of different hull shapes on waves* |

shape and degree of the rocker is important, as a beam wind can use the deepest part of the rockered hull as a pivot on which to spin the boat. One of the problems associated with fitting fixed skegs to the rear of white-water kayaks, in order to help them run straight, is the alteration of the pivot point.

The trouble occurs in high winds, when the skeg immediately moves the pivot point from amidships to the stern. This will cause the bow of the kayak to blow downwind, making it almost impossible to maintain a straight course or turn back into the wind.

Skegs and rudders

SKEGS

Sea kayaks are designed to run straight. Unfortunately, in strong beam winds nearly all kayaks have a tendency to 'weathercock', i.e. their bows tend to swing round into the wind, causing the paddler to make tiring corrective strokes on the upwind side. The Eskimos were aware of this problem and many traditional Greenland kayaks had a temporary *skeg* or fin fastened to the underside of the hull. In some cases the skeg was built into the frame during construction. Some modern designers have improved on this idea and a number of sea kayaks are now fitted with retractable skegs as part of their integral construction.

The controls which work the skeg should be positioned within easy reach. These controls usually take the form of a sliding toggle, held in a recess at the side of the cockpit. When the skeg is not needed it can be pulled up into its boxed housing inside the rear compartment. When needed, the skeg is simple to operate and effective in use.

If the fin is in the 'up' position, the kayak will follow its natural tendency and 'weathercock' into the wind (Figure 4A). In the 'down' position, the fin will grip the water and allow the bow to be blown downwind (Figure 4B). The paddler can gradually drop the skeg until it reaches a position where the influence of the wind is cancelled out completely (Figure 4C). Only occasionally may it be necessary to 'fine tune' the controls in order to compensate for any major changes in the wind speed.

The drag created by the skeg through the water is

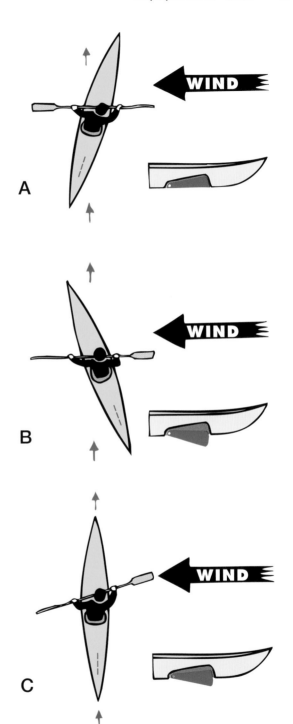

| Figure 4 | *Effects of drop-down skeg* |

hardly noticeable. The mechanism is easy to repair, and the only problem I have ever had was caused by a pebble jamming in the fin box. If the fin is made of plastic it can snap if struck sideways by rocks. Those made of aluminium will bend but they can always be bent back or knocked reasonably straight again. Skegs that are raised and lowered by means of a concealed steel cable deploy in a more positive manner than those which are operated by a stretchable rope which extends back along the rear deck.

Relying on a skeg can make you lazy, so learn how to handle your kayak in the wind without the skeg. I mean – we all know that mechanical things can never go wrong... but...

RUDDERS

A rudder is another mechanical means of maintaining a course in awkward seas. Thin wire or nylon cord leads in from the rudder mechanism, through the deck either behind or to the side of the cockpit. These wires are then connected to foot-operated peddles or to a T-bar, both worked in the same way – by knocking the bar from one side to the other with the feet. Although rudders can be a help, they bring with them added problems:

1　Any one of the deep-water rescues can damage the wires or the actual rudder mechanism. During rescues, injuries inflicted by rudders are not uncommon.

2　Rudders make seal landings and especially seal launchings very difficult.

3　Any towing will need to be done from the body of the paddler and not from the kayak, because tow lines anchored to the boat will foul the rudder mechanism.

4　If you capsize in surf, you will discover that a rudder means that there is no safe place to hold the kayak near the stern, which would also allow the kayak to rotate in your hand.

5　In my experience, when rudders break or bend they usually do so at a time and in such a way that makes paddling ten times worse than it would be with no rudder at all. Remember, learn to handle your kayak with your paddle and your body. Look upon skegs and rudders as expendable extras.

6　The presence of rudder pedals can affect your forward paddling stroke. To be efficient, you need to be able to push your feet down onto a firm footrest. The foot pedals which control your rudder will tend to give a spongy foot support.

Spray cover or skirt

A spray cover or spray deck (Figure 5) is absolutely essential for kayaking. The paddler sits in the only open hole in the boat, almost filling it, and wearing a shaped skirt with an elastic around the hem. The hole is effectively sealed when the cover is pulled over the cockpit coaming. Skirts made of thin neoprene material are probably the most watertight. I use one with a very long funnel which helps to keep me warm and which can be rolled down in warm weather. But for calm summer paddling I prefer one made of neoprene-

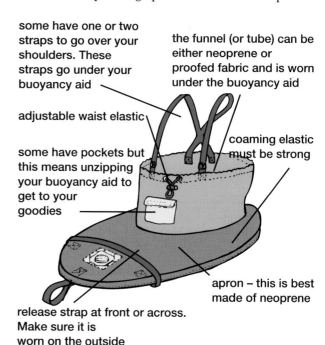

some have one or two straps to go over your shoulders. These straps go under your buoyancy aid

the funnel (or tube) can be either neoprene or proofed fabric and is worn under the buoyancy aid

adjustable waist elastic

some have pockets but this means unzipping your buoyancy aid to get to your goodies

coaming elastic must be strong

apron – this is best made of neoprene

release strap at front or across. Make sure it is worn on the outside

Figure 5　*Spray cover or spray skirt. I prefer a high tube made from proofed nylon linked to a tight-fitting neoprene apron. Some paddlers like their compass fastened onto the apron, either by 'velcro' or by an open-sided neoprene pocket*

covered nylon with an adjustable elastic waist fitting. I find it does not cause condensation round my waist and if it gets really warm I can slacken the waistband. A spray cover must have a release strap, loop or toggle so that its removal can be quick and trouble-free.

Backrest and footbrace

You might have to sit in your kayak for many hours so it is in your best interest to be nice and comfortable. Choose a seat that is not too contoured. If you look at one and it appears it was obviously shaped to someone's behind, you can bet your life it wasn't yours! My own seat designs have come a long way since I sat on wet plaster covered by a sheet of polythene. I have found that long seat pans that rise slightly upwards towards the front are usually the most comfortable; that is because they don't have that unpleasant tendency to exert pressure underneath my thighs thus causing pins and needles.

During the forward paddling stroke it is essential that you are able to exert pressure on some kind of foot brace. Fail safe swing out footrests have given way to sliding, adjustable foot braces, that have a notched rack which can be locked into any number of positions to fit the length of your legs. When you are sitting comfortably in the kayak with the balls of your feet on the footbrace, your heels should be pointing inwards towards the centre of the hull. Without moving the ball of your foot, you should be able to hook your thighs under the shaped supports that are situated on either side, under the cockpit coaming. You should also be able to straighten your leg out, so that your calf is almost touching the bottom of the hull.

Kayak flotation

If you wet-exit from an empty kayak, keep it upside down. The air trapped inside the hull will support you. In rough seas or surf the kayak will be rolled over; it will then take in water and sink unless you have filled it with some kind of buoyancy. This will keep it afloat, and if you hang on to the end toggles it will help to keep you alive. It is also more economical not to have your kayak sink out of sight.

Buoyancy can be supplied by any of the following.

PILLAR BUOYANCY
Long vertical blocks of polystyrene foam can be fixed into position fore and aft. This type of flotation, known as *pillar buoyancy*, is useful in that it can support and give rigidity to the deck. Pillar buoyancy can make repairs difficult and take up space that is needed for equipment. It is used extensively in some plastic kayaks.

INFLATABLE AIR BAGS
Kayaks, that for one reason or another fill with water, either sink or become hopelessly unstable. This is less than desirable.

If you are unfortunate enough to own a kayak that does not have a bulkhead system, you will have to fill every available space with large, specially shaped buoyancy bags. These should be placed well inside the boat, at least one in front of the footrest and the other behind the cockpit. These bags are usually inflated by means of long tubes. This means they can be pushed down inside the boat after you have loaded your camping equipment and then blown up to hold the gear firmly in place. However, before pushing your air bags in place, I suggest you make sure that there are no jagged projections inside the hull. You neglect this at your peril. And remember, all bags should be checked frequently for wear and small holes.

SEALED AIR COMPARTMENTS
These are formed by fitting bulkheads. One is usually in front of the footrest and the other one behind the seat. The watertightness of these compartments depends upon the method of securing the bulkheads, and on the type and shape of the hatch lids and how they are fixed. Avoid hatch covers which are secured in a perfunctory manner and which can easily become dislodged during deep-water rescues.

PACKED EQUIPMENT
Waterproof bags filled with equipment, properly sealed and secured inside your kayak, will provide ample flotation. Any large spaces around the bags can be filled with items such as empty water containers, small blocks of foam, or indeed anything that is light and buoyant and will not float out in a capsize.

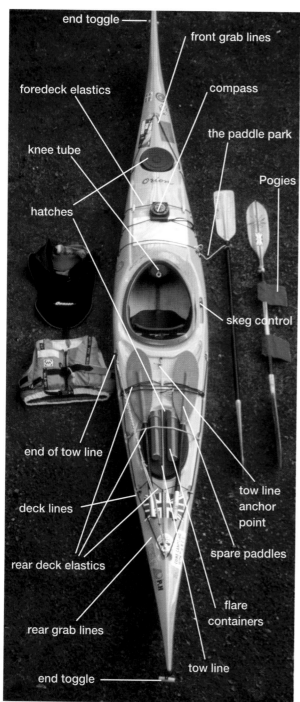

end toggle

front grab lines

foredeck elastics

compass

the paddle park

knee tube

Pogies

hatches

skeg control

end of tow line

tow line
anchor
point

deck lines

spare paddles

rear deck elastics

flare
containers

rear grab lines

tow line

end toggle

Plate 2 *A sea kayak showing equipment and decklines. Note the spray skirt, paddle and buoyancy-aid normally used by the author* (Photograph: the Author)

THE DECK LAYOUT

Deck lines

These are the grab lines. They can be run round the outside of the foredeck, rear deck or both. Situated just above the gunwale line, they have various uses. They can be used for assisting during rescues, for hauling and pulling the wet slippery kayak, or for holding on to in the water. These lines should not be allowed to sag or become slack. My line is tensioned by a lorry driver's hitch on the left side, just in front of the cockpit.

There are a number of ways the deck lines can be secured. The most efficient and most up-to-date method is by means of the recessed deck fitting. Some fittings are drilled with two holes so that the extra holes can be used to secure deck elastics as well as to take deck lines. Back in the dark ages, when I decided to put deck lines on my first sea kayak, I had to use small stainless steel clips fastened to the deck by pop rivets (blank end of course). These clips did well at holding the lines in place, and all but destroyed everything else they came into contact with. This included spray skirts, knuckles and skin. Their protrusion on the inside tended to harpoon anything that attempted to be waterproof. Unfortunately, some manufacturers still use this system.

On no account must lines be allowed to hang or stretch round under the lip of the cockpit coaming. These can become slack and effectively tangle with the paddle during an Eskimo roll, or with the paddler in the event of a capsize and wet exit.

The tow line

A tow line fitted as part of the kayaks deck-line system is very handy for everyone, and doubly necessary for those leading or guiding groups. In theory, the most efficient point to tow from is behind the cockpit; however, in practice this can prove to be the worst position. Towing often has to be done when conditions are bad. To swing round at right angles to the kayak being towed, and then capsize and have to perform an Eskimo roll, could cause the line to wrap round the paddle or the paddler with tragic results.

Any equipment carried under the rear elastics could be sheared off the deck and into the water by the sweeping action of the line.

My tow-line anchor point is a small rope loop, glassed in place, centrally situated immediately behind the cockpit. The tow line is fastened to this loop and then fed along the rear deck, through the white plastic ring (a rope ring would do) then forwards again. The line then terminates at another anchor point with a quick-release shackle. This shackle or clip is fastened near at hand for quick release. A loop of shock cord is incorporated into the tow line. This is to absorb the shocks and jerks generated when towing in anything but a calm sea. Make your tow line at least 15 ft. long. Notice how the long line on my own towing system is kept tidy with a row of quick-release 'chain stitch'.
Some kayaks, in particular those constructed of polyethylene, cannot be customised in this way. In such cases paddlers may prefer to use a waist-belt-anchored tow line. I have dealt with this under 'Auxiliary equipment' (pp. 43–8). See also 'Rescues' (page 116).

Hatches

The round, black, rubber hatch on the foredeck and the larger oval hatch on the rear deck are used as a means of access to the fore and rear watertight compartments. These compartments are formed by two bulkheads, one just in front of the footrest, the other either immediately behind the cockpit or about 2 ft. behind it, to allow more space behind the paddler for items which need to be instantly accessible (such as a first-aid and repair kit).

Hatches which allow access into the main compartments should never be removed out on the open sea. Hatches can blow away or get dropped overboard accidentally. Boats can swamp, and in anything but a calm sea, this can be a major disaster. Most good quality kayaks now come with a small day hatch situated on the rear deck, directly behind the cockpit. This allows access to a small enclosed compartment, which is isolated from the rest of the interior. You will find that there is enough room in here to carry all those immediate items which you may need on the water. In the unlikely event of the hatch cover becoming lost, any water taken in will make little difference to the performance of the boat, or your life expectancy.

Another alternative is to have a sloping bulkhead: the top almost touches the rear of the cockpit coaming and the bulkhead then slopes away at an angle so that its base is about a foot behind the cockpit. This gives a small space for emergency equipment. Paddlers who prefer the sloping bulkhead do so because when the boat is upside-down in the water, a slight pressure on the upturned bow will cause the cockpit to become an almost self-draining unit.

Whether or not a hatch is watertight often depends on its shape. Round is always watertight (frogs' ears are round!). Oval is usually watertight (if you place the lid in exactly the right place on the rim). Hatches in any one of the other multitude of shapes and securing systems mean that you take your chance.

Beware of those hatches that have lids over neoprene seals. People naturally remove the rubber seals during storage but they then forget to replace them before going out onto the water. Check inside the hatch rim to see if the rim has been fitted properly and that the finish is smooth. You should not be able to feel any ragged strands of glass. Be careful when you do this.

All hatch covers should be tethered to the boat in some way to prevent them from blowing back out to sea whilst you are unloading gear on the beach. Yes they really do blow away!

Foredeck elastics

These elastics, usually three in number, are to hold your chart and compass. You should try and resist the temptation to store your hand pump, paddle float, sunglasses, water bottle, sun screen, VHF radio, hat, mobile phone and items of medication under the elastics. These ornaments will certainly inhibit you using your paddle at a low angle and might make it difficult for you to perform a number of the more advanced bracing and directional paddle strokes.

Spare paddles

Spare paddles to be used in an emergency are usually

carried on the rear deck and are held in place by shock-cord elastics. I have never considered carrying paddles on the foredeck because any water that swills down the deck is then often deflected up your nose. Their presence would also clutter my view from the 'bridge' – a situation which, as a purist, I would find quite unacceptable.

Leaders, beware! Without a set of spares, you may find yourself paddling with the broken stump belonging to one of your party.

The paddle park

Do not fasten the paddle you are using permanently to your kayak. A capsize when landing in surf or in any rough water could cause you to find yourself irre-vocably tangled to a tumbling sledgehammer. A foot or so of cord fastened to a broom-clip will provide you with a means of retaining your paddle while resting. I prefer the system shown in Figure 6. Whilst paddling in high winds, I can have the paddle leash fastened to my wrist with a loose loop of thin shock cord. If I wish to rest or take part in a rescue, the little ball on the end can be tucked under a deck elastic. When my wrist leash is not being used it can be wrapped round my paddle shaft and kept out of the way until I need it. (See Plate 2. Notice the tiny red ball near the neck of the wooden Toksook paddle.)

The paddle leash

The leash is made from a piece of thin shock-cord elastic with a loop and some kind of toggle or ball at either end. One of these ends is fastened to the paddle. If the paddle has to be anchored to the kayak, this toggle enables the leash to be held in place under the deck elastics. Because there is no knot or fastening, the leash can be pulled free of the boat with one hand. In rough or windy weather one loop is held over the wrist of the controlling hand. I have my leash about 26 in. long so that, if necessary, I can hold my paddle in the extended position.

Additional deck elastics

Do not feel you must accept as permanent the way

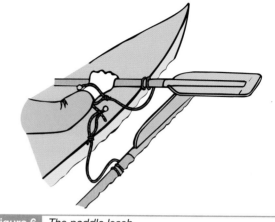

| Figure 6 | *The paddle leash* |

in which the deck elastics have been positioned on your new kayak when you buy it. Many kayaks are built to meet the demands of a rapidly increasing market in what is a relatively new sport, and – unfor-tunately – are often fitted out by manufacturers who are not themselves sea kayakers. To make their products 'look the part', and to copy what may seem to them simply a 'fashion', they place their deck elas-tics in criss-cross patterns with no apparent thought as to their ultimate function.

The addition of new deck elastics is a simple matter. I usually try to make do with the existing fit-tings and thread new elastics through to hold such items as flares, hand-held pump or other pieces of equipment. If there are no existing fittings suitably placed, you will have to create new anchor points.

If your kayak is made of glassfibre, small rope loops can be glassed into place; but if you do not wish to work with glassfibre, the easiest method is to fit the skin-shredding stainless steel clips. You will be obliged to drill two holes in your deck for each fitting, then pop-rivet them in place. Use blank-end rivets and cover over the piece that sticks out on the inside. If your kayak is made of polyethylene this method is probably the only option open to you. To ensure a watertight seal you will have to make a little backing plate out of aluminium or stainless steel. Cut a piece of rubber (insertion rubber or bicycle inner tube) to make a joint between the plate and the hull. An alternative is to squeeze silicone rubber solution on to the plate before fitting it into place.

End toggles

The toggles at the bow and the stern are the handles used for lifting and carrying the kayak. You also need to hang on to them when you are swimming your kayak ashore after a capsize. Towing a kayak in surf is not easy, and your boat will twist – sometimes over and over again while you are trying to maintain your grip. For the best results you should have small-diameter toggles, as close to the ends of the kayak as possible and with the cord holes about three-quarters of an inch apart. These will allow your boat to rotate without the tourniquet effect of a twisting loop damaging your fingers, or without the end of the kayak thrashing your forearm and wrist. If you are ever towed by another kayak, the rescuer's tow line will be attached to your toggle loop. You should therefore inspect the cords holding the toggles regularly, and renew them when necessary.

Leaders, you should inspect the toggles of all your group's kayaks. This is especially necessary when people are using their own kayaks and equipment. I used to carry about 9 in. of thin strong cord just in case one of my group had a frayed or weak toggle loop.

Learn to splice! It makes a neat job of lines and loops.

Pumps

During your ventures on the sea you will eventually need some method of removing accumulated water. In other words, you will need to bail out the boat. Everyone should carry a sponge to keep the kayak nice and dry. Any small plastic cup or container is also handy. For larger quantities of water you will need some kind of pump: there are a number of varieties from which to choose, for example portable, foot-operated, hand-operated and electrically driven.

PORTABLE

The cheapest and most popular pump is the hand-held type made by Whale. It can be carried on the rear deck when not in use. To remove water, you merely stick the suction end of the pump into the water that has accumulated in the bottom of the boat

and slide the handle up and down – like a bicycle pump. The water will then gush over the side of the boat out of the nozzle at the top of the pump. Mechanically it is foolproof and it will remove large quantities of water in a short space of time. However, in order to use the pump you must remove your spray skirt – hardly a safe practice in choppy seas!

HAND-OPERATED (FIXED)

I have always favoured the hand-operated pump manufactured by Chimp. I have mine positioned on the rear deck, immediately behind my back. It can be a little awkward to operate, but then it is not often used. I have never needed to use my own pump to empty other people's boats, and so I have removed the surplus tube from my suction hose, fitted a plumber's elbow and fastened it at 'floor' level just behind my seat.

Chimp also make a pump with a shape suitable for mounting under the foredeck with no part showing above. The handle is detachable and is stored separately – naturally on a length of cord! This foredeck position certainly makes the pump handle more accessible to the paddler. However, under normal touring conditions, pumps are not normally used enough to justify having the pump and its associated pipework intrude into the cockpit space. This is especially so if, like me, you enjoy the convenience of having a knee-tube for storage.

I find foot operated pumps are very useful. They are fixed either to a front bulkhead, although this would have to be reinforced, or to a wood cross beam fixed in place above the footrest. The joy is that the spray skirt does not have to be removed nor is there any need to let go of your paddle.

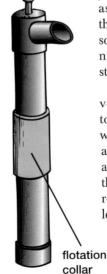

flotation collar

Figure 7 | *Portable hand-pump*

ELECTRICALLY OPERATED

I remember once being very impressed by a couple who came to an assessment course, each with their kayak equipped with small, expensive electric pumps. These pumps were positioned directly behind the cockpit and were driven by a motorcycle lead-acid
battery. Re-entering their kayaks after completing some exercise or other, they merely pressed a water-proof rubber button behind the seat and the tiny submersible pump then emptied the kayak quite happily at a speed of about 4 gallons per minute. All this took place without any effort or contortions on behalf of the occupants. I thought to myself, 'This is for me. Never mind the weight. I want one.' Later that day, in conditions that had deteriorated, one of the pumps failed. I decided to stick to my hand-pump.

Leaders

Regardless of your own fixed pump system, I suggest you carry a portable hand-pump somewhere on the deck. You can use this to empty out any kayak belonging to your group *without removing your own spray skirt*. The pump can also be passed round for others to use.

Knowing that some member of your group will eventually drop your pump into the sea, I suggest you wrap a little floatable foam around its barrel.

PACKING

When packing the kayak, try to keep all the heavy gear near the centre, away from the bow and stern. If the weight is at the extremities, some inertia will be produced when the kayak is turning.

Reasonable care must be exercised in balancing the kayak, by distributing the weight fore and aft, but it is surprising how little the trim of the kayak is affected by quite heavy loads.

A small space should be left behind the seat for emergency gear (first aid, repair kit, exposure bag and any odd items of clothing needed during the trip). These should all be held in place by shock cord stretched across the inside of the kayak and attached to small loops glassed on to the inside of the hull.

If the kayak is not fitted with bulkheads, all bags should be secured with either rope or shock cord or else stored behind inflated, tailored air bags, so that they will not float out in the event of a capsize.

CHOOSING A KAYAK

Choosing a kayak is a big decision. Once you enter the kayak retail stores you can be thrown into utter confusion. Racks and racks of beautiful kayaks in flamboyant colours will cry out for your attention. The best thing to do first is to get some advice from your paddling friends. Ask questions like, 'What don't you like about your boat?', and 'If you hadn't bought that one, which one would you have bought?'

Desirable qualities

You will be pleased to know, dear reader, that we all want the same type of kayak. It must be stable enough to stand up in and narrow enough to be fast. It must run straight regardless of the strength and direction of the wind but it must turn without effort. Hatches must be large enough to pack the kitchen sink in and be completely watertight no matter what shape they may be... and so the list goes on.

STABILITY

Probably the main concern of the novice is stability. 'Will I tip over? Will I be forced to swim in that ghastly, dark, cold water? Can I choose a boat wide enough to remain dry forever?' Well, the bad news is that if you want to learn to kayak you're going to get wet – at least in the beginning. The good news is – *kayaking is a dry sport*, unless it's raining or the wind throws up spray. Once you've learnt just a few skills *you will stay upright*. Keep thinking – a bicycle is only *one inch wide*! And remember the Eskimos, who started all this kayaking business, did not wear life-jackets, did not wear wet-suits... nor could they swim!

However, stability is important. Unless you are experienced, you probably will not be able to tell if a hull is stable merely by looking at it. A 25-in. hull can be unbearably unstable, while a 23-in. hull can feel like an armchair.

The feeling you get when you are sitting upright in your kayak is known as *initial stability*. Perhaps a more important type of stability to you as a paddler is the boat's 'reserve' of stability or *secondary stability*. In other words, as the boat is leaned over and you anticipate a capsize, the kayak does not feel any more unstable than it did when you were sitting upright. An almost round hull will feel unstable at first, but if the hull shape flares outwards as it rises up towards the gunwales the change of shape will inhibit the kayak leaning too far and can thus prevent a capsize.

Although they may feel a little tippy at first, sea kayaks with a good reserve of secondary stability generally make better rough-water sea boats. A kayak that feels very stable during the first half hour may paddle like a lifeless plank after four weeks.

LENGTH

Most sea kayaks are between 16 ft. and 19 ft. long. Generally speaking, long kayaks are faster than short kayaks but they are more difficult to turn. Long boats tend to bridge small wave troughs, while short boats can make for a wetter ride unless careful thought is given to their bow and hull shape. However, some people prefer the manoeuvrability of short kayaks.

THE COCKPIT

Cockpit size is another preoccupation of the novice. I remember my own thoughts: 'That hole is too small! A dwarf couldn't get *into* it... let alone get *out of* it!' Luckily, they were all groundless fears. With a little experience you will find that *staying in* is the difficult part.

So when you try the seat in a kayak, always start by sitting on the rear deck. Lift your legs into the cockpit, straighten your legs and then slide forwards. Getting out is the same movement in reverse.

Sitting on the seat with your back comfortably supported and your feet resting on the footbraces, you should be able to hook your knees under the cockpit coaming or under specially made knee-grips that protrude inwards from the side of the coaming. You

should feel snug and comfortable. You don't sit in a kayak – you wear it. Is the cockpit smooth and well finished? You should feel round the underside of the coaming to make sure that there are no jagged edges. Take special notice of the area where the top side of the seat meets or joins on to the underside of the coaming.

If the kayak does not have a back-strap or support, these can be bought separately and fitted afterwards.

If you are a person of ample proportions you may have to enquire if the seat comes in two sizes. It is quite easy to cut out an original seat as I have done and fit a soft, warm, foam seat in its place.

COLOUR

Some people may think pastel shades are sweet. It's also fashionable to be colour co-ordinated and have all your equipment in tune with your dark blue or purple lifejacket. If, however, you find yourself in a busy shipping lane, you may wish that even your nose was day-glow red so that you could put it on a stick and wave it. For safety's sake, and so that you can be easily spotted in time of trouble, make sure that either the deck of your kayak or at least some large piece of your equipment – like your lifejacket or your paddle – is brightly coloured or incorporates some day-glow, fluorescent colours as part of its design.

In general

If you intend to undertake lots of long-duration camping trips and you plan to carry large quantities of equipment, or if you are, shall we say, a large-volume person, you should choose a large-volume kayak for your needs. For most paddlers, however, a medium-volume kayak will carry enough equipment for two-week trips and can also be used as a 'day boat'.

Considering the valuable equipment you are going to pack, such as your sleeping bag, look inside the hatches. See if your waterproof bags will be in danger from any jagged edges of any unsmoothed fibreglass, or from the screws that hold the hatch rim, or from the blank end of long pop rivets. Check and see that the inside of your waterproof compartment is smooth all over. Try and choose a kayak with recessed deck fittings. These have no projections on the inside and do not shred human skin on the outside.

End-toggles should be comfortable to hold. You should not be able to put your fingers through rope loops. These could act as a tourniquet while you are trying to tow your boat to shore.

All else aside, you want to enjoy your kayak. You want to feel good when you sit in it. Most people are drawn to choose a boat which appeals aesthetically. Fortunately, with a sea kayak, this consideration goes hand in hand with the qualities we have already outlined. Graceful lines mean graceful performance; clumsy lines mean clumsy performance.

MODERN SEA KAYAKS

In tracing the history of the modern sea kayak, it becomes apparent that over the years many different types of boats have been used – but that few of these have been purpose built. Most of the individuals who explored the delights of sea kayaking made 'one-off' boats. They then duplicated them for a few friends. Others paddled standard kayaks currently in use, sometimes adapting them. Many bought plans and built their kayaks in lath and fabric. The Tyne Single Kayak was very popular and so were some of the longer boats designed by Percy Blandford.

My own first kayak, designed by Blandford, is well worth a mention. Known as the PBK 10, Blandford's description of it reads: 'This decked, kayak-type canoe is the smallest craft capable of carrying a man and camping kit on rivers and canals and the open sea in moderate conditions. Construction is simple and economical and well within the capabilities of the average practical boy – or girl (several PBK 10 canoes are already in use by the girls who built them).'[1]

The Rob Roy canoe, (Figure 8), popularised by John McGregor, was often used for sea and estuary work and even surfing. It was built of overlapping wooden planks which were fastened to the steam-bent frames by copper nails clinched home in the traditional clinker-built rowing boat style. These boats were very strong and heavy; whether they were true canoes in that they could be portaged by the one-man crew is debatable. Note the unfeathered paddle

blades, the cockpit coaming with no provision for a spray cover, the hole in the foredeck to take a mast for a small lugsail, and the rather bizarre backrest. When under sail the paddle was used to steer.[2]

In the old type of sea kayak (Figure 8) the bow and stern were reinforced by a brass strip extending about 1 ft. along the bottom of the keel. The boats were either made rigid or with a folding frame and skin which fitted into 2 bags, one about 5 ft. long for the frame, the other rather more square for the rubber-proofed canvas hull covering. The large press-studs illustrated around the cockpit coaming were used to secure the spray cover until it was found that they corroded and filled with sand, becoming quite useless.

Some firms started producing boats modelled very closely on Eskimo designs, but which demanded a very high degree of skill from the men paddling them. The Tyne Greenland, the Ottersports Angmagssalik (Figure 9) and the Klepper Eskimo were all of this type.

Scotland with its wild, lonely offshore islands has been a home of sea kayaking for many years and has consistently produced many good designs. In the 1930s John Marshal designed the Queensferry, which was still popular in 1955. Boats in this range were about 14 ft. long with a beam of 30 in. The hull was of hard chine form, the heavy frame covered in canvas. Another popular boat at that time was the Loch Lomond, designed by H.A.Y. Stevenson. This was light in build with more stringers (i.e. longitudinal laths), giving a rounder hull form. A couple of years later came the Clyde Single; a graceful kayak designed by Joe Reid (16'3" x 25½"), it was a hard chine form with a short V. Duncan Winning designed the Kempock and Cloch single kayaks; then he and Joe Reid combined to produce R. and W. Canoe Plans, the first being the 16 ft. long Gantock Single (Figure 10). Ken Taylor, a fellow club member with Duncan Winning, brought a kayak back from Greenland that inspired Andrew

[1] *Boat Building*, Percy W. Blandford, Foyles Handbooks, 1957

[2] *A Short History of Canoeing in Britain*, O. J. Cock, *BCU, 1974.*

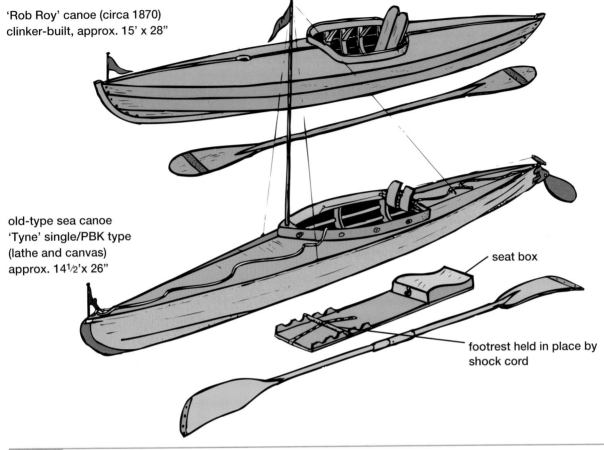

'Rob Roy' canoe (circa 1870)
clinker-built, approx. 15' x 28"

old-type sea canoe
'Tyne' single/PBK type
(lathe and canvas)
approx. 14½'x 26"

seat box

footrest held in place by
shock cord

Figure 8 | *Early sea kayaks*

Figure 9 | *Angmagssalik (kit from Ganta Boats)*

Figure 10 | *Gantock Single. Length: 16ft. width: approx. 24 in.*
Plywood, joined at keel and chine with glassfibre. Watertight bulkheads fore and aft

Carnuff to produce the Skua, approximately 15½ ft. long by 23 in. wide, which was then reproduced in glassfibre by John Flett, eventually to find its way into the fields of education and coaching. The Ken Taylor kayak from Igdlorssuit was also to have its influence on kayak design much farther afield. Duncan Winning sent the drawings of his boat down to Geoff Blackford on the south coast of England. When Geoff later produced his Anas Acuta sea kayak he succeeded in combining the hull design of the Ken Taylor kayak with a modified deck specifically aimed at accommodating a European adult.

Over the last few years the popularity of the sport of sea kayaking has increased beyond all bounds, with the result that many new firms have sprung up to reap the benefit of an ever-increasing market. Sea kayaks are now being produced in large numbers commercially, and new models seem to appear at a rate which leaves me bewildered. A few years ago the sea kayaking world was a relatively small one, so that if a kayak came on to the market and had obvious faults the word was passed round among paddlers by word of mouth. If the boat was a bad one, it usually fell by the wayside and was never heard of again. This is not so today, and the bad designs stand next to the good in the retail stores – *caveat emptor*!

MY OWN CONTRIBUTION TO DESIGN

My venture into kayak design started at a time during the early 60s when there were no sea kayak designs on the market. It's hard to believe, but very true. So you see, I was driven to design my first kayak in a fit of desperation. I had been introduced to the sport of kayaking after signing up for an introductory course run by my local Education Authority. The affair was held on a local river and I took to the sport like a duck to water. Unfortunately, I happened to live right next to the sea and the idea of using a river boat on the open North Sea did not seem the best way to go. The use of Fibreglass had just been introduced onto the sporting scene, but only a few nondescript kayaks made of that material had began to appear on the market.

As I have mentioned earlier in this book, the handful of people who actually ventured out onto the sea did so in boats made from plywood or canvas stretched over a wooden frame. These boats tended to be wide and stable with huge, long cockpits. My own prized possession was a kayak just over 10 feet long and 36 inches wide. It was known as a PBK 10 after its designer, Percy Blandford. I sat on a wooden, box-type seat which was loosely fixed to

Plate 3 *The author in his Ice Floe. Turning is made much easier if you can take advantage of a wave passing underneath. The Ice Floe, which is a large volume expedition kayak, has a capacity of 55 litres in the front compartment, 100 litres in the rear compartment and 175 litres in the cockpit area. it was the success of the large volume Ice Floe which 20 years later, formed the basis for the Gulfstream.*

(Photograph: Alan Ainslie)

the bottom boards by two wooden turn-buttons. The support given to my behind could be compared to that given to a pea on a drum and in the event of a capsize and bail out, I would find myself swimming in the middle of a mass of floating debris; this would include the wooden plywood seat, its now loose cushion, together with the swivel wooden backrest, the bottom boards together and the foot rest. The bailer, and any other valuable items which had been placed strategically between my legs, such as my chart, compass and lunch, would also have exited the boat. The various ropes and painters, which I had taken the care and time to coil up neatly on the bottom deck boards, would now be floating out in all directions. It was hardly a satisfactory state of affairs but if I wanted something more seaworthy, I would have to design and build it myself.

In the early '60s I had turned my back on the world of industry, and instead I taught Craft, Design and Technology in a Secondary Modern School for boys. I suppose I was fortunate in that my design background included five years at the Marine and Technical College as well as two years at Art College. This meant that when I turned my attention to kayak design, besides being no stranger to a drawing board, I was also able to approach the challenge by looking at it more as a piece of sculptured kinetic art, rather than a technical exercise.

At this time, I was involved, with the enthusiastic aid of the older boys at my school, in the building of a modified river kayak design that could be used by my local Volunteer Lifeguard Club as a 'rescue' craft close inshore and in surf. This grew out of the fact that I was spending two evenings a week, as well as weekends, putting the lifeguards through an intensive kayak handling programme.

Meanwhile, back in my own garage, I began experimenting with various hull shapes all made of fibreglass. I coupled these hulls with decks of either plywood or wood and canvas. My results were anything but encouraging until I happened on a copy of '*The Bark Canoes and Skin Boats of North America*' by Adney & Chapelle. This delightful and informative book, together with the lines of the Oseberg Viking longship, which had been dug up some years previously, gave me plenty of inspiration. Amusingly however,

due to the length of my garage, any kayak I designed and built would have to finish up with a maximum length of 16 feet 10 inches. Not daunted by these limitations, I devoted myself totally to designing and building a kayak that would not only look the part but would also be at home on the open sea.

Basing my design loosely on the Mackenzie Delta kayak and the kayaks of West Greenland, I sculptured the 'plug' (that's the full size model), from a combination of plywood, cardboard, chicken wire and plaster. I gave the rear end of the hull a cross section very similar to that of the Viking longship. This gave the boat remarkable stability and the undercut leading to the rear part of the keel also prevented the stern from squatting at high speed. In plan view I made the hull 'Swede Form', i.e. the widest part of the hull was slightly behind the seating position of the paddler. This gave me speed and also stability to a narrow boat. Once the plug was polished and finished, I allowed it to 'cure' (set hard) for a few days. It was then that I was able to make my first deck and hull.

My method of joining the deck and the hull together was primitive to say the least. Up until that time, I had joined the 'Rescue' boats together by screwing in a wooden strip around the top edge of the hull on the inside. The deck was then fitted in place by using an exterior overlap, very like the lid on a tin. The overlap was then screwed into place. To make the joint watertight, I sealed the inside with strips of resin-impregnated, glass matt by using a brush on a long stick. The trouble was, that in the long sea kayak I hadn't worked out a system of getting the 'whetted out' glass strips into position up in the extremities of the bow and stern. I needn't have worried because the problem was solved for me. The deck would not fit into place over the hull, so in order to get the parts to meet together I was obliged to cut off an inch from the bow and stern. This created an inch wide hole at both ends of the boat and I was able to use these holes to feed in the whetted glass draped round a wire coat hanger. To finish off the joint, all I had to do was stick a couple of tennis balls filled with glass and coloured resin over the holes and wait for it to go hard. Then I merely peeled off the rubber and I was left with two

Plate 4 *The 'North Sea' kayak was my first successful design. It was a stormy day and I had been doing some rolling so I was wearing my nose clip and a neoprene hood under my helmet. The paddles were made from a plywood kit and glued into an aluminium shaft. In order to carry small items, I stitched a pocket on the cover of my life jacket. I had fixed some elastics on the rear deck for my spare paddles and two across the fore deck for my chart and compass. However, lifting toggles and decklines were yet to come.*

The white disc on the foredeck is not a hatch cover but a number disc. In my very first sea race I would draw number 13 – and win.

(Photograph: the Author)

coloured ball ends. They protected what would have been sharp ends and gave me something to hold onto when carrying.

The kayak was fast, and, for a boat that was just over 20 inches wide, it was very stable. The slightly raised fore-deck and the flat rear-deck, together with a pronounced sheer-line, gave the kayak a streamlined appearance. I made the cockpit small but not unpleasantly so. I called my new kayak 'Kiska', after one of the Aleutian Islands, and I tested the new boat in rough seas and high winds in my local harbour. The boat handled beautifully and I delighted in the knowledge that I now possessed what I felt was a rocket ship. As far as the boat's speed was concerned, I decided to put my beliefs to the test and enter for an open water kayak race. It was held on the sea from Sandsend to Whitby (the traditional home of Dracula) and I remember I drew number 13. The wind was strong, the sea was rough and during the 'Le Mans

Start' I had trouble getting my spray skirt over the cockpit coaming. Nevertheless, in spite of my lack of experience and the fact I was competing against kayaks that had been designed for racing, I came in first place. My credibility as a kayak designer was established and it wasn't long after this that I was approached by a local boat builder who wanted to build the *North Sea Tourer* on a commercial basis.

The kayak was to be a very popular touring boat for many years, but in 1974 and in the light of what was now considerable experience, I felt that I could give the boat more stability and a little more room inside for long legged paddlers. I also modified the seat and the cockpit. After listening to some bad advice, I also cut off some of the boats graceful stern, so that a rudder could be fitted if the need arose – which it never did. To give the updated image a new name, I called the updated design the 'Baidarka' in tribute to the Aleut kayaks which I admired so much. However,

there was another big problem to overcome.

Fibreglass had become popular over a decade earlier, but to prevent this non-floating material from sinking, paddlers had been forced to fill their hulls with some kind of flotation. This was to prevent the very real danger of boats swamping and sinking after an accidental capsize. This internal buoyancy was usually in the form of inflatable bags of one kind or another, (I used wine casks with a tube attached) or strategically placed blocks of closed-cell foam. The reality was that air bags were prone to puncture, valves had a habit of leaking and foam floated out unless it was well fixed in place. Because of this, any deep water rescue, no matter how well practiced, could swiftly become a drama. However, being something of an innovator, I felt I had the solution to this problem.

During rescues, it was customary to lift the bow first. I decided to fit a bulkhead behind the seat to form a watertight compartment. Access would have to be by means of some kind of watertight hatch. I settled on a design used on sail boats. It was large in circumference and locked into its frame with a quarter turn. I even designed a recessed moulding in the rear deck of the *Baidarka* to accommodate this hatch. Sadly, after doing all that work, the hatch was nowhere near watertight, and I had to blank off the huge hole and look for a more suitable cover. I

settled on the type which I remembered having seen as a small boy on the life boats and life rafts which littered my local beach immediately after the Second World War. After prising open these hatches we discovered that the goodies and Horlicks tablets inside were still dry and fit to eat. I traced this hatch, which was still in production, and used it on the rear deck of the *Baidarka*. I tested the new kayak in the Tyne Estuary on March 10th 1974. The day was memorable in another way because during the storm, large vessel called the *Oregis* was blown onto the Black Midden Rocks with some loss of life. I sat and watched all this with water breaking over my decks whilst hanging onto my paddle. When I finally got to shore I discovered that the new hatch was totally watertight. It didn't take me long to cut out a hole in the fore deck and create a second watertight compartment at the front.

The result of all this effort, was that I now had a fast, roomy, eminently seaworthy kayak (Plates 4, 6, 24). The next thing was to cast my restless eyes round for a suitable challenge. The North Sea was on my doorstep so I decided to cross it and attempt to reach mainland Europe. After 34 hours on the water, my first attempt in the summer of 1975 almost finished in disaster. The following year however, I launched from Felixstowe Ferry with two companions, all paddling *Baidarkas*. We set off at six o' clock in the morning

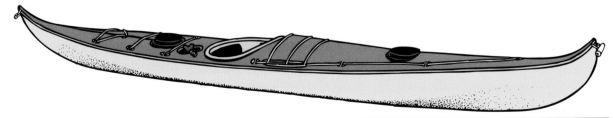

Figure 11   *The Biadarka Explorer. Length: 16'10", beam 21"*

Figure 12 | *The Andromeda*

and landed on the beach at Ostend 31 hours later.

In 1977 I modified the *Baidarka* even further. It was given more volume, the tip of the bow was extended up vertically, and the cutaway stern was remodelled with a graceful upward sweep to balance any windage fore and aft. Thus the *Baidarka Explorer* took on its distinctive shape. All kayaks used for deep-sea work should behave well when they are paddled into oncoming seas. With its added buoyancy, the *Explorer* behaved exceptionally well. The boat's length, together with the narrow 'V' section at the bow, caused the boat to rise gently to the waves so that very little water came over the bow. Straight running was assured by the integral keelson that ran the whole length of the boat.

The *Baidarka Explorer* was made even more famous in 1978 by the HTV film '*Canoeing into the Past*'. This was an account of the expedition I organised along the Aleutian Islands in 1978. We covered a distance of some 300 miles during which time we were self-sufficient and lived off the supplies we carried inside the boats.

Several design modifications later, it was in 2001 that I went right back to my original design. I accentuated the keel and this time, because I was no longer constrained by the length of my garage, I was able to give the kayak the kind of sculptured clipper bow and overhanging stern shape that I'd always dreamed of. The result is the *Andromeda*. It has a sleek, graceful look, but what makes it really beautiful is the unmistakable influence of the East Greenland kayaks. It is one of the fastest and most comfortable, long-distance touring kayaks on the market and the more gear you put into it the better it handles.

Interestingly enough, another famous kayak design of mine, the *Gulfstream*, was also the product of slow evolvement over a period of many years.

When I returned from the Aleutian Islands, I reconsidered some of my ideas on kayak design. The *Baidarka Explorer* which we used on the expedition worked perfectly well, but I also felt I needed an expedition kayak that was manoeuvrable as well as stable, and which would handle as well when it was empty as the *Baidarka* did when it was loaded with gear. It was at a time when I was preparing to do a good deal of filming so I needed a boat which would

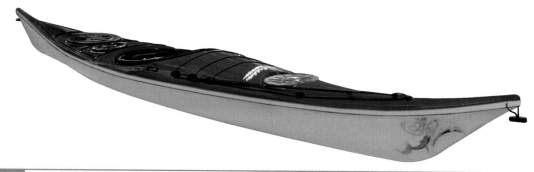

Figure 13 | *The Gulfstream*

allow me to be towed backwards in rough seas using a hand held camera.

Influenced by illustrations and dimensional drawings of single kayaks used by the Aleuts in the late 18th and early 19th centuries, I began to design a new boat. I decided to do the job in two stages. First, I would concentrate on a general purpose sea boat. As far as room for equipment was concerned it would be low volume, but I planned to use it as the basis for a larger volume, deep sea expedition kayak.

I called the new kayak the '*Umnak*' after the Aleutian Island of the same name. The length of the new boat was 159 feet long with a beam of 24 inches. It had a rockered hull so that it would turn well without difficulty and an amidships cross section that would give good rough water stability. In some ways the bow and stern of the *Umnak* resembled that of the *Baidarka* but it was not quite as high or as sharp. I placed most of the buoyancy in the *Umnak*'s hull in the centre, directly under the seat; this gave the paddler a feeling of balanced security. I discovered that I could take the *Umnak* on any water where I could take an open canoe and this included White Water Rivers. Although I never designed the *Umnak* to take a rudder, a number of ambitious owners decided that they wanted to adapt theirs and make them more suitable for short-range expedition work. The shape of the kayak's stern made it quite easy to make a slip over moulding that would carry a rudder assembly. In blustery conditions, this adaptation was found to improve the handling of the rockered hull while still retaining the versatility of a kayak only 15'6" long.

Based on the *Umnak*, I designed the '*Ice Floe*' as a fast, long range, deep sea, expedition kayak capable of withstanding the severe storm conditions which can be found on the open ocean.

I used the stable mid-section of the *Umnak* but I lengthened the boat and gave it an almost straight keel and a specially moulded stern, to hold the boat on track in quartering seas. I designed the *Ice Floe* as a straight runner. By simply leaning the kayak over, the gunwale in the area of the wide mid-section, helped to make turning or track-correction an easy matter. It was even possible to lean the kayak right over, so that the skeg on the hull at the stern cleared

the water. This, coupled with a good sweep stroke, allows the kayak to almost spin round during the turn. As an illustration of the hull's stability, a great deal of my cine-filming during the expedition to Alaska's Prince William Sound in 1978 was done whilst being towed backwards in quite choppy seas.

Not everyone wanted to carry vast quantities of equipment or to be self-sufficient for a month at a time, so I decided to redesign the hull giving the new kayak a sleeker more streamlined look. This made it a medium volume kayak suitable for the beginner as well as for the more experienced paddler. I called this new kayak the *Orion*. I gave it a semi-elliptical, cross-sectional hull for stability and placed most of the volume amidships. In comparison, the bow and stern were low in volume. I wanted to give the boat stability even in rough seas, so that when the kayak lies at rest, in a trough, and at right angles to a steep swell, the narrow less buoyant bow and stern will tend to sink down into the wave. This allows the buoyant middle section to settle into the trough giving maximum support to the paddler. When the kayak is perched on the crest of a wave, with the bow and stern hanging in space, the most buoyant part of the kayak is still fully supported by the water. This ensures stability and comfort for the paddler.

This hull configuration gives the kayak straight running qualities when touring, whilst the rockered hull, combined with the wide middle section, makes the boat very manoeuvrable when the hull is edged. The rear deck is low enough to allow an experienced paddler to perform any of the Eskimo Rolls that require the paddler to lie back as close to the deck as possible. In general terms, the kayak could be described as pleasantly docile, in that it does not make any moves which are sudden, unpredictable or in any other way frightening to the occupant.

I designed the high powerful bow so that it would slice down and through oncoming seas and then slice cleanly out again without throwing water into the face of the paddler. This helps the paddler maintain a good consistent speed, even when paddling into wind and oncoming seas. The *Orion* has been a popular design and was successful for many years but in a weak moment, and after some persuasion, I allowed a manufacturer to alter my original rear-

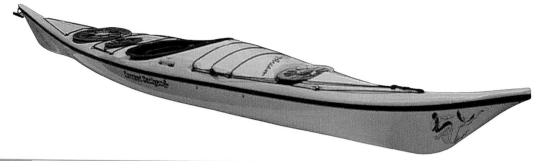

| Figure 14 | *The Slipstream* |

deck and replace it with one into which they had moulded a special recess to carry the spare paddle. It was a modification that I never liked, so after more than a decade, I decided to do some redesigning and fine tuning. I redesigned the rear deck, incorporating a day hatch immediately behind the cockpit. I gave the boat a more comfortable seat and made some modifications to the hull. The result was a kayak I decided to call the '*Gulfstream*'.

Since its launch in 1996, the *Gulfstream* has become one of the world's most popular, open-water touring kayaks. Due to the boat's success, by popular request in 1997, I introduced a scaled-down version called the *Slipstream*. I made it a foot shorter and two inches narrower than its big sister. The *Slipstream* has proved ideal for smaller, lightweight paddlers who want all the deep-sea qualities of the *Gulfstream* but without the larger volume.

In 2001, I had the joy of seeing my *Gulfstream* produced in Polyethylene. The kayak was called the *Sirocco* and it was my first venture into the wonders of plastic. Everyone who knows me will tell you that I have always been concerned about the lack of rigidity of many of the plastic kayaks at present on the market. The problems are usually in the area of the fore deck and the under-side of the hull along the keel. I need not have worried, because the hull shape, together with the convex curves and recesses of the *Gulfstream* gave the plastic *Sirocco* a stiffness and lack of flex that was far more than I could have expected. The real test came on the day when I had to try out the first *Sirocco*. I remember, I shut my eyes and I discovered it was impossible to tell from the handling characteristics that I was in a kayak made of plastic.

In all, I have designed sixteen deep-sea kayaks but I wanted only to include two of my earliest and most popular designs that have influenced the shape of kayaks internationally over the last twenty years.

Many people ask me why all my kayak designs have decals on the bow. Well, I consider all my kayaks to be true deep sea craft in the traditional sense. Since I sculpture my kayaks to be things of beauty and grace, then why not embrace tradition and have a figure head!

The Reiver

The *Reiver* (Figure 16) is an extremely fast, medium,

| Figure 15 | *The Sirocco* |

| **Figure 16** | *The Reiver (17'1½" x 22")* |

sea-touring kayak. Modelled in the style of West Greenland Eskimo kayaks, it has an almost flat rear deck which rises up to a graceful stern. The boat has a small, well-fitting and comfortable cockpit with good support for the knees. The foredeck has a pronounced sheer which rises to a high, powerful, straight bow. A keel, which runs the full length of the hull, gives effortless straight running, and the fast hull seems to respond to the slightest touch of the paddle. Beam winds have hardly any weathercocking effect upon the boat.

The Reiver was the first kayak I designed completely in the United States. The boat is 22 in. wide and, considering its traditional narrow beam, has comfortable initial stability and excellent secondary stability. Since it is a kayak's deck shape that governs its rolling qualities, the sheerline fore and aft make the Reiver one of the easiest boats to roll.

The Border 'Reivers' were bands of robbers and cutthroats that terrorised the region between England and Scotland 400 years ago.

CHOOSING A KAYAK

In the last edition of this book, I wrote (may I bite off the offending hand) 'North American designs appear strange and unfamiliar.' I have to say that in the '90s this was certainly true, especially when viewed from the standpoint of a British paddler who was be used to a narrow, sleek kayak with a very small cockpit and a system of deck line and safety toggles. The cry at the time was 'all British boats are tippy and therefore unsafe', while 'all North American sea kayaks are wide, stable and safe.' My own view at that time was that all sea kayaks should have small cockpits. Looking back, I suppose I was thinking in romantic

terms about the Inuit boats. However, when I finally gave this subject some deep, sensible thought, I could not escape the fact that my white water kayak had a large cockpit and yet it did not take in any more water because of it. I designed my next sea kayak with a white-water sized cockpit and discovered that the only disadvantage was that my compass and chart, when placed under the fore-deck elastics, were further away from my myopic eyes than they had been previously. During this drastic rethinking, I also gave the new boat a beam of 24 inches, which was also the same as my river boat. The modifications were just fine and I now had a kayak in which I could relax and twist around in when taking photographs, without the fear of diving into the drink with a load of expensive equipment wrapped around my neck.

So where does the sport stand at present? Well, over the last few years, the cockpits seem to have taken on a universal size. Rudders, which were often a standard feature, seem to be giving way to skegs of one sort or another, and the only way you can discern the national origins of a sea kayak is to look for the name of the designer (good quality sea kayaks should carry the name of the designer somewhere on, or inside, the hull). Unfortunately, I have to say that there are many kayaks on the market today that look as if they have been designed by a committee.

Choosing a kayak is a big decision, and apart from the house you live in or the car you drive this could be the most important purchase of your life. The trouble is that the advice you will receive on the subject could range from the bizarre to the absurd. The first pearl of wisdom you'll hear is that you should buy a kayak that feels comfortable for you. Well, if you did that and you've never been in a kayak before, you'll finish up with a wide stable barge that you will grow out of in a couple of weeks.

I made this mistake myself in the early days. The person who advises you to choose a kayak the same as that of your best friend, isn't providing much help either, especially if your friend is a nervous, timid soul who has only limited horizons. It is vitally important to choose a boat design with features that will allow you to do what you want to do with your kayak. However, at this stage of the game you will have no idea what you want to do or the particular type of craft you want to do it in. If you don't mix with paddlers and you don't have anyone to advise you, the real trouble starts in the in the kayak store. Here you will be assailed by all manner of shiny craft in flamboyant colours, which hang bewilderingly from the walls or ceilings. They all cry out for your attention (and your money). You will immediately notice that they come in a variety of lengths, widths and colours, which range from weird to the absolutely impractical. I have to say that many of these craft will have originated from manufacturers with little or no experience of the sea.

Roughly speaking, the boats you see will fall into two categories. They can be classed as Sea Kayaks or Recreational Boats. Although both these craft are used for touring, it is there that the similarity ends.

Recreational boats

The short, stubby, little recreational boats with their huge, wide cockpits are not kayaks in the true sense of the word. Most have flat bottoms, which make them very stable on flat water and almost impossible to stabilize or manoeuvre in rough seas. They are slow and don't track (paddle in a straight line) very well. The seat is usually fixed to the bottom of the hull. There will certainly be no support for your thighs or for your visible, unprotected white knees.

Because of their 'homely' qualities, recreational boats are very limited in the type of journeys they can undertake. To keep the price low, recreational boats are not fitted out with the basic safety features we have come to expect. These include watertight compartments and deck lines. Because of their limited use, recreational boats rarely have options such as skegs or rudders.

Sea kayaks

For the most part, sea kayaks are long, sleek and straight running; and you don't sit in them, you wear them. All good makes will have hatches and watertight compartments that make them unsinkable. They will have fixed deck lines for you to grab, and toggles at both ends for carrying. The cockpit must be of a kind that can be sealed off with some kind of a spray cover when you are sitting on the seat. No part of the seat should be loose.

There are a number ways in which you can try out some of the various designs. You could always attend one of the Sea Kayak Symposiums where the various manufacturers line boats up along the beach for you to 'test drive'. You could also enrol on a sea-kayaking course with a reputable outfitter or Outdoor Centre. You might be able to rent a boat or try those belonging to your friends. Many people have been introduced to kayaking by taking a short, guided tour. Of course, you could always find out who is selling a boat – not so you can buy theirs, but to learn why they are selling it and which new model they are going to buy and why!

Let us suppose that you are fortunate enough to be able to try your selected sea kayak out on the water. It is best if you can test the kayak you are thinking to buy while it's stationary and afloat. In other words you're going to test the hull for stability.

Your first priority is to see how the boat feels when you sit in it. The seat should be nice and comfortable with room for your thighs. This is a serious consideration because as you make progress, you will be sitting in your kayak for many hours at a stretch. As I mentioned earlier in 'Stability' as a novice your main and natural concern will be stability; 'Will I tip over?' 'Will I be forced to swim in that ghastly, dark, cold water?' 'Can I choose a boat that will allow me to remain dry forever?' Well, the bad news is that if you are going to learn to kayak, you are going to get wet – at least in the beginning. The good news is that once you know what you are doing, and unless it's raining or the wind throws up spray, kayak touring is a dry sport. Once you've learned a few very basic skills you will stay upright. Remind yourself that a bicycle is only an inch wide!

Let us suppose that you are going to try out a boat.

First you will need to adjust the footrest so that your legs are slightly bent. Get someone to steady the boat and then sit in it next to a low dock. (See fig 36.1 and 36.2) If no dock is available, use the bow of a friend's kayak positioned at right angles to you. What you are looking for is something solid to lean upon. Support the nearest hand lightly on the dock (or bow) and lean slowly over. The knee on the high side should be bent upwards and hooked underneath the cockpit coaming. The leg nearest the dock should be straight and pushing down on the footrest. As you start to lean, you should feel some resistance. This is what is known as primary stability and it's what gives you that comfortable, secure feeling when you're paddling normally on flat water. Now lift your support hand a fraction of an inch above the dock and keep on leaning. You should be able to take the gunwale line of your kayak slightly past the point where it touches the water, and still not have to support yourself. This is known as secondary stability. Suddenly there will come a point when the boat will go over and you have to use your hand for support once again. This is known as the moment of capsize.

As a little exercise, using only your hips, try wobbling the boat from side to side to the limit of its secondary stability. Keep your hand poised above the dock, just in case. Keep on doing this for a few minutes. Through repetition, the kayak's stability will be registered on your nervous system and the balance mechanism of your brain. Very soon your balance will be instinctive. A point to remember is that your stability will be affected by your centre of gravity. If you are a paddler with a long torso and a good deal of upper body weight you will be more unstable than a person of the same height but whose weight is spread lower down. (See 'fixed ballast' page 47.)

Your skill level will start to improve the moment you sit in the boat, so the kayak you thought was a little tippy the first time you sat in it could feel like a lifeless plank in a week's time. Don't delude yourself into thinking that width brings stability. Many boats have been bought with flat bottoms and wide beams with the mistaken idea that this type of stability is seaworthy. In a flat sea, the kayak does sit flat on the water; but because the hull shape follows the wave slope (Fig 3A) it is unsuitable for anything but flat calm water.

The other cross-sectional hull shapes you will meet up with are the Chine or V-shaped hull, the round hull and the semi-elliptical hull. The V-shaped or Chine hull (Fig 2), is the traditional shape of many Greenland Eskimo kayaks; as long as the amount of rocker is not too excessive these hulls can have good directional stability. Chine boats are not as fast as those with round bilges but as long as the bottom V is not too acute these boats can be extremely stable and comfortable. The multi-chine, round hull is the traditional shape of the Aleutian Island kayaks. It is a faster hull than the Greenland kayaks and the rounded hull gives a softer ride in beam seas. The true round hull is certainly the fastest through the water. This is why racing kayaks have this kind of hull shape. Unfortunately, they are also frighteningly unstable so if you fancy racing (See chapter 5) when mastering this instability could become a life-long pursuit.

Being very practically minded, I have always based my hull designs on a semi-elliptical cross section. I found that this compromise between speed and stability gives me a feeling of security in rough water and a smooth fast ride. The sad news is that you, dear reader, are faced with something of a dilemma. You will also be pleased to know that we all want the same qualities in a kayak. It must be light enough to lift up onto the top of a vehicle (see fig 34.2), yet strong enough to withstand the battering of rough usage. It must run straight at all times – even in the most trying conditions – yet turn easily when the need arises. It must be stable enough to give the timid confidence, but versatile enough to allow bracing strokes to be performed easily. The hull must have enough space to accommodate a mountain of equipment, but the amount of freeboard (the area between the water line and the lowest point of the gunwale) must be kept to a minimum. High seats give extra speed but less stability. Low seats give stability but can also provide the paddler with wet elbows and skinned knuckles. Decisions, decisions!

The following points will help make your decisions better informed:

LENGTH

Most sea kayaks are between 16 ft and 19 ft long. The

length of a kayak has a huge effect on its tracking ability, manoeuvrability, stability and speed. Long kayaks take less effort to paddle than those which are short and stubby because the flow of water past the hull, known as laminar flow, is offered less resistance. This allows long boats to glide farther with each stroke, and they are also able to bridge the smaller wave troughs thus giving you a smoother, faster, drier ride. Shorter boats, i.e. those less than 16 ft long, are easier to turn but they are slower, and will cause you to expend more energy – especially in wind tossed waves.

Naturally, you don't want a boat that feels too 'tippy', but nor do you want to buy a boat that will not grow with you as your skill level increases. I always tell people that the only difference between a stable or an unstable kayak is the difference between a good haircut and a bad haircut. I know this is an over simplification but you must remember that you will be a novice for only a very short period of time.

WEIGHT
Sea kayaks, depending on their dimensions, usually weigh in at around 50–55 lbs. A kayak that is a bit on the heavy side can be a pain when you have to lift it unassisted off your car, or face a long carry to reach the water. Once you are afloat however, the weight should not bother you at all. I would go so far as to say that a little extra weight should give you quite a comfortable feeling, especially when you are going up and down on the waves. You will find that the weight will also give you momentum when you have to punch through waves, and you will not be blown out of control in high winds.

SEATS
The first thing you will look for is a boat that has a comfortable seat. This is vital when you consider that the time you spend in the cockpit may run into many hours. The back of your seat rest should not be too high, nor should you be able to dislodge it if it happens to be located into a preformed slot. Semi-rigid back straps or back bands are best. These should be slung to give your back plenty of support but they should also be flexible enough to allow you to lean back onto the rear deck. If you cannot lean back onto the rear deck, a number of advanced techniques will be closed to you. Remember that awkward, narrow or uncomfortable seats can be cut out and replaced by very comfortable alternatives made of pre-shaped foam. These can be easily fitted with the help of a sharp knife and impact cement. Back bands can also be retro-fitted.

CHOOSE A KAYAK THAT WILL GROW WITH YOU – NOT ONE WHICH YOU WILL GROW OUT OF.

THE COCKPIT

As a novice the cockpit size will be another of your preoccupations. I remember my own thoughts on this: That hole is too small! A dwarf couldn't get into it – let alone get out of it! Luckily they were all groundless fears. With even a little experience you'll find that staying in is the difficult part.

Most cockpits these days are quite large and you can actually sit on the seat before you lift your legs inside. However if you have a kayak with a small cockpit, start by sitting on the rear deck. Lift your legs into the cockpit, straighten your legs and then slide forwards and onto the seat. Getting out is the same movement in reverse.

Sitting on the seat with your back comfortably supported and your feet resting on the foot braces, you should be able to hook your knees under the cockpit coaming, or under the specially shaped thigh supports that protrude inwards from the side of the coaming. You should feel snug and comfortable. Is the cockpit smooth and well finished? Feel around the under side of the coaming to make sure there are no jagged edges. Take special notice of the area where the top side of the seat meets or joins on the underside of the coaming.

If you are a person of ample proportions you may have to enquire if the seat comes in two sizes. It is quite easy to cut out an original seat and fit a soft, warm, foam seat in its place.

COAMING

This is the raised flange between one to two inches wide around the top of the cocking (Figure 1.1). This is what the spray skirt fits over in order to keep out the water. Run you fingers carefully around its rim. If it is very thin and sharp, it could damage your expensive new spray skirt (as well as your fingers). In cross section, the best coamings are slightly convex (raised up). This allows the material of the spray skirt to press firmly against surface of the coaming giving you a more watertight seal.

GENERAL SHAPE

There are some points that are worth looking for. As I mentioned previously in 'seats', you should be able to lie back onto the rear deck even if this means raising your posterior off the seat. Because of this,

you are looking for a boat with the rear deck lower than the fore deck. However the height of the front deck should not be so high that it prevents you for placing your paddle at a low angle to the water. It is for this reason that I advise against very high peaked fore decks. The sales pitch is that it helps to shed water; in reality oncoming water never gets that far up the deck unless you're in surf.

This brings us to the question of bow shapes. Rising bows and V shaped hulls slice through the water when running through large waves or short steep seas. Bows which, in cross section, widen out in a concave sweep as they rise upwards towards the deck tend to look graceful. However, in a boat as small as a kayak, as a flared bow plunges downwards, it will throw water upwards and outwards. This water then hits you in the face at around three miles per hour. Fine, narrow, upswept bows on the other hand, allow the front of the boat to plunge cleanly into an oncoming wave and then slice upwards and out again, with a minimum amount of water thrown into the face of the paddler.

ROCKER

When you look at a boat from the side, the rocker is the curve of the keel from the bow to the stern. This rockering tends to govern directional stability making the kayak easier to turn. The amount of rockering in sea kayaks has to be limited as it causes stern drag and hence a reduction in forward speed. The shape and degree of rocker is important. For instance, you may see kayaks where the gentle curve of the bow starts somewhere near amidships but the rocker at the rear of the boat is hardly discernable and may even be formed into the shape of a continuous skeg or fin. This means that in any kind of a cross wind, the rear of the boat will lock itself into the water while the front end will blow uncontrollably down wind. (Sometimes called lee-cocking). In other words the kayak cannot be turned to face into a strong side wind even with the use of a rudder. This is probably one of the most dangerous faults a hull can have especially if the winds are off-shore. The good news is that most kayaks with well balanced rocker will tend to 'weathercock' or blow slightly into the wind and this can be easily corrected by the use of a skeg. Kayaks that 'lee-cock' are bad news because they are almost impossible to correct, either with a skeg or even with a rudder.

SEA KAYAKS: WHAT ARE THEY MADE OF AND HOW ARE THEY MADE?

The modern solo kayak can be made from a wide range of materials, but in the main they fall into two categories. The most popular are those made from fibreglass (composite). Running a close second are the boats made from roto-moulded Polyethylene.

I remember when the first fibreglass kayaks came on the scene in the early 1960s, and it's a testimony to the material that many of these boats are still going strong today. If you are looking for a long term investment, fibreglass is your best bet.

Fibreglass is an ideal material for small boats. It is lightweight, and the weight of individual kayaks can be controlled during manufacture; it is durable, rigid and it will resist impact. If you are unfortunate enough to get a hole in your boat, it is not beyond any handy paddler to accomplish an invisible repair. Deep scratches to the surface gel coat will not affect the boats performance to any extent, and they can easily be filled in and smoothed off, making the hull look as good as new.

Composite kayaks are made from layers of woven glass, graphite or Kevlar cloth and are 'laid up' in two female moulds – one for the hull and one for the deck. After both these moulds have been prepared, i.e. waxed and polished, a coat of thick, coloured resin gel is applied – giving the kayak its hard surface and shiny coloured finish. Once the surface gel coat is dry, matting, pre-cut to shape and made from any of the materials mentioned, is carefully laid inside a mould together with strategically placed reinforcing material – usually of Kevlar. Liquid Resin is then forced into the fibres either by hand stippling with a brush or a roller, or by a process known as vacuum bagging where the resin is sucked through the fibres with the aid of special machinery. Both these methods bond the fibres together, before setting rock hard. When the hull and deck have hardened or 'cured', the two mouldings are removed. The edges then trimmed and then joined together using fibreglass tape and resin or a shaped plastic extrusion. This jointing or gunwale line is then reinforced from the inside. Once this is hard, the kayak is ready to receive its cockpit, bulkheads and hatch rims. All that is left to do then is the finishing process. This is when the boat receives all its necessary fittings, lines and other additions that go to make it safe and seaworthy.

No maintenance is necessary. Leaving the kayak out in the sun for a few years may cause some gel coat colours to fade a little, and hatch covers that are made from a rubber composition have been known to degrade after a while if they are not protected. This does not seem to apply to pure rubber hatches. The joy of fibreglass is that kayaks can be cut, altered, customised and repaired very easily.

Kevlar

Another type of material that is also popular with composite boats is Kevlar. This tremendously strong synthetic fibre is woven into a cloth is laid up with resin in the same way as fibreglass. It might be interesting to note that it is used in the manufacture of flak jackets and bullet proof vests. Because Kevlar is stiffer than the ordinary woven glass, kayaks can be made much lighter, with a weight saving of 5–10 pounds, yet still exhibit an incredible rigidity. The only problem with Kevlar is that it's dreadfully expensive, although this makes it a bit of a status symbol. Kevlar is also notoriously difficult to cut and repair, and it also makes these boats awkward to customise. Kevlar boats can be easily identified as the cloth weave is golden brown, and some manufacturers exploit this by giving their Kevlar kayaks a coat of clear gel. If you have to haul your kayak about without assistance then Kevlar could be the material for you.

Plastic or rotomoulded polyethylene

There was a time when the most serious paddlers of my acquaintance would not have contemplated changing to plastic. However, the hirer who watches the novice group dragging their kayaks over rocks and mussel beds, then bouncing them against stone jetties, will be offering up a prayer of thanks to the scientist who invented polyethylene.

I have to admit that in the early days of plastic, I did not give these kayaks a very good press. Because of the lack of stiffness, which was often due to poor design, I tended to think of them as an aesthetic nightmare. Since then however, science and care on the part of some designers, has solved many of the problems that haunted the earlier craft. Kayaks are now more rigid and also more resistant to UV sunlight, although they are still heavier than their composite counterparts.

Rotomoulded kayaks are manufactured in huge, two piece, heated metal moulds. Pea sized pieces of coloured plastic are poured in. The mould is then clamped shut, heated, and then rotated and seesawed. This coats the whole of the mould with hot, liquid plastic. (This is why plastic kayaks are all one colour.) The complete process takes about half an hour and after some initial cooling, the finished kayak is removed from the still hot mould and placed in jigs to prevent it warping and twisting as it cools. Once cold, the kayak is finished off with hatches, bulkheads, cockpit furniture, deck fittings and lines.

Kayaks are Rotomolded from either linear or crosslinked polyethylene. Kayaks made from linear polyethylene do not scratch or gouge as easily as a crosslinked boat. The linear boat is more rigid and it is possible to repair damage by welding. At the end of its life, it can be sent back to the factory, recycled and used again. Cross-linked boats have better impact resistance but due to their increased flexibility they need more support. It also takes an expert to execute a good weld. Cross-linked kayaks cannot be recycled and have to be disposed of as with so much trash.

Because Rotomolded kayaks are heavier than composite boats, the question of weight might be an issue when it comes to carrying the boat or lifting it on top of your vehicle. However, this extra weight will have no bearing on the kayak's performance once it's afloat.

Polyethylene kayaks are very reasonably priced. They resist accidental impact like no other kayaks can, and they are certainly a godsend when landing on mussel beds, bouncing off rocky shore lines, or when hired out to careless members of the public. However, these boats do have a definite life-span. When plastic boats are new they resist impact damage very well. The newer the boat, the more kindly it receives the blows. After three to six years, depending upon how much your boat has been used and the amount of strong sunshine it has been exposed to, your kayak will start to chemically degrade. The ultraviolet stabilisers and plasticizers will begin to loose their effect. The colour will start to fade; the boat will become less flexible and thus more susceptible to impact damage. Welding repairs will become much more difficult.

Plastic does soften with heat, so never fasten your Rotomolded kayak down onto your roof rack by pulling it down tightly at both ends. It certainly won't enhance the boats appearance even where the air is cool, and in hot climates your kayak may well finish up like a 17 foot long, soft plastic banana.

To sum up, I would have to revise my thoughts on how plastic kayaks compare with those made of composites. If there is a weakness it would be in the design of many plastic kayaks rather than the materials from which they are made. Poorly shaped decks still dent inwards during rescues and many boats, although functional, still look as if they have been designed by a committee. Beauty appears to be a quality which some designers feel is unimportant so long as the boat floats and exhibits all the usual accoutrements. As a final piece of general advice to the potential buyer I might suggest that you choose a plastic kayak that has already proved itself on the open sea in its composite form. As an example, the *Sirocco* (Fig. 15) is my own contribution to the Polyethylene scene and is the plastic version of my successful *Gulfstream* design.

Polycarbonate

Polycarbonate would seem to be the newest method of kayak construction and as yet those that employ this method are in the minority. However, this could well change in the future. Most people are familiar with polycarbonate as the material used in the manu-

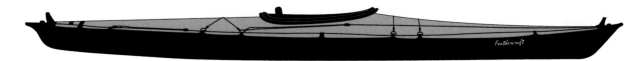

Figure 17 *The Feathercraft Kahuna*

facture of industrial eye protection goggles. It has a more highly polished finish than Polyethylene. It retains its rigidity, is more abrasion resistant and from a distance it cannot be distinguished from one of its shiny composite cousins.

Polycarbonate is supplied from the manufacturers in sheet form and in a manner not dissimilar to the way composite kayaks are vacuum bagged, the polycarbonate sheets are vacuum shaped into separate hull and deck moulds. Unlike plastic boats, the hulls and decks can therefore be in different colours. Polycarbonate kayaks can also be built using a Kevlar and resin layup on the inside giving an interesting mix of the two materials at a slightly cheaper price than composites. However, Polycarbonate is still more expensive than Polyethylene.

Repairs can be carried out using resin and fibreglass, and the manufacturers claim that Polycarbonate is more resistant to destructive effects of UV sunlight. However, the material has not really been around long enough yet for us to make valued judgements on its long term properties.

Folding kayaks

Folding kayaks have been around for a very long time. *Nauteraide, Tyne and Folbot* have all manufactured kayaks of excellent quality. *Klepper*, probably the most famous firm, introduced their first kayak before the First World War. Their most famous model, the *Arius*, had inflated airsponsons incorporated into the gunwales. This made the kayak unsinkable and left all the room inside for the stowage of equipment. The double version of this design gained immortality after the Atlantic crossings of Captain Romer in 1928 and Hans Lindemann in 1956. *Kleppers* are still beautifully made and can be supplied with a sail rig.

The early folding boats were beautiful craft but assembling and maintaining these, wide, stable,

folding kayaks was something of an adventure. The canvas skins suffered abrasion, the brass fittings tended to corrode and the wooden frames and stringers had their weaknesses and needed work with the varnish brush from time to time. However, when all is said and done, there is an undeniable appeal in being able to pack your kayak into a bag and backpack it or have it accompany you, even on a small aeroplane, to some remote paddling paradise.

The Canadian firm *Feathercraft* have certainly taken a more space-age approach to the manufacture of the folding kayak. As an example, the (figure 17) designed by Doug Simpson is a modern folding boat in the very best tradition of soft-skinned kayaks. Gone are the varnished wooden stringers and the ply-wood frames. The brass fittings are also a thing of the past. This kayak uses anodised aluminium tubing for its longitudinal stringers and heavy duty polycarbonate for its frames. The fun in putting one of these boats together is that all the tubes are colour-coded, and like tent poles, they all jump together with the assistance of thin, elasticised shock cord, however, care must be taken not to let sand get into the joints. The *Kahuna* has a rigid cockpit coaming which gives the paddler the same rough-water dryness and rolling qualities that are enjoyed in a good quality, rigid sea kayak. The *Kahuna*, like their other models, is covered with a specially formulated urethane material called Duratek which is welded together with solid urethane reinforcing strips.

There are few common sense considerations regarding long term storage and it is as well to rinse with fresh water after a long trip, or before packing the boat away, in order to remove any residual salt.

Like their other models, the *Kahuna*'s rigidity comes from a stretch-and-lock lever system situated at the centre, while the two inflatable sponsons which are built into the gunwales help to give the final tension to the skin. Optional extras include a rudder and hatches to the front and rear which makes the

Plate 5 *The author executing a one-hand moving turn during part of an on-water demonstration. The kayak is a Chesapeake Lightcraft 16 made by the plywood, stitch and glue method. (Photograph Carol T. Harris)*

positioning of equipment inside the hull much easier.

Stitch and glue

One of the most popular, and probably the easiest, way to build you own kayak is by means of a plywood kit – there are plenty of imaginative and graceful designs to choose from. Even with the most basic of woodworking skills, success can be yours. You'll find that everything is supplied. The shapes you need are pre-cut from top grade marine plywood and all you have to do is follow the simple instructions and 'stitch' the flat sections together using the wire provided. Once the kayak is sewn together, you merely reinforce and seal the seams with fibreglass and filler.

Kayaks made of wood are usually finished with a coat of epoxy, paint, or marine varnish, and any damage which exposes the wood must be repaired immediately when the area is dry. Repairing boats of this kind means that you will also restore the appearance as well as the hole. Getting wood repairs to look 'invisible' can be a time consuming process, but the result is well worth the effort. A finished and var-

nished plywood kayak is a joy to behold but to get the best out of your kayak it should be dried out thoroughly after use, stored in a dry place and maintained by rubbing down and varnishing at least one every two years. The frequency of varnishing will depend on the amount of use your boat gets. I once did an on water demonstration in a *Chesapeake Light Craft 16* (Plate 5) and I have chosen this boat as a good example of this type of construction.

The traditional school

We are now talking about kayaks that are built by what is called skin-on-frame or lathe and fabric construction. These boats are usually modelled on either Greenland type kayaks or those from those of the Aleutian Islands. The ones I have seen all look as if they have been put together with the loving care of a gold watch. The wooden frames are delicately carved and the longitudinal stringers are bound to them using waxed or synthetic twin. Instead of skins, the covering can be of fine glass cloth impregnated with a light coating of clear resin.

YOUR PADDLE

When considering the viability of various paddle shapes, it is worth remembering that when John McGregor, A.K.A. Rob Roy, popularised the use of the 'English Canoe' in Britain during Victorian times, it is probable that he based his paddle shape on the oar, used at that time for rowing. I remember that when I first started paddling, the blades I used certainly bore more resemblance to a double ended oar, than to the sleek paddles which are now accepted as part of today's kayaking scene.

Apart from your lovely kayak, the paddle will probably be the most important piece of equipment you will have to choose, and believe me, your choice is important. It is the paddle that propels your kayak forward through the water and enables you to perform all the wonderful and diverse strokes and manoeuvres that are part of kayaking at sea. My paddle is so important to me personally, that on my frequent trips abroad, I always carry two of my favourite sets of blades in my luggage. These have been specially made so that each can dismantle into four pieces.

When you are touring on the sea, or open water, you need a paddle that will allow you to cruise along at a steady rhythm for hours on end. It must be mechanically efficient and its design must minimise any tendency the blade might have to *flutter* (where the blade wobbles up and down during the pull stage) or *slice* (where the blade cuts sideways through the water without giving you any support).

One of the biggest decisions you will have to face is whether to paddle feathered or unfeathered. Feathered means that the paddle blades situated at either end of the shaft are set at right angles to each other. Unfeathered, on the other hand, means that the blades are set in line with each other, rather like a double ended oar. When you are a beginner, an unfeathered paddle appears less complicated and you will think, quite naturally, that you are only going to paddle very short distances on your local and, therefore, friendly piece of water. Staying upright is the most exciting achievement you anticipate, and going out in bad weather or when the wind is strong is not even a consideration. This is understandable, but in a matter of weeks your confidence and skill level will increase by leaps and bounds. You will become more ambitious and soon you may well get caught out in changing weather. Happily, you will discover that rough water will bother you a lot less than you thought. This is when you will wish you had feathered paddles. The trouble is that it is much harder to break the habit of paddling unfeathered once a few months have passed. Believe me, it is best to start off as you mean to go on and paddle with blades feathered at 90 degrees from the very beginning.

There are numerous advantages to using a paddle feathered to 90 degrees.

1 Handled correctly, feathered blades are less likely to cause you tendonitis (tenosynovitis or Repetitive Stress Injury), because there is less chance of a side to side movement of the wrist, which would force your wrists to their maximum (and unnatural) sideways extension of 20 degrees inward and 30 degrees outward. Difficulties can also be encountered if you cock your wrist up and down too vigorously *instead of lifting your control hand when you plant the paddle into the water* (See Fig.40)

2 During the normal paddling stroke, the feathered paddle presents the *edge* of the upper blade to the wind. This allows the blade to *slice* forward during the forward thrust, thus minimising fatigue.

3 During the forward stroke, the *upper forward moving blade* is at the correct angle should an emergency brace be needed on the non-stroke side.

4 At the end of the stroke cycle, the correct exit angle of the feathered lower blade automatically places the downward moving, upper blade in the most efficient position for the next *catch*, and ready to begin the next stroke cycle.

5 For extended paddle rolls, it is easier to 'wind up' under water into the starting position when the paddle is feathered to 90 degrees. Some extended rolls are impossible with unfeathered paddles.

The paddle shaft

Your paddle shaft should not be completely round at the handgrip but slightly oval in shape. This is usually referred to as *indexing*. This will provide you with a recognisable handgrip and give you the security of knowing that your hands are positioned properly, relative to the blade's angle to the water.

I always use two-piece break-apart paddles. This allows me to fit a personalised hand grip if the paddle does not already have one and the two piece also enables me to replace the worn shrink wrap covering when it gets scuffed or damaged. It's an infuriating fact of life that my paddles always seem to acquire sharp scuffs or nicks just where I need a smooth, comfortable surface for my hands.

Paddle blade shapes

As you can see in fig.18, kayak paddles come in a number of shapes and sizes. Asymmetric blades were designed in the late 1960s to give racing paddlers maximum power during the 'catch' phase of the forward paddling stroke.

Asymmetric blades are now used extensively by recreational paddlers and are sold in a variety of widths. I find the easiest to control are those with a longer blade and a width of about 5 inches. Asymmetric blades are at their most efficient while paddling forwards but there is a slight loss of efficiency when these blades are used for drawing or sculling strokes. If you do choose an asymmetric paddle, look for one that has a raised spine down the centre of the driving face as well as the one that usually exists for support on the back of the blade. With these ridges, you will find that the blades will grip the water more efficiently, slowing down the escape of water from the face of the blade and decreasing any tendency to *flutter* or *slice*.

My own preference for many years was a Seamaster paddle. The blades were made of wood fixed into a plastic covered aluminium shaft. In the early 1980s I developed another design. This was also

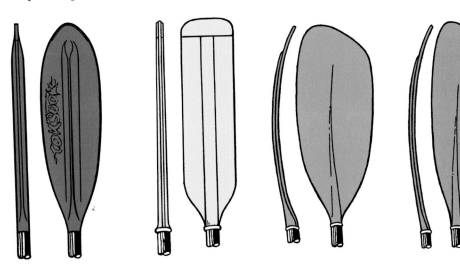

Figure 18   *Some assorted paddle shapes used by sea kayakers:*
(1) Toksook. (2) Seamaster. (3) Asymmetric spoon blade. (3) Narrow asymmetric spoon blade.
The most popular materials are: wood (hand carved or marine plywood); composite, this includes carbon fibre, graphite, or glass matt reinforced with resin (hand lay-up or injection moulding); ABS (plastic and polypropylene injection); RIM (Reaction Injection Moulding – foam polyurethane injected under pressure).
   I find the most efficient and forgiving paddle blades are those which have a pronounced spine travelling down the centre of the driving face of the blade as well as the support which runs down the middle of the back of the blade. You will find that whilst paddling forwards, this raised ridge slows down the water as it tries to escape off the face of the blade. It also makes the paddle blade easier to control when performing any bracing or support strokes, especially those which involve sculling.

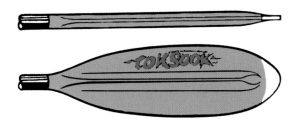

> **Figure 18.2** *The Toksook paddle:*
> *The unique design of the Toksook paddle is based on the willow leaf shape used by numerous Alaskan native kayak hunters. (Kotzebue, Nootak, Nunivak Island etc. see plate 39). The modern Toksook (pronounced took-sook) is made of graphite or carbon fibre. Its hollow interior is filled with a light buoyant foam so that it handles in much the same manner as one made from a light wood. A small aluminium insert protects the tip of the paddle from accidental damage.*

made of wood and was based on the willow-leaf-shaped blade used by the Nootak and Nunivak Inuit paddlers (fig. 18.2). I called the design the Toksook (after the Inuit village of the same name). To keep up with the times, the Toksook is now manufactured in graphite and carbon fibre. The blades are hollow and have a raised spine down both faces. This makes the Toksook a very forgiving paddle and during the forward stroke, I find it almost as efficient as a racing 'Wing' blade.

What size paddle?

In times past, it was always accepted and recommended that the correct length for a paddle was arrived at by standing upright, fully extending one arm above the head and hooking one's fingers over an imaginary vertical paddle, and then measuring that height from the ground. Although this is fine for general purpose surfing or river paddling, it's not a guide for paddling on open water or the sea. It was found that short people needed a paddle perhaps 3–9 inches above their normal reach while very tall people would paddle better with the top of the upright blade level with their wrist.

The area of a normal paddle blade is about 108 sq. ins. If this is placed on the end of a longer shaft, the strain at the joint between the blade and the shaft is

increased. But if, while preserving this area of 108 sq. ins., the blade is shaped longer and narrower – even if the shaft is no longer – the stroke is lengthened. Because the water pressure is much more gradual on the blade as it is pulled through the water, it is rather like paddling in low gear. The propulsion is the same but the effort seems to be less and, with the increase in length, the upper blade is lower during the stroke, presenting not only a better angle to any wind there might be but also offering

PADDLE SIZE TABLE

Height	Kayak Beam	Paddle Length (cm)
Less than 5'4"	17"–22"	210–220
"	23"–26"	215–230
"	27"–34"	230–245
5'4" to 5'9" (Average)	17"–22"	215–230
"	23"–26"	215–240
"	27"–34"	225–250
5'9" and over	17"–22"	220–240
"	23"–26"	220–240
"	27"–34"	230–250

less resistance because of the thinner shape.

Because sea paddles are generally longer than whitewater paddles, the variations become much greater. We now have a situation where a person, say 5 ft tall, would be quite happy with a paddle 230–240 cms (paddles are usually measured in centimetres) which would also suit someone say 5 ft 10 ins tall. I am 5 ft 7 ins tall and I use a 240 cm Toksook. However, I also know a sea kayak coach who is only 5 feet tall and has great success using a Toksook paddle 240 cms long.

The length of your paddle will also influence the speed of your paddle stroke (this cyclic movement is known as the *cadence*). A high cadence is easier to maintain with a short paddle, while a slower touring stroke is less strenuous with a longer paddle. I find that using a long, narrow blade on the end of a normal shaft length is much kinder to my arm muscles. If you choose to use a Toksook type blade that has its area lengthwise rather that width wise, do not be tempted to shorten your paddle shaft. If you do, you might find that you now have a tendency to clip the blade against the gunwale during the forward paddling stroke.

Paddle weight

There is a school of thought that says that lighter is better. For marathon racing this is undoubtedly true, but for touring in all weathers, I prefer a paddle with some weight. It is interesting that paddles of the same weight can have different handling characteristics. This is caused by how heavy the blades are in relation to the shafts. The weight of the blades is often referred to as *swing weight* or *throw weight.* It's an important consideration which unfortunately, is not really something you can try in the shop. This is because the second there is water pressure on the *lower* blade the whole paddle becomes *weightless.* Try this the next time you are in your boat on the water and you will see that any pressure you exert, as in the forward paddling stroke, supports the weight of the paddle. You can prove this to yourself and suspend your paddle while it is in the water. Do not hold the paddle, but merely exert a gentle pressure on the shaft using only one finger of each hand.

What are they made of?

Paddles are made from all manner of materials. The earliest were made from driftwood. Even today, wooden paddles are still very popular but the wood that was found lying on arctic beaches has now been replaced with beautifully seasoned Western Red Cedar, Ash and Sitka Spruce. Paddles are made first by glueing or laminating strips of these and various other woods together before being carved. Carving is now done by cutting machines which are controlled by computer programmes. Wooden paddles have a certain aesthetic appeal and there are some who would say that a wooden shaft flexes, is warmer to hold and is kinder for long distances. Paddles are usually varnished while more expensive models are covered with a protective layer of fibreglass with their end tips capped with metal or hard plastic. Wooden paddles need a coat of varnish occasionally

and don't fare well with very rough usage.

Composite paddles are now made from all manner of space-age materials such as carbon-fibre, graphite and fibreglass. Fibreglass is the most reasonably priced. It is durable and can be easily repaired. Some blades are very thin, causing them to slice uncontrollably through the water. Carbon-fibre is lighter, more rigid and wears better than fibreglass, but is usually more expensive. At the top of the range are the paddles made from graphite. These are the lightest and most durable, and of course they are the most expensive. My own preference is a Toksook paddle made of graphite. The tips of these hollow, willow-leaf-shaped paddles are protected by a light metal insert.

The most inexpensive, yet still reliable and enjoyable paddles are made from polypropylene, reinforced with either epoxy or fibreglass. Shafts in this price range are usually made from aluminium tubing covered with PVC.

No matter what your paddle is made from, you will find that in cold weather, rubber drip rings prevent your hands from becoming numbed by the constant trickle of cold water.

In bad weather, using a paddle leash of some kind is safer than pushing the paddle underneath one of the deck elastics. This is because if the kayak were to swing round in a high wind and then capsize, the paddle would be effectively trapped under the deck elastic, foiling any attempt to roll up again.

Spare paddles *of the type you normally use* should always be carried, even on short trips. These spare paddles can be carried on the rear deck, held firmly in place by elasticated shock cord (Plate 2) Mind you, I have a number of friends who prefer to carry their spare paddles stowed under the fore-deck elastics. They say that if they are needed, they can be quickly to hand. For my part, I feel that paddles placed on the fore-deck clutter the view I have from the 'bridge', and have an unpleasant tendency to direct water up my nose when I'm paddling through oncoming waves. Like many things in Kayaking, it's a personal choice.

CLOTHING

Eskimos had no trouble keeping warm in their kayaks. Keeping cool was their big problem. You will soon discover that paddling a kayak, even in cold weather, can be a warm business. Your clothing should therefore be comfortable and it should keep you dry. If the worst happens and you do get wet, your clothing should still keep you warm. When things are bad it will be the cold that kills you.

Long gone are the days when everyone improvised their paddling clothing from cast-offs and church sales. Besides being practical, sportswear is now technologically efficient. Many fashion-conscious kayakers even have their equipment colour coordinated. It is a pity, however, that some paddlers will opt for cosmetic hues and disregard those which would be more easily seen in an emergency. If the weather prospects are bad, if you have any doubts about your capabilities, and if the water temperature is cold, dress for survival and never mind the colour.

Natural materials have now been superseded by man-made fibres such as polypropylene. Because the fibres of polypropylene are plastic they do not absorb water; any perspiration or moisture is carried through the fibres and away from the body. The advent of these materials has almost eliminated that clammy, sticky feeling we used to know so well.

The big problem, therefore, is to find an outfit that is comfortable to paddle in and which is also suitable for the accidental capsize. Your question is, do you dress for the water temperature, the air temperature, or both? There are three main options.

Your body

1 *The dry-suit.* Dry-suits are designed to keep you dry and warm, so they are made from thin waterproof fabric. They should fit loosely over the arms and body and have thin latex seals at the neck, wrist and feet. The suits can be bought as one- or two-piece. Dry-suits do not usually allow perspiration to escape, although some suits now on the market are made of waterproof 'breathable' fabrics such as Gortex which do –

they are comparatively expensive but well worth the outlay. No matter what sort of dry-suit you buy, you can wear what you like underneath. Beware of overdressing: thin polypropylene will be sufficient to transport any moisture away from the surface of your skin, but even in cold conditions two layers should be quite sufficient. Cotton does not do so well because it tends to absorb moisture and is slow to dry.

Remember that the whole principle of the dry-suit is lost if you happen to sit on a thorn or a jagged piece of rock. The good news is that it is easy to locate the leak once you are in the water – and the suits can be patched and repaired.

2 *The wet-suit.* Wet-suits are designed to keep you wet and warm. They are made of a closed-cell foam called *neoprene* which also provides a certain amount of buoyancy. The suits come in various thicknesses and are designed to fit snugly over the skin. In the event of immersion the suit allows a tiny amount of water to enter between your skin and the suit; your body then heats up this water (which does not circulate) so that you keep warm. For maximum benefit your wet-suit should be a made-to-measure fit with no large air pockets between you and the material.

The most popular style for kayakers is known as the 'Long John' or 'Farmer John'. This is a sleeveless one-piece with roomy arm-holes and a vest-type neckline. The shoulders are adjustable, being 'Velcro' fastened. Worn over a short-or long-sleeved polypropylene shirt the neoprene will not impede your arms. A paddle jacket, with or without hood, can be worn to keep the polypropylene shirt dry. Some paddling jackets have neoprene cuffs and neckbands. Unlike the dry-suit, you do not need to worry too much about any tiny holes that may appear in your wet-suit.

3 Your third option is to dress for the air temperature and not for immersion. This is appropriate mainly for those who are paddling in warm climates, on warm water and in experienced company. Amongst those who paddle in cold climates and on cold water this option applies only to accompanied paddlers with a high degree of skill.

Once this level has been reached and surfing is not contemplated as part of the trip, paddlers seem to turn a full circle in their ideas of clothing. They may still wear their polypropylene undergarments or they may revert to old ideas of comfort – warm, baggy trousers and sloppy woollen pullovers over easy-fitting shirts, all covered with high-waisted waterproof fisherman's trousers and a paddling jacket. (Instead of the baggy pants, wet-suit trousers can still be worn as part of the outfit.) However, these choices are really open only to those paddlers who have reached an advanced stage in the sport. Only then can they decide whether, in order to be prepared for an unlikely capsize, they wish to paddle long distances stinking, sweating, steaming and prickling in rubber equipment like an out-of-work frogman or whether they prefer to dress like sensibly turned out hill-walkers, depending more on their skill and expertise to keep dry and worrying about meeting the freezing rescue when and if the time comes.

Interchanging the separate components of these three options should help you finally settle on the outfit that you 'cannot live without'. On a personal level I have to admit that my outlook changed a few years ago when I became the owner of a Kokatat *two piece* dry suit which gives me a versatility I never thought possible. The whole suit is made from lightweight Gortex and it is joined at the midriff with an interlocking roll. The joy is that I can wear the top separately in conjunction with a Farmer John, or on a warm day I can wear the waterproof bottoms with any top I choose. I had my trousers made as a special so that instead of finishing off the legs with the usual latex gasket or bootee, I had heavy duty, shorty gum boots fitted. I can now walk over rocks and mussel beds with complete immunity and my feet are always snug and dry.

Gortex clothing must have any residual salt rinsed off straight after use if the pores of the material are to retain their 'breathing' capacity.

Your head

You will need appropriate headgear. In cold weather you can lose most of your body-heat through the top of your head, so when surfing or practising in cold water wear a neoprene helmet under your crash-hat. For ordinary paddling in cold weather a woolly hat should be sufficient. Hot sun will burn you or give you sun-stroke so a big-brimmed hat is a good idea. Hats with big peaks are ideal for deflecting water when you are paddling head on into waves. Merely bend your head; the oncoming water, which is approaching at at least 3 mph, is deflected away from your face. The wooden hats worn by the Aleuts when paddling were the classic solution to this face-stinging problem.

The traditional Sou'wester is still tops for torrential rain and it can also be worn back-to-front if you feel the need for the large peak.

Your feet

I hate having cold feet so I always keep mine warm and dry. Your footwear should also enable you to walk over sharp rocks, slippery rocks and mud. Neoprene socks can be worn for warmth but you will need to wear plastic sandals to give the sole some strength (some neoprene bootees have thick durable soles). If you are not in the water and you wear neoprene for many hours your feet can finish up looking – and smelling – like decomposed tripe. I favour more sociable footwear – normal socks under knee-

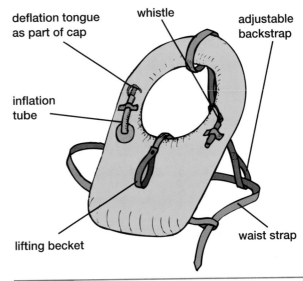

Figure 19 *Lifejacket B.S.I. 3595*

| Figure 20 | *Beware of badly fitting buoyancy aids* |

length rubber boots. I do not wear this combination if I anticipate a ducking.

Your hands

If your arms and body are warm, your hands will usually arrive at the same temperature after a short period of paddling. However, there are a number of ways in which you can prevent your digits from dropping off with the cold. Try to keep your hands dry. Wet hands soon freeze in cold winds, but drip-rings on the paddle shaft will prevent water from dribbling down. Even wet hands can be kept warm by open-palm mitts made of neoprene. These are good because they still allow you to retain the 'feel' of the shaft against your palm. In a cold wind I prefer loose-fitting Pogies. In these your hand is cocooned inside a type of mitten that fits around the paddle shaft. You merely slide your hand inside and grip the shaft without any hindrance. I do not recommend Pogies that fit tightly around the wrist; they will keep you no warmer and there is always a problem in getting your hands in and out quickly. Take care when wearing rubber kitchen gloves over woollen ones. It is easy to lose the feeling of the paddle and you might also have difficulty locating your release strap when you need it most.

In general, what you wear is governed by your own skill-level and by what you intend to do on a particular day. Remember – you are dressing not only for comfort but also for survival. It is perhaps of interest to mention that the Eskimos did not wear wet-suits. But then they didn't wear lifejackets either – the majority could not swim because there was nowhere for them to learn!

BASIC EQUIPMENT

Lifejackets

Figure 19 shows an inflated lifejacket, buoyant at the front and in the halter around the neck. It is a *two-stage lifejacket*; that is, it has a piece of sponge enclosed in a thin polythene bag inside the main front compartment, and this combined with a piece of sponge inside the neck halter gives an 'inherent' buoyancy of about 14 lb whilst uninflated for the first stage. The second stage, after the lifejacket has been inflated, gives a buoyancy of more than 35 lb which can twist the body of a helpless swimmer around from the face-down position to a survival position of about 45° to the water with mouth and nose clear *under normal conditions*. The lifejacket is worn deflated in the kayak and blown up only in case of emergency *in the water*. If, in the event of a capsize in very cold water, you should lose consciousness through hypothermia, an *inflated* lifejacket will keep your face out of the water, so long as the sea is not too rough, thus increasing your chances of survival.

As a member of the British Canoe Union's Coaching Scheme I advise all those about to embark on the sport of kayaking to wear a BSI 3595 lifejacket. However, certain other aspects must be taken into consideration. *The lifejacket must be blown up before it becomes a true lifejacket.* Until then, it is just a rather inefficient buoyancy aid. People tend to chew and destroy the deflation tongue.

The lifejacket gives no thermal or any other type of protection to the back. One has a choice of tying either a quick-release knot that always comes undone at the wrong time or a knot that is difficult to untie quickly (buckles were tried and then for some reason rejected). The bottom of the waterproof outer case tends to wear and should be worn with a special

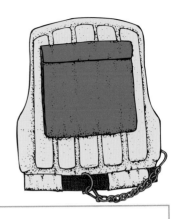

cover to extend and possibly even double the life of the main casing. If the outer casing is ripped and the inner polythene envelope is also damaged, the inner sponge, which is not closed-cell, soaks up the water, forming a millstone round the neck of the swimmer.

I was carried from the sea one cold Sunday in December 1966 while training a group of lifeguards in surf techniques. I 'drowned' into unconsciousness over a period of about 15 minutes out in the surf. Exhausted, breathless and confused, I was prevented from turning my head to one side to vomit by the same lifejacket which kept bringing me to the surface in the huge tumbling stormwater waves. By the time I used my failing energy to twist sideways, clear my blocked throat and suck another breath, the next wave sent me choking underneath. I must have blacked out several times until I awoke standing against a wet wall, I thought. It was no wall, but the sand by the water's edge where I had been dragged after being taken from the water.

Buoyancy aids or PFDs (Personal Flotation Devices)

The thing to remember about a buoyancy aid is that it will not turn and hold the body in the lean-back survival position, but rather hold it in an upright position, allowing the head to loll forwards if it wants.

The majority of the advanced paddlers I associate with all wear buoyancy aids of one type or another. I have worn both types illustrated in Figure 21 and found them satisfactory. They are comfortable to wear, help to keep the body warm and are easy to

swim in. Any zips are the heavy diving-suit type. The foam is closed-cell, and they can also serve as a seat or pillow without any damage to their efficiency. In lifeguard and in beach rescue work, and as an aid to swimming, I consider them invaluable. I once had to enter the water amongst rocks in surf; although I damaged my legs and arms the buoyancy aid protected my spine and chest. Without it I would have been badly injured.

The construction of the modern PFDs used for open water kayaking is far more complex than it was a decade ago. This is due to the fact that we now demand much more from a garment, which is primarily designed to keep us afloat. We now require pockets to carry all the small items that have to be kept close to hand. It is obvious, therefore, that lots of pockets of varying sizes are desirable and indeed many manufacturers supply extra pockets which can be added to the original garment. Knives can also be carried in pockets, although most PFDs now have some kind of external 'frog' or fastener fitted on the front of the vest, which is able to hold the sheath of a quick release knife. A large rear pocket can be used to carry just about anything. I found that mine is exactly the right size to hold my platypus water container (I feed the tube over my shoulder, through various rope loops and under one of the front pocket flaps, into a position where it is out of the way but ready to be sucked on when needed).

The external shell of the modern PFD is usually made of a 500 denier rip stop material, which will stand up to years of constant wear. The incorporation of broad pieces of retro-reflective tape gives a high degree of night visibility. The inside fabric, on the other hand, is usually made of a softer material, making it more comfortable to wear next to the skin. The brightly coloured outer covering (yellow, red and orange are the most easily seen), forms the base for a skeletal harness of webbing. This can be used as the anchor points for any add-on accessories, or for any rings or fasteners needed for either hoisting or lifting the wearer during an on-water emergency, or as a secure anchor-fastening for a personal towing system. In many cases, this supportive harness includes padded and adjustable shoulder straps which allow the body of the PFD to be raised or lowered on the upper torso as the need arises.

In many cases, a broad, towline belt can be run through webbing loops on the outside of the garment. In this way, the buoyancy foam will form the cushion that will protect your ribs during any rough water towing. Any tow line must have its own quick-release mechanism. Compression straps should be fitted under the arms, so that the tightness of the PFD can be adjusted at will.

Some points to consider

Your Life-vest PFD should give you between 16–17 lbs of buoyancy.

Always test a new PFD in the sitting position, so that when you are sitting in your kayak it will not ride up level with your ears. Remember that any foam which goes over your shoulders, or is higher than the top of your chest, will not help you one little bit when you are in the water.

Your arms should be completely unrestricted and your PFD should allow you to swim quite freely, without riding up under your armpits. With this in mind, you should avoid PFDs with only elastic around the waist.

On pockets, avoid zip fasteners that have small teeth. Even rinsing will not prevent them from seizing up with salt water. If you wish to access 'stuff' in your large rear pocket, either fasten it to tapes that are looped over your shoulder or – wait for it – get your paddling partner to fish it out for you.

The choice of buoyancy aid/PFD or life jacket will always be a personal one but it is a choice only of type. One kind or another must be worn at all times. Find a safe piece of *shallow water* and *in the company of a friend*, try and put your PFD on in the water. Try and keep your feet off the bottom!

Waterproof bags and containers (or 'Oh God – my sleeping bag's wet!')

'The only thing that's really waterproof is a frog's ear.' Remember this when you consider protecting anything from the penetrating effects of salt water.

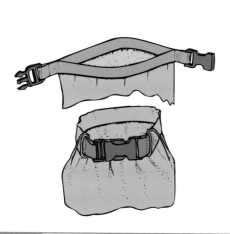
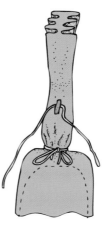

Figure 22 | *Methods of securing the necks of waterproof bags*

As with many items of equipment, the best and most satisfying results can be achieved either by improvising or by making your own waterproof bags and containers. I made my first bags from the waterproof material of ex-army groundsheets, but there are now numerous very good custom-made bags on the market. The best are those with a roll-seal at the neck. This seal is accomplished by rolling the top down about four times. The roll is then bent round (with the roll on the outside), and the ends are fastened by the two halves of a clip-together buckle (Figure 22).

These bags can be obtained in various diameters and lengths. The width you choose will depend upon the size of your hatch opening. If you have the small (7½-inch) opening you will require some of the long thin bags. Whatever size the bag, however, fill it about two-thirds full and squeeze out as much air as you can. This will allow you enough room to roll the neck over and make the seal.

People sometimes complain that access is difficult when loading equipment into kayaks with small hatches, especially when some items are bulky – such as sleeping bags or tents. When buying your waterproof bags, take this into consideration. Transfer your sleeping bag from a bulky ball into a long thin sausage. It doesn't matter if your tent is in four different bags as long as when they are packed they can all go through the holes and be stowed. I tend to keep the canopy of my tent dry while the poles and pegs are carried in the cockpit area. Many small bags are better than a few large ones, as it is easier to balance and stow gear; and, of course, if you do find that your hatch has let water in, all your eggs will not have been in the same waterproof basket.

If your kayak has watertight compartments, remember it is not a good idea to ask companions to remove the hatches for you when out at sea in order to pass out items of gear. If the hatch lids are not secured with a long piece of cord they can finish up

helping to swell Davy Jones' locker, and this will leave you with a lost friend and a gaping hole in your deck.

Plastic waterproof containers are a big help and they come in a variety of sizes. A little petroleum jelly or grease on the threads will help maintain the waterproof seal when the lid is screwed down.

Carry a compass ('Didn't we see that headland about half an hour ago?')

Unlike dinghy sailors and yachtsmen, kayakers have never had compasses specially manufactured for their particular needs.

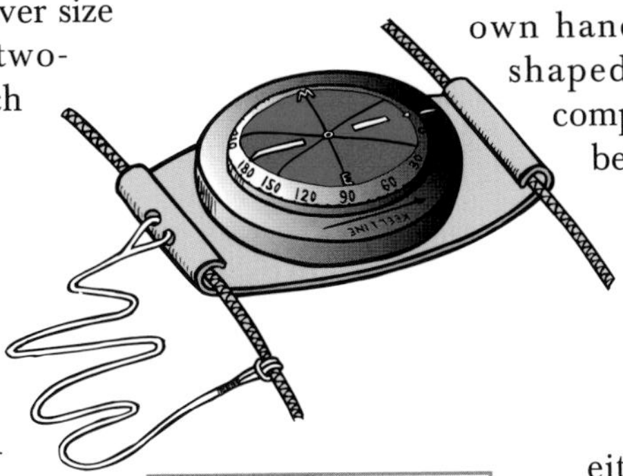

Confidence is usually best inspired by one's own handiwork. Armed with a dome-shaped car compass, or any small compass for that matter – it need not be waterproof – and a moulding kit of the clear plastic that is so popular with children, it is possible with a bit of ingenuity to produce a compass which will take the exact shape of the deck. This can have either lugs or a hole for straps or cord, and will be unbreakable and easily seen. If, however, one wishes to buy the ready-made article, there are now numerous small compasses on the market which are suitable for the kayak paddler and which can be fixed to the boat in a variety of different ways.

Figure 23 Compass

The choice of shape and size of your compass will depend upon where on the 'bridge' you wish to have it placed. Compasses can be fixed to the deck or the apron of the spray skirt using self-adhesive Velcro. (Make sure you have a cord attached.) Some kayaks have a recessed fitting in the foredeck, but with them you are restricted to a specific type of compass. If your eyesight is good, the dome-shape type of compass can be fixed on to the top of the round, rubber front-hatch-cover. Some paddlers prefer a compass with gimbal mounting. This will keep the compass horizontal and independent of the motion of the boat, but the trouble is that any compass on a

Plate 6 *4.30 a.m. on the morning of 3rd June 1976 and three kayaks lie ready for what proved a successful attempt to cross the North Sea from Felixstowe Ferry to Ostend in Belgium. Each of us had our own compass arrangement. During the first hours of darkness poor Tom Caskey lost his overboard – it wasn't tied on!*

fixed mount is liable to become damaged or lost during rescues.

Orienteering compasses are clear and easy to read and are small enough to be slipped into a pocket fixed to the apron of the spray skirt. They can also be carried in the pocket of your buoyancy aid when not in use. Suunto of Finland make some particularly good examples of this type. In the event of complicated island-hopping in bad visibility, it is advisable to have an orienteering compass hanging around the neck, or at least somewhere handy so that it can be used in conjunction with the main compass on the deck when plotting the course from a chart.

For normal paddling in bad visibility or at night, I, being even more short-sighted than ever, have discarded my Suunto diving compass and taken to the yachtsman's flat competition compass. The dial is large and the luminous figures stand out against a black, green and red background (Figure 23). The needle is slowed right down by the thick liquid filling, and the course is easily set by means of a moving bezel. I rarely use the figures on the dial because I find I can hold my course by merely keeping the colours in the predetermined position. At night the luminous bezel and calibrations fairly glow in the dark. I use this compass fixed on to a base which is curled up at both ends. These curled-up ends loop round the deck elastics so that the compass is held firmly in position and on top of my chart if necessary.

My compass is kept on looped cord fastened through one of the deck elastics. In the event of my having to rescue someone, I can either lay the compass on top of my spray skirt or let it hang over the side in the water out of harm's way.

EMERGENCY EQUIPMENT

Even on short trips, emergency equipment should be carried inside the kayak, where it can be reached in a hurry.

Repair kit

The minimum repair kit has been said to be a roll of wide, waterproof, self-adhesive tape for patching the kayak. However, it is foolhardy to go to sea with the minimum amount of equipment: consider some of the things you may have to do either for yourself or for some other unfortunate paddler.

1 Join spray-cover elastic by crimping pieces of wire with pliers.
2 Patch a buoyancy bag with a piece of PVC (PVC glue) or a lifejacket with a piece of rubberised cloth (Impact adhesive).
3 Repair a hole in a spray cover.
4 Stitch something together (waxed thread and needles with a sailor's palm).
5 Dry your boat or stick tape on to it.
6 Clean the surface (Acetone).
7 Require some string, cord or wire.
8 Burn the fraying end of a splice (waterproof matches/lighter) or light a stove.
9 Open a tin (small ex-WD-type opener is the best).
10 Make a phone call or buy a pint and a pie for, say, four people.
11 Need some toilet paper (kitchen roll is more substantial when damp).
12 Fasten something with a safety pin or tighten a screw.
13 Cut something (scissors or a sharp knife).
14 Repair a hole in a wet-suit (carry a patch).
15 Repair a tent (needles and some spare pieces of material).
16 Need a pencil and paper or a spare set of tide tables.

First Aid

Just as the roll of tape is the minimum repair kit for the kayak, I suppose a roll of medicated plaster is a comparable repair kit for the human body. While kayaking I have been faced with the following small problems:

Scalding tea over knees and hands
Jellyfish or wasp and bee stings (Anthisan antihistamine cream)
Burnt hands
Fish hooks in fingers (pliers from repair kit)
Headaches and toothache
Sickness and nausea
Both mild and severe glass-bottle cuts to the feet
Midges and seeds in the eyes or spines from sea urchins embedded in fingers
Severe sunburn
Splinter of glassfibre up fingernail
Dislocated shoulder (lifejacket can be fastened under the arm for support)
Damaged ribs or pelvis
Severely cut hands
Drowning and cardiac arrest
Diabetic coma
End of little finger severed
Dehydration
Ticks under the skin (long nose tweezers or methylated spirit)
Mosquito bites
Poison Oak rash to both legs
Mild exposure and severe hypothermia
Severe chest cramp
Exhaustion and fear
A sprained ankle
Multiple injuries from a cliff fall

Accidents are those unexpected things which perhaps happen only once. A member of one party caught her head on a fish hook which had been left dangling over the water. On another occasion a man at the end of a kayak was playfully trying to capsize it and its occupant in a swimming pool, unaware that his nose clip was hanging through the sternloop. The man in the boat chose just then to demonstrate how fast he could roll round and round. Try explaining this kind of strangulation to a coroner.

Flares

If you are in trouble – real trouble – you want to be

seen to be in trouble easily and very quickly.

All the hand flares in the world are useless if the people on shore are fastening shoe-laces or walking head down into the wind and rain. *You must make them turn round and look.* Your first signal, therefore, must be audible as well as visual. I carry two Pains Wessex Yachtshutes for this purpose. These fire a rocket or star shell into the air to approximately 1000 ft.; a grenade then explodes and a bright red flare floats slowly to the surface of the sea giving people plenty of time to see it. Sometimes called a Maroon, this is one of the international signals of distress. Unless visibility is bad or you are a long way out to sea, the Maroon will probably also pin-point your position, especially if your kayak is painted in bright colours. But carry hand flares too. These will help rescuers to locate your position in bad visibility, especially if you have drifted a long way since sending up the star shell. I also carry three 2-star red flares. Not the exploding type, they send two bright red flares high into the air, with about a 5-second pause between.

Unfortunately, if your pyrotechnics don't work through contact with salt water the manufacturers won't accept responsibility, and the polythene bags they are wrapped in cannot be trusted. Rather sad when one considers that they are for use at sea.

I carry my small flares separately in long plastic screw-top containers within reach on the deck. I have protected even the largest parachute flares by making special containers out of glassfibre, using a piece of pipe as a former. I have also seen very effective containers made from plumbers' plastic waste-pipe.

Pockets stitched to your personal buoyancy are an ideal place for carrying flares on your person, but it must be remembered that in this position they can be badly affected by the action of the salt water. It is quite pointless having your flares packed away inside the kayak. When you need them, the last thing you will want to do is to remove your spray cover or dig deep down into your equipment.

A Very pistol might be an additional useful piece of equipment. Because this would not float, it would be advisable to secure it by a lanyard. Cartridges in assorted colours should be kept handy. The possession of a Very pistol requires a firearms certificate in the United Kingdom.

An essential piece of emergency equipment is the exposure bag (a polythene bag, approximately 6 ft. by 3 ft) used to protect hypothermia cases from wind and cold. Their usual bright orange colour also makes them helpful in rescue spotting. I have now taken to carrying a brightly coloured poleless shelter. It has two draw string windows which can also be used to put your head through – one for you and one for a friend. I suppose it could be described as a voluminous double poncho. It keeps out the wind and rain and talking of *emergencies*, it is very handy for hiding calls of nature in treeless areas!

VHF radios

When the first edition of this book went into print, those who ventured on to Britain's coastal waters did so warm in the knowledge that there were manned coastguard stations placed at regular intervals around the shores. Because of this, any parachute flare directed heavenwards had a good chance of being seen first-hand by some sharp-eyed coastguard. Unhappily, this is no longer the case. Visual watch has given way to a different system, so that monitoring is now done on VHF radio distress frequencies, i.e. channel 16 (See Figure 24).

In those early days when sea kayaking was really beginning to develop, many considered it a heresy to carry a VHF radio in a sea kayak. Even now there are those who would argue that this equipment detracts from the sense of freedom and self-sufficiency that is the essence of the sport. There are, however, many instances when help has to be summoned quickly. Apart from personal need, the observant paddler

Figure 24 │ *VHF radio*

may wish to radio for help on behalf of some other water-user in distress. Paddling with a group some years ago, on a miserable day – the clouds were low and visibility was poor – we saw a single distress flare fall slowly out of the cloud and into the sea. It appeared to have originated from a solitary fishing boat, which was wallowing way off in the white-topped distance. We had no way of informing any-one, so I had to perform a hull-crunching sea landing on some rocks at the base of a lighthouse and then slip and slither to the entrance in order to let someone know what had happened. We had been the only people to see and report the flare. If I had possessed a VHF radio it would have been much simpler for me to alert the rescue services.

I do not intend to go into all the technicalities here, but anyone who wishes to use a VHF radio at sea must hold an operator's license and a Ship Licence. The former is a Restricted Certificate of Competence in Radiotelephony (VHF only). The examination for this certificate consists of a written test followed by a practical test on VHF procedures. The Ship Licence authorises the use of the radio and, like a television licence, must be renewed each year. For paddlers living in the United Kingdom, application should be made to the *Department of Trade and Industry, Licensing Branch, Radio Regulatory Division, Waterloo Bridge House, London SE1 8UA.*

The VHF radio is clearly a very useful emergency item. Every serious kayaker – and especially every group leader – should give careful consideration to the carrying of a small VHF radio. Voice contact can be maintained with the coastguard and with Emergency Services if things get out of hand. That in itself is a morale booster. The range is limited and is usually little more than line-of-sight, so remember that the height of your aerial is critical for the range of your transmission. In a sea kayak, being low in the water, you start with a distinct disadvantage. However, in communication with the coastguard your signal will often be picked up by a local booster station or any passing vessel or fishing boat and then relayed to one of the coastguard's district HQs. Remember that VHF radios are most useful where there is an abundance of water traffic or monitoring stations on land which can pick up your message.

Sadly, in remote areas, your signal might well shoot off into space. In certain parts of the Canadian Arctic, automatic repeater stations have been set up which can relay signals up to a hundred miles in some cases.

The equipment itself must always be used with care. And remember, once you initiate a distress call using a VHF radio *you cannot change your mind.* Any decisions will now be taken by the coastguard, the SAR helicopter crew, or the coxswain of the lifeboat or rescuing vessel.

Routine communications consist mainly of inform-ing the coastguard of your movements, obtaining weather information, and listening to Port operations for traffic movements and informing them of your movements. This is especially important in busy ports where the movement of large vessels is inhibited. Ship-to-ship contact can sometimes be useful, and lis-tening to local fishermen on Channel 10 is good for live entertainment. There are many good, small, sophisticated handsets on the market that are reason-ably waterproof, and waterproof cases are also avail-able that will enable you to carry your VHF radio per-manently on the deck of your kayak. I would recom-mend a brightly coloured float fastened to the water-proof case. This will prevent it from sinking and make it easy to locate as it either floats away or sits beside you on the rock while you eat your lunch.

Rules for the operation of VHF radios may differ in various parts of the world. It is incumbent on pad-dlers to acquaint themselves with any regulations, necessary qualifications or local restrictions that reg-ulate the use of this type of radio equipment in their own country. In Canada, for instance, paddlers must pass a test and pay a fee to the Department of Com-munications. In the United States there are no such limitations and a station-operator's licence can be obtained free from the Federal Communications Commission.

AUXILIARY EQUIPMENT

Liquid refreshment

By the time your brain tells you that you are thirsty,

you are already two pints into dehydration. Hydrate your body before you set off on a trip. Even on short trips take a hot sweet drink of some sort in a thermos flask. The sugar will help to restore your blood sugar level after strenuous activity. Remember that if you make it with powdered milk the drink will stay hot much longer. Some 'Thermos' flasks are unbreakable, but if yours is the delicate kind protect it with some padding taped on or slipped over the outside; flasks never seem to last long otherwise. Some people prefer to take a small stove and have the hot drink or soup fresh; it all depends on personal fancy. A fact not commonly known is that a hot drink will keep you cool in hot weather.

Emergency food may lie in the container for some time so choose something that doesn't go off – barley sugar, glucose sweets or the eternal Mars bar. Health food shops sell blocks of concentrated compressed fruit and vegetable compounds which last a long time and are very tasty as well as filling. Mountaineering shops also usually carry a good line in emergency and dried food.

Food and drink needed for the trip can be carried on the rear deck or inside the kayak, but if you carry it on the rear deck it means that if you wish you can keep picking as you get hungry and have a quick gulp of warm orange juice as your thirst increases. However, if you want the drink to stay cool and your chocolate biscuits to look like biscuits, not like some disgusting dark-brown soup, under the deck is the place for them.

Radio

For short one-day paddles a radio is rather pointless, but for kayak camping, listening to the weather forecast for your area can be helpful. One does not necessarily have to choose the smallest radio in the world for kayaking. Space is not usually so limited, and it is quite possible to find oneself in a mountainous position where reception on a miniature radio is rather restricted.

Ensure that your piece of oriental electronics is well protected from water and is also well padded! Trying two or three Eskimo rolls or even executing a normal deep-water rescue with the radio rattling round unprotected inside the kayak will not exactly enhance the general performance or improve the reception of your radio.

One last important warning:

KEEP ALL BATTERY-OPERATED PARAPHERNALIA AWAY FROM YOUR COMPASS!

Waterproof torch/flashlight

This is just what it says, except that some torches are only 'water resistant' and hardly suitable for having water constantly breaking over them, let alone for being dropped into water. The type obtainable from diving shops, if not too large and heavy, can be taped to your helmet and used for night paddling, enabling you to work at the chart or compass without a break in your paddling. It is surprising how the luminosity of your compass will fade unless you keep giving it a flash from your torch to liven it up every now and then. I find a caver's headlamp ideal for this purpose. It dispenses with the need for a helmet and is much lighter to wear, leaving the torch on deck free for other things such as letting other water-users know your position (see also 'Navigation at night', page 172).

Sunglasses

Paddling directly into the sun not only affects your view ahead; it can also give you a severe headache. When not in use, sunglasses can be worn either around the neck on a cord or tucked under the deck elastics, in a plastic case perhaps.

The Eskimos use a solid, filled-in type of eye shield with thin slits cut out for each eye, allowing only a limited amount of sunlight to enter. I have experimented with this type of protection by filing a narrow slot in industrial protective spectacles and then painting them matt-black, and I have found them very satisfactory.

Watch

You'll need a watch to time trips or work out the tides if nothing else, and it must be waterproof. An expanding strap is useful so that the watch can be worn over neoprene cuffs. There was a time when a good waterproof watch cost a fortune. However, these days a good one can be had very reasonably from your local garage.

Whistles and signals

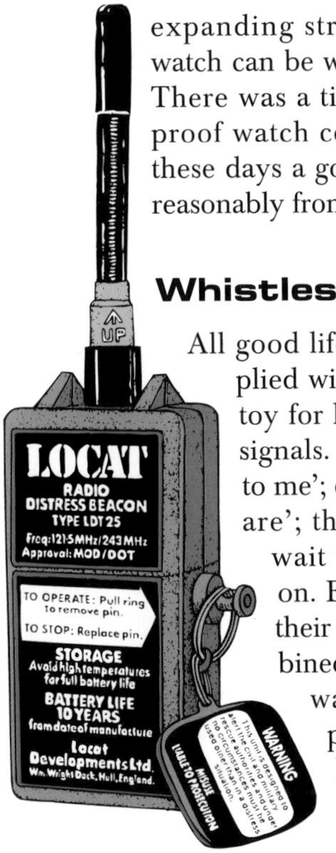

All good lifejackets seem to be supplied with a whistle, a wonderful toy for leaders who love audible signals. Two short blasts, 'Come to me'; one long, 'Stay where you are'; three blasts, 'Raft up and wait for me'... and so it goes on. Each guide seems to have their own system, which, combined with one hand held up, waved side to side, or the paddle held above the head, makes some kayak expedition leaders look like continental traffic policemen. When audible signals are

Figure 25 EPIRB

really needed it is usually windy, and unless the people for whom your blast is intended are downwind they'll probably never hear it anyway. Instead you will just have to paddle very fast and catch them up. As for an exhausted swimmer trying to blow a whistle in the water to attract attention, I think that if they are within whistle range they will probably be seen anyway.

It may seem ludicrous to dwell upon the merits of the pea-operated and non-pea-operated whistle. Lifejackets are fitted out with the non-pea type, which gives a low tone rather like the old-fashioned policeman's whistle, while the pea-operated whistle gives a shrill piercing blast familiar to all school playgrounds. The pea-operated type is ideal for leaders and instructors who wish to control large groups from the vantage point of the beach. Unfortunately, unless the pea is of the non-perishable, non-waterlogging type, you'll soon find yourself blowing through noiseless pulp.

Learn to whistle by pursing the lips. It carries just as far if not further than an ordinary whistle, and can be done while you are paddling because you don't have to take your hand off the paddle to do it.

Emergency Position-Indicating Radio Beacon (EPIRB)

When you feel that all is lost and the shadow of the Grim Reaper falls across your foredeck (or upturned hull!), all you need to do is to pull the pin on your little box. The radio beacon housed therein will immediately start to transmit your position on the International Aviation Distress Frequency. No matter where you are in the world, this signal will be picked up by a Search and Rescue (SAR) satellite. Your cry for help is then bounced back to earth to a Local User Terminal (LUT), or to a Mission Control Centre (MCC). These nerve centres will then initiate the necessary procedures for your rescue.

Your Emergency Position-Indicating Beacon (EPIRB) (Figure 25) will keep transmitting for about 36 hours. It has a range of 200 miles and will give your position to within about $4\frac{1}{2}$ miles. If you intend to paddle in remote areas, this is your most effective means of summoning help. But be warned. Once you 'pull the pin' the rescue machinery is irreversible. As soon as your distress is confirmed by a second satellite signal, the search for you will be under way. Bear in mind that no expense will be spared to reach you.

At present EPIRBS have a 90% false alarm rate. In one instance an SAR helicopter chased a van down one of Britain's motorways. Another time, a rescue helicopter hovered above an apartment block in Glasgow at 3 a.m. When the police finally gained access and

Figure 26 *'Global Positioning System'*

woke the sleeping inhabitants, the offending electronics were discovered on top of a wardrobe. (They were also found to have been stolen from an oil rig.)

Global Positioning System (GPS)

With 60 miles of open sea behind us and 40 miles of haze in front, I declared with some feeling, 'I wish I had a little magic box so that I could just press a button and we'd know exactly where we were!' That was in 1975.

Well, it had to happen and the little box has arrived. For those long, open crossings or trips along wilderness coastlines, there is now a small, hand-held, battery-operated piece of electronics that will pinpoint your position on land or sea to within 100 yards.

The Global Positioning System (Figure 26) works in conjunction with a number of satellites which circle round the earth in six different orbits. These satellites send out signals which are picked up by your little receiver. As long as your GPS receives the signals from at least three satellites, it can give you your longitude and latitude. The only information that it needs, and which you feed in beforehand, is your starting point, your destination and your chart datum. There is a model known as the Multichannel GPS which can receive input from a larger number of satellites. It then selects the best three signals from those offered.

We can thank the Armed Forces for the GPS. They needed an accurate system for directing long-range missiles and now it is in the public domain. So whether you're paddling in the fog of Scotland's Outer Hebrides or in the maze of Florida's Ten Thousand Islands, you will be able to pinpoint your exact position to within one metre. It will also enable you to paddle on a course to another predetermined position that you have already programmed into the machine. You can determine the speed you are paddling, how far you have already travelled and the distance between fixed points.

Don't forget to carry some spare batteries, however, make sure you can still use your chart and compass when all else fails.

The GPS will only work if the satellites are in line-of-sight, so you must be careful not to shield the signal with your body or that of anyone rafting up to you.

Its size – about that of a small transistor radio – makes it possible for the GPS to be carried in the pocket of a buoyancy aid. Some models are waterproof, while others are merely 'splashproof' and would therefore require some kind of waterproof bag or container.

Nose clip

This very important piece of equipment consists simply of a steel or plastic spring which holds and presses two rubber disc-shaped pads against both sides of the nose. Before condemning it as being only for beginners, bear in mind that without doubt in some cases sudden death has been caused by water being driven up the nose. This has either slowed or arrested the heart through a reflex action involving the vagus nerve.[3] Capsizing a kayak is not like diving into water; the forces and pressures are different. If a man pauses upside-down while rolling, the pressure is sustained; and the sudden rush of water up the nose can be very painful.

When novices are doing their initial capsize or training for rolling, the nose clip can protect the paddler from a great deal of discomfort and give him time, when upside-down, to think of the more important aspects of what he is doing. During surf acrobatics, or even while learning to surf, capsizes may come with some violence without time to take the necessary quick intake of air. If a nose clip is worn and if the mouth is kept shut this will stop an involuntary and dangerous inhalation of water through the nose.

Folding kayak trolley

The folding kayak trolley, an oft-neglected piece of equipment, can be made from a pair of small pram-like wheels attached to a folding wooden cradle, which has webbing straps allowing it to be fixed under the fore end of a kayak. It enables the kayak,

[3]W. R. Keatinge, *Survival in Cold Water*, Blackwell Scientific Publishers, 1969.

fully packed with camping gear, to be perambulated rather than portaged across long distances from loch to loch or bay to bay, perhaps avoiding dangerous headlands. If one is forced to make an unwanted landing, the trolley is readily available to take all the equipment to a different launching place, perhaps a number of miles away. When not in use it folds up, the wheels detach and it can be packed either on or under the deck.

Bilge pump

A small, hand-operated bilge pump situated behind the paddler enables the centre section of the kayak between the bulkheads to be pumped dry (in the event of a capsize with a fully loaded expedition kayak in a situation where a normal deep-water rescue would be impossible). The most popular pump in this country is the Henderson Chimp. Figure 7 on page 9 shows the position of the suction and discharge tubes.

Personal belt tow-line

Plastic kayaks, whether they are for the open sea or for white water, seldom have any provision for anchoring or carrying a tow line.

A belt tow-line is portable (Figure 27). You take it with you and use it with any boat you happen to be paddling at the time. Many personal towing systems are designed for white-water use, so if you want to use one of these from a sea kayak you might have to extend the line. This line, carried in a Velcro-fastened pouch on the belt, should incorporate a piece of shock cord. When fully opened out, the line should extend at least one boat's length from the stern of your kayak. Too long is better than too short, and you can always take up the spare length by chain-'knitting'. This can be undone quickly when you need the extra length.

Try and get a waist belt long enough to go around the outside of your buoyancy aid. The flotation foam in the jacket will effectively absorb any sudden jerks.

This belt should have some quick-release mechanism. I have occasionally seen paddlers capsize while towing from the waist; the roll attempt which follows then wraps them in their own tow line. This

is a distressing sight especially when they try and exit from the boat and find that their own tow line is preventing this.

I prefer old-fashioned rope. Some tow lines, I have discovered, can have a mind of their own, especially those made from narrow webbing. It looks good and it's colourful, but in high winds and up-draughts this thin webbing can take on an aerodynamic property and fly about in the air like some demented snake. The trouble then is that the moment the wind drops, the tape falls in limp coils around the necks of all those nearby.

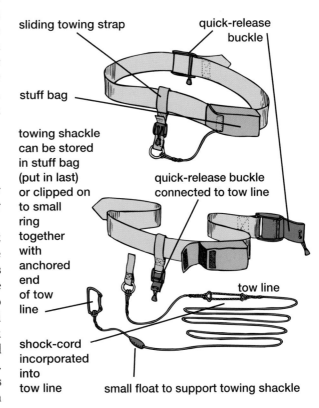

Figure 27 *Personal belt tow-line*

Fixed ballast

There are often times when we could all do with that little extra stability. Some expedition kayaks, when completely empty, can be very unwieldy in strong winds. Some paddlers may feel they are too light for their kayak; others may have bought a kayak which now feels a little unstable. Potential paddlers may look longingly at the beautiful lines of a particular kayak, only to be informed by friends that it's unstable. However, if the kayak is made from fibreglass all these problems can be solved.

I once needed extra stability while I was involved in some filming from my kayak. I found that the only way to get continuous head-on footage of kayaks being paddled towards me was to be towed backwards, during which time I panned the camera across from one paddler to another. Now, when seas are rough and the equipment is expensive, this pastime is anything but restful on the nerves. What I needed was:

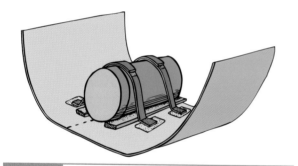

Figure 28 *Fixed ballast – situated immediately behind your seat*

(a) some kind of ballast that was so fixed that it could not slide about;

(b) something portable;

(c) something that would not affect the handling of the boat;

(d) something to provide the type of stability found in those little round-bottomed toys which are weighted so that when they are pushed over they immediately rock back into the upright position again.

My solution worked a treat and it really is simplicity itself. All you need is a small round plastic container (a BDH bottle which is four inches in diameter by eight inches is ideal). I filled the container with small, chopped-up pieces of lead pipe. I fixed two thin 8-inch strips of wood to the bottom of the hull, parallel to one another, at either side of the centre support. This formed a cradle for the container. The two strips of wood also held in place two thin webbing straps which could be passed over the container and fastened by Velcro. I merely placed the weighted container on the cradle and fastened the straps. The result was a small, heavy, localised and immovable ballast weight.

When paddling the kayak I found the effect of all this quite remarkable. Although I could still lean my kayak right over on to its side in order to perform the various strokes, the weight, which was fixed dead centre, was constantly trying to bring the kayak upright again. The further I leant the kayak over, the more it tried to pull me back again.

Depending upon what you are doing and how much ballast you need, you can reduce the weight of your container by replacing some of the lead with sand. If you are transporting your kayak to the water alone, you might be wise to carry your boat and the ballast separately. Remember, your ballast may weigh 20–30 lbs.

For those who have a suspect Eskimo roll the fixed ballast is a godsend.

The Eskimos often needed ballast in their empty, large-volume, load-carrying kayaks. For this purpose they used smooth, rounded stones. This worked well most of the time, but the kayak could not be rolled, and the paddler could not lean over too far.

Basic strokes and techniques

2

When I first sat down to write this book in 1974, it seemed that most people took up sea 'canoeing' after first having been introduced to the sport on inland waters. Most seemed to have had the advantage of some kind of basic instruction in the use of the paddle before they ever wandered down a beach or clambered over seaweed. If they were not fortunate enough to have had qualified instruction first hand, they probably gained their expertise by mixing with the 'right people' so to speak – by attaching themselves to an experienced friend or group.

Being a lazy writer, this made things very easy for me. I assumed a pre-experience on the part of my readers, and geared my passages on the basic strokes accordingly.

However, it has become evident over the years that more and more people wishing to experience the delights of paddling on open water now come to it directly, with no paddling background. Because of this they require instruction and guidance as complete beginners.

In the following pages, therefore, I have adjusted the text on basic strokes and techniques to include, as far as is possible, all the fundamental information. With the same aim in mind I have tried to follow the procedures, content and format of my basic practical outdoor classes.

The basic strokes

A kayak is a water vehicle powered by a person wielding a paddle. Every movement of the craft, in whatever direction, is due to the paddle being held in a certain position and moved in a certain manner. We call these manoeuvres the *basic strokes*. The term can be misleading, because it invites the reader to suppose that there are other strokes which are more advanced; whereas, in fact, when we refer to *advanced strokes* we are really only talking about the basic strokes performed in a more professional manner, in a smooth sequence, or in a more demanding or 'advanced' situation.

If you can, take the time to watch an experienced paddler on the water. Notice how the strokes merge. One fluid movement flows into the next, and the paddler appears to be at one with the craft and the paddle. To reach this high level of competence, however, all these movements must be broken down into their separate components. It is these separate components which are referred to as the basic strokes.

In the following pages some of the strokes may look daunting; however, they will soon become second nature to you. Your first hesitant attempts will soon become confident and productive, while your forward paddle stroke will develop power and rhythm. You will become aware that you no longer have to *think* about doing the strokes; your only thought will be of the *conditions* in which they are done. Your movements, although founded on the basic strokes, will become more complex. You will lean without thought and move your paddle instinctively without hesitation. Your movements will become economical and you will *no longer get tired*. Your grounding in the basic strokes will have paid off.

The correct paddle length

This is dealt with in detail on page 31 but as a general rule, if you stand behind the paddle with its bottom blade next to your toes and reach up, and if you can just hook your fingers over the top of the blade without stretching your body or your arm then the length is about right for you. The same size paddle would be suitable for surfing and white water. True sea-touring paddles can be anything from 9 in to 1 ft longer than a general-purpose paddle.

Left- or right-hand control

To find the correct control position, stand with the driving face of the lower blade facing your feet (Figure 29).

Now look at the upper blade. If the power face is on the right, then it is a *right-hand control* for *right-*

Figure 29 | Left- or right-hand control

Figure 30 | Basic paddling position

Figure 31 | Simple paddle control exercise

handed paddlers. If the power face is looking the opposite way, then it is a *left-hand control* for *left-handed paddlers.*

The basic paddling position

Whether you are paddling forwards or backwards, or performing one of the many different paddling manoeuvres, the paddle is held in what is known as the *basic paddling position.* In this book, all instructions and illustrations assume that the paddler is right handed and the paddles are set for right-hand control.

Hold your paddle with your hands slightly more than shoulder-width apart (Figure 30). Your palms should be on top of the shaft with your thumbs underneath. Your hands should be equidistant from the centre of the shaft. The knuckles of your right hand are in line with the top edge of the right-hand blade. The power face is looking backwards. If your shaft is oval towards one end only, then that will be the grip for your right hand.

Now try this simple exercise (Figure 31). Hold your paddle at arms' length. Grasp it firmly in your right (controlling) hand, whilst leaving your left hand relaxed.

Drop your right wrist so that the knuckles are

facing back over your shoulder. Do this several times, allowing your paddle to rotate through 90° so that the left power face also faces to the rear. I have heard this movement likened to twisting the throttle on a motor cycle.

Remember that your right, controlling hand moves the shaft by dropping the wrist, bending the elbow, or doing both at the same time. *The shaft never moves inside the fingers of the right hand.* In other words, no matter what weird contortions you may get the paddle into, once you return your hands to the basic paddling position the paddle should be ready for the next stroke. You should not have to twist the shaft back into its correct position.

The paddle blade

To make recognition easy, all the various parts of a paddle are distinguished by name. To help confuse the novice, however, some of the parts have more than one name! Familiarity will soon dispel any confusion and in Figure 32:1 I have named those parts that are referred to in the text.

THE LEADING EDGE

In the following pages I make repeated reference to the fact that the leading edge of the paddle blade must be *high* for certain manoeuvres. If the paddle is moved through the water sideways, with its leading edge high, the blade will act in a manner similar to that of a water-ski. It will stay on the surface or at a chosen depth – but only for the duration of its forward movement. For example, plane your extended paddle flat along the surface of the water. Keep the leading edge high and the blade will skim across the water like a flat stone. Tilt the leading edge slightly *down*, and the blade will *stop* abruptly and *sink*.

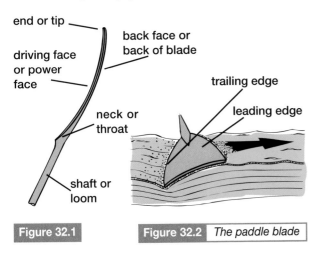

end or tip

back face or back of blade

driving face or power face

trailing edge

neck or throat

leading edge

shaft or loom

Figure 32.1

Figure 32.2 | *The paddle blade*

You will see from Figure 32.2 that once the leading edge is high the blade becomes aerodynamic, and like an aeroplane's wing takes on a climbing angle and supplies *lift* and thus *support* for the paddler's weight.

It will soon become apparent to you as you perform some of the basic strokes that a slight alteration in the angle of the paddle will give you support as well as propulsion. As an example, forward paddling with a backward tilt to the blade's upper edge

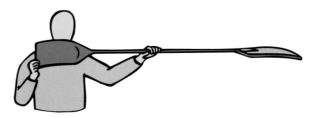

Figure 32.3 | *Extended paddle position*

will give you enough support to allow you to lean over from side to side on every stroke. *All strokes should be supportive as well as propulsive.*

Extended paddle position

As a matter of course, it was quite natural for the Eskimo hunter to slide his hands along to one end of his paddle, thereby gaining extra length and leverage to help with the variety of strokes and braces which he used as part of his daily work.

The modern paddler will also often find an advantage in the added leverage gained by holding the paddle in what is now known as the *extended paddle position*. It will help to give you confidence when practising any of the supporting or bracing strokes, and it is especially useful for such manoeuvres as turning a kayak in high winds. There are a number of Eskimo rolls which require the paddle to be held in the extended position.

Figure 32:3 shows the extended paddle position on the left side. The *cupped palm* of the right hand is supporting the *lower corner* of the held blade.

The left hand is a *forearm's distance* from the neck of the held blade. The knuckles of the left hand are facing *backwards*.

The outer blade has its *driving face* looking *down*, *parallel* to the surface of the water.

You will notice that when this stroke is applied on the *right side*, the held blade will have its driving face towards you.

Edging, leaning and the knee-hang

Kayaks built for use on open water do not turn easily. You will be relieved to know that this has little to do with your level of ability. The answer is really quite simple: *sea kayaks are designed to run straight.* To make turning easier, you must lean the boat over on to its side so as to place the more manoeuvrable part of the hull (i.e. the gunwale) under the water. There are two ways of doing this; edging or tilting, and leaning.

EDGING OR TILTING

This is the most controlled method of getting the boat over on to its side, and it is therefore kinder on the nerves of the novice. Keep your body as perpen-

| Figure 33.1 | *Edging or tilting* |

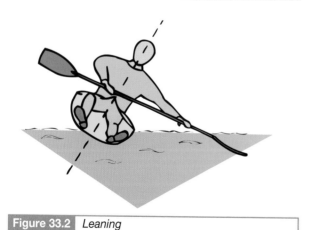

| Figure 33.2 | *Leaning* |

Note: the paddler's right knee is raised, enabling him to knee-hang on the right side

dicular as possible, flex your hips, keep your balance and dip the gunwale into the water.

The high-side knee, in Figure 33:1 the right knee, is raised and pressed upwards, either against the knee-braces or underneath the cockpit coaming – hence the expression 'knee hanging'. You should feel quite stable when you do this, and once you get used to keeping your centre of gravity over the kayak you will be surprised how far over you can dip the gunwale without losing your balance.

LEANING

This is when you allow your upper-body lean to follow the angle of the lean of the kayak (Figure 33:2). The paddler and the boat become one unit, very much like when a cyclist goes round a corner. Because your weight is off-balance you need the support that the paddle gives during the stroke.

LIFTING AND CARRYING YOUR KAYAK

The easiest way to carry your kayak from one place to another is to persuade a friend to help you. One of you holds the rear, one holds the front toggle and off you go. Always try and leave the awkward, heavy rear end for your friend. If your kayak is well balanced, you might find it less of a strain if you carry it by yourself. I know I certainly do.

For a right handed lift, stand next to the boat's point of balance. This should be an inch or so in front of the seat. With your legs slightly apart, your back straight and the bow to your left, reach down and take hold of the coaming with your right hand, palm uppermost. Using your legs to help you lift, hoist the kayak up your knee and then onto your shoulder (fig. 34:1A). Because you lift the boat slightly in front of the centre, the stern will remain supported on the ground (fig. 34:1B). Hitch the boat slightly forward until you find its point of balance and the stern pivots up. Bring the paddle up to your hand with a deft movement of your left foot (fig. 34:1C). The kayak should rest comfortably on your shoulder and be easy to carry (fig. 34:1D).

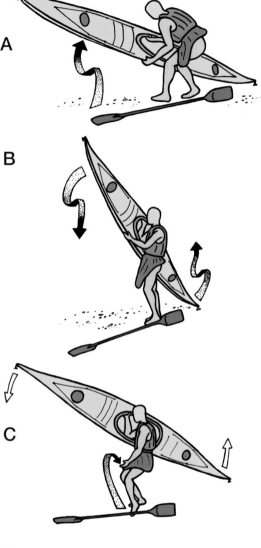

Loading onto a vehicle

This is much easier than it first appears because you are not going to try to lift the boat all in one go.

In the absence of those roof rack cradles that have those tiny roll-on wheels, you will have to do what I do and use a piece of old carpet. You will need this piece of carpet to protect the back of your car. The pile side faces down. This is important, as the burlap backing will damage your vehicle's paint work.

Lift or carry your kayak until you can rest the bow on the roofrack or the trunk of your car (fig. 34.2A). Then walk to the stern and lift it high in the air. Now push the kayak forward into position on the roofrack (fig. 34.2B). Fasten the kayak onto the roofrack with ropes or straps, and then secure the bow and stern so that the boat cannot swing about (bungee elastics are not strong enough to hold a sea kayak down on a moving vehicle). Do not forget your piece of carpet. You can stand on it while you get changed.

Note: If your kayak is made of polyethylene, move the bars of your roofrack as far apart as possible. This is especially important in hot climates, where the heat can soften the plastic, thus causing your kayak to sag into something resembling a banana!

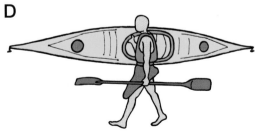

| Figure 34.1 | *Lifting and carrying your kayak step by step* |

| Figure 34.2 | *Loading on to a vehicle* |

Figure 35 | *Launching from a flat beach.*
Spot the car keys!

Launching from a flat beach

This is usually quite easy, especially in a glassfibre or plastic kayak. Watch and judge how far the waves swill up the beach. Choose a lull, climb into the cockpit, and position yourself while the boat rests on the sand. Secure the spray cover *with the release strap on the outside*. The next wave washing up the beach should put enough water under your hull to enable you to push off and paddle into open water. With experience you will be tackling quite large waves. When that day arrives, do not raise your paddle above your head; rather keep on paddling straight through with your head down.

On a very flat beach it is possible to sit in your kayak ready for the big moment only to find that the sea appears to have receded. Should this occur, there are some who advocate knuckling down towards the water using a hand on either side of the kayak. Unfortunately my arms are rather short, and when I clench my fists the knuckles do not reach the sand together. I prefer to use an upright paddle on one side and, by leaning over, put my flat palm on the other. Then by a series of lifts and ungainly forward jerks I make my awkward way to the water's edge, leaving a trail in the sand reminiscent of that of a one-armed mermaid (Figure 35).

Launching from rocks

Taking care not to fall as you carry your kayak over the slippery rocks, find some water that is deep enough to float your boat clear. Watch out that the surge doesn't lift it up and settle it down on a sharp rock. Now, suppose you are positioned on the left side of the kayak (Figure 36).

1 Lay the paddle across the deck just behind the cockpit and across a convenient rock, thus forming a linking bridge.
2 Hook your right-hand thumb around the paddle shaft while your fingers hold on to the cockpit rim.
3 Grasp the shaft with your left hand. Keeping your weight mainly on this hand, sit on the shaft almost where it meets the kayak's deck, and lift your legs into the cockpit. Straighten your legs, then slide yourself on to the seat.
4 Transfer the paddle to the front of the cockpit or a paddle park and adjust the spray cover *with the release strap on the outside*.

Note: This is also the method you would use to launch from a low floating dock or a sloping concrete ramp. Another method of launching from a shallow dock is to get into the seated position. Merely sit on the dock. Put both feet in the centre of the boat and lower yourself onto the seat, keeping all of your weight on your arms (figure 36.1).

When disembarking, do this in reverse; but as you leave the boat and stand up remember to hook your paddle into the cockpit in case the kayak drifts away. Many good paddlers have prized their stiff limbs from the cockpit, straightened up and stretched with

Figure 36 | *Method of entry from rocks or landing stage*

relief, only to turn round and see their boat bobbing in about 5 ft. of water just out of paddle reach.

Launching from a high dock

This launch involves climbing into your boat from a high dock. The high dock support probably needs more care than any other method of entry. You will find that the boat is too low down for you to steady it with either your paddle or hand. Personally, I always try to get someone to hold my boat when I do a high entry. First make a little test. Sit on the edge of the dock with your legs dangling into the cockpit. If you can place the soles of your feet into the cockpit, then you should be alright – any higher and you could finish up in the water.

Sit on the edge of the dock facing the bow. Prevent the kayak from drifting by placing your feet in the cockpit. Twist sideways towards the dock, keeping your weight on your hands. Roll over onto your stomach so that your behind is suspended over your cockpit. Keeping your feet in the centre of the boat, bend your knees and lower yourself gingerly onto the seat. Your weight should be supported by your hands on the dock (see Figure 36:2). If your kayak has a small cockpit, you will have to sit on the rear deck before sliding into the boat.

Getting out next to a high dock can also be tricky. I usually position myself as close to the side of the dock as possible and keep my paddle fastened to the boat. With a deft piece of balancing, I place both hands on the back of my cockpit coaming and totally unsupported, I slide out and sit on the rear deck. With the speed of light, I bring the nearest hand onto the dock for support. I then hoist my body upwards and twist so that I'm lying on my stomach, all the time keeping one foot in the boat as an anchor.

Capsize drill or the wet exit (Figure 37)

I tell everyone that kayaking on the sea is a dry sport – and, unless you are involved in surfing or some such pursuit, it usually is. You should, however, resign yourself to a couple of capsizes during your learning period. I remember that I was somewhat apprehensive before my first capsize, upset by the thought of getting stuck in the cockpit. In fact, this turned out to be a groundless fear: the big problem is actually *staying in* the cockpit. Without thigh braces and padding you will fall out of the boat. It is diffi-

Figure 36.1 | *Another way to launch from a low dock*

Figure 36.2 | *Launching from a high dock can be tricky*

cult to convince novices of this.

PREPARATION

For your first attempt choose a piece of calm, sheltered water and enlist a friend for moral support. Unless you are lucky enough to practice this in a swimming pool you should wear some kind of flotation device. You should not be eating. Remember, *chewing-gum and water sports do not mix!* To prevent water from getting up their nose, some people prefer to wear a nose clip. Without a nose clip you will soon discover that breathing out slowly through your nose will prevent the water from going in.

THE EXIT

1 *Make sure that the spray-skirt release-strap is on the outside.*

2 Take a breath and capsize. Now let go of the paddle.

3 Sit still until you are completely upside-down.

4 Locate the release-strap on your spray skirt. It doesn't matter whether or not you can open your eyes; most people find the strap by groping for it.

5 Pull the strap forward towards the bows, then upwards to clear the coaming (Figure 37A).

6 *Lean forwards.* Place both hands behind you on either side of the boat (Figure 37B).

7 Straighten your legs, then push up and away in the direction of the small arrow (Figure 37C).

Once on the surface, grab the boat's toggle and then retrieve the paddle. *Take the boat with you while you do this.* If you hold on to the nearest lifting toggle while you swim to the paddle you will find the boat easy to tow; it will also help to support your weight. Remember: if you leave the boat even for an instant the wind may blow it away faster than you can swim after it.

It is natural for you to feel some slight lack of confidence prior to your first wet exit. By all means do the first one without the spray skirt in place. In this case, bang three times on the upturned hull with your hands before allowing yourself to make the exit. Hanging upside-down for these few added seconds will give you confidence so that you will not panic when you need to remove the spray deck. It will also be a signal to your friendly onlooker that

Figure 37 | *A wet exit – Capsize Drill (or how to fall out!)*

you have not expired and are in fact in complete control of the situation.

Remember: the first movement of your exit is like taking off a pair of trousers – you lean forwards. (Nobody leans backwards when they remove their pants!) Do not practice this after a full meal.

EMPTYING OUT

Stand in about a foot of water and flip your kayak onto its right side. If you do this quickly you shouldn't scoop too much water into the boat. Now lift the bow upward and twist the boat upside down. Most of the water should drain out. Any water that is left in can be removed by using your pump or sponge.

If you swamp your kayak but manage to swim it to shore, do not try and pull the boat onto land while it is full of water; the pressure will probably split the seams. To prevent this, when the boat is in about a foot of water, turn it onto its side. This should drain

| Figure 38 | *Emptying your kayak* |

out most of the water. Now with your friend supporting the other end, turn the boat completely upside down and see-saw it until it is empty.

The Forward Paddling Stroke

The paddle stroke we use for touring on the sea, based on the traditional racing stroke that was used before the advent of the 'wing' paddle (see Chapter 5). The stroke was an art form itself and was developed over many years as the most efficient method of propelling a kayak forwards. In its purest form however, it has only limited use when paddling on the open sea. As Figure 39 shows, the paddler leans aggressively forwards. His back is unsupported. His right arm pushes forwards and will finish up straight out at maximum stretch with his right shoulder twisted forwards. During the stroke his right hand is relaxed, perhaps open, the fingers facing forwards. His left arm pulls the paddle backwards, bringing the blade close to the hull.

Note the height of the upper blade. This is a sure

| Figure 39 | *The Forward Paddle Stroke showing complete breakdown of movements* |

beam-wind catcher. The lower blade is purely propulsive, giving hardly any support in rough conditions.

Sea kayaking method

The stroke may have to be continued over many hours, so it is as well to get comfortable. Sit in a relaxed manner with your feet on the footrest. In rough conditions you should wedge your knees up underneath the cockpit coaming, but for normal flat-water paddling the legs can be almost straight (Figure 40:1).

The back should be supported in any way which suits the individual. I prefer a wide, padded backstrap so that the lower half of my body is braced between the footrest and the backrest. The body should be upright and curved slightly forwards. *Never lean backwards.*

The Forward Paddle Stroke really consists of two parts, both of which occur simultaneously. They are the *pulling phase* and the *pushing phase.*

THE STARTING POSITION
Hold the paddle with your right hand at a height approximately level with your ear. Your lower (left) hand places the power blade in the water, as far forwards as is comfortably possible.

THE STROKE – PUSHING PHASE
Begin by moving your hip and the right side of your

Figure 40.1

Figure 40.2

Figure 40.3

Figure 40.4

chest forwards. At the same time, push your right hand forwards at eye-level, following the line of the gunwale. Avoid crossing your hand over towards the centre line of the boat. During this forward push the paddle shaft is not gripped tightly but is cradled in the curved hollow between the thumb and forefinger. The fingers are relaxed and curved slightly forwards. With your *wrist slightly dropped*, push the shaft by the *upper part of your palm* (Figures 40.1 and 40.2).

THE STROKE – PULLING PHASE

During the pulling phase the shaft is held firmly by the left hand. As this lower hand starts to travel backwards, the grip changes to facilitate a 'pulling' action with hooked rather than clenched fingers and a *relaxed thumb*. This grip change, combined with a hip rotation, ensures that the wrist remains in an almost straight line in relation to the arm (Figure 42.3). Failure to relax the grip and *swing the body* will cause the wrist to bend to its limit. This is dangerous and could cause an inflammatory condition of the tendons known as tenosynovitis (otherwise known as the 'kiss of death' to paddling!). The action of tightening and relaxing the hands 'milks' fresh oxygenated blood to the muscles and helps to prevent any tendency towards cramp.

THE TRANSITION

Once the lower hand is pulled back to a position level with the hip, the upper arm is straight and the body is fully rotated forwards from the waist. The upper, forwards hand – with the paddle – is brought straight down to coincide with the *rotation of the body* and the lower blade being clipped from the water (Figure 40.4).

In the instant before the right-hand blade touches the water, it is turned through 90° into the correct angle for the catch, by raising the left arm so that from the shoulder to the elbow, it is parallel to the water. In this manner the fully extended feathered blade will be presented almost vertically to the water. If the shaft is oval at the handgrip, this backward flick of the left hand will cause the paddle to fall into the correct position due to the cradling shape of the palm. However this will not happen if the paddle is gripped too tightly.

This pulling phase is the most important in the

whole stroke cycle. It is vital that the *body* and arm are fully rotated forwards. The paddle must be dipped into the water cleanly, at boat speed and without a splash, in a position immediately outside the wave that runs from the bow.

The most productive part of the pulling phase is the time during which the immersed blade covers the first third of its backward movement. It is important, therefore, that the paddle blade is placed well forwards. It is then propelled backwards with a vigorous pulling movement involving the shoulder and the hip muscles – indeed the whole of the upper torso. This is also referred to as 'upper-body rotation'. The pulling action ends when the lower hand is level with the hips. The speed with which this pulling blade is lifted from the water is governed by the rotation of your body.

The paddle is placed further out from the side of the hull than it is during the racing stroke, giving the stroke a slight sweep outwards rather than a downwards plunge. The upper blade presents a more acute and therefore more favourable angle to any beam wind, with hardly any likelihood of the paddle being snatched or twisted from the upper hand by the wind. Moreover, because the paddle action is lower, it is less tiring on the arms and shoulders.

Opening and closing alternate hands during the stroke cycle allows fresh blood and oxygen to circulate into the muscles, thus preventing cramp. It also helps to keep the hands from becoming numb in cold weather. Pressing on the footrest during the stroke cycle does the same for the muscles in the feet, legs and thighs.

When worn by the paddler the kayak is propelled not only by the movement of the trunk and arms, but by the *whole body right to the tips of the toes.*

Paddling a kayak without a firm footrest makes it necessary for the occupant to brace with the thighs, without a firm support for the feet. This is inefficient from the point of view of propulsion, and causes bad circulation, 'pins and needles' and, eventually, severe cramp.

Paddlers should be able to alter their forward stroke to suit prevailing conditions, such as an approaching danger, an adverse wind or tide race, or a need for speed.

Remember, the paddling effort is not constant when you are in a following sea (Figure 96:2 on page 141). As the wave passes underneath, ease your efforts; build them up again when the boat is in the trough; and aim to reach maximum when the hull is on the face of the wave slope. Ease off again as the crest is reached and passes underneath the boat.

In calm conditions, as a novice you should be able to paddle three or four miles without any problems. If you grip the paddles too tightly however, blisters may form inside your thumb. You may find four to five miles an ordeal at first, but after a few months of practice and if conditions are calm, you should be able to paddle between twenty and twenty five miles quite easily.

Proficient paddlers can usually cope with distances of between 12 to 30 miles (depending on such things as age, general fitness and muscle mass). Advanced paddlers should achieve significantly in excess of this. However, all these distances may be increased if a strong wind is favourable, or cut down to a mere couple of miles – even for an advanced paddler – if conditions are bad.

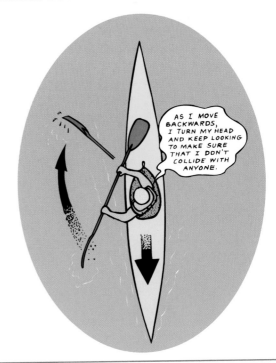

As I move backwards, I turn my head and keep looking to make sure that I don't collide with anyone.

Figure 41.1 *Basic reverse paddling*

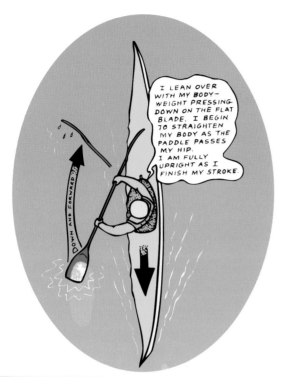

Figure 41.2 *Advanced reverse paddling*

Reverse paddling

There will be many occasions on which the quickest way to position your kayak will be by moving backwards. For instance, one of your group may capsize behind you. Turning around in fresh winds can be a time-consuming business. Fortunately, some vigorous reverse paddling will get you into position faster and enable you to give more immediate help.

When inexperienced paddlers propel themselves backwards they tend to place the paddle blades in the water vertically – or, in other words, in the 'slicing' position. This is unproductive and gives the paddler no stability (Figure 41:1).

When reverse paddling in rough seas the stroke should give you support as well as propulsion. For it to do this, the *back of the blade* should be presented to the water as *flat* as possible and at an angle of about 45° to the side of the boat (Figure 41:2). With practice you will be able to lean over as you press down and present the flat blade to the water. At the same time you should thrust down and forwards onto the foot pedal on the same side as the stroke. You then

quickly transfer your weight onto the opposite side and repeat the stroke, now pressing down on the other foot. What it really amounts to is that you will finish up paddling backwards by using a series of *reverse sweep strokes*. In this way you will be supporting yourself as well as propelling yourself backwards. You will find that the power you exert is much greater and the stability much more reassuring than if you were to present the blade vertically to the water. A strong powerful reverse stroke takes a good deal of practice to perfect. Use this lean and your *body weight* to exert pressure *downwards* then *forwards* during the stroke.

Warning: over the years I have watched paddlers drive themselves backwards, with considerable violence, into other kayaks, speedboats, the heavy beams of wooden jetties, and concrete breakwaters. In the light of these expensive and often painful mishaps may I offer this advice: *when travelling backwards, look backwards!*

Stopping

Once, during a practice session out at sea, I remember hanging upside-down waiting for an Eskimo rescue (Figure 79.1, pp. 116-17). The sea was choppy and I had an unfamiliar partner. Time dragged by – as it tends to when you are holding your breath. After what seemed like a long time I am afraid I lost faith and dog-paddled up to the surface to get a gulp of air. I was aware of a kayak's bow flashing past my eyes as my head broke the surface. The pointed front end of my rescuer's kayak went straight through the deck of my boat in a position level with my knees. Positioning himself for the rescue had taken longer than he thought. His concern for me and the sight of my upturned hull then spurred him into high-speed action. In retrospect, perhaps we should have practised emergency stops *before* the Eskimo rescue!

At full speed you will not be moving at much more than 5 mph. However, the combined weight of you and your kayak gives the mass considerable momentum. To stop yourself moving forwards it will take *four* paddle strokes and a surprising amount of effort. The Stopping Stroke is identical to the stroke that is used for reverse paddling. If you happen to be practising in a short river boat, use short strokes to minimise any turning effect you may generate. You will not have this problem in a long sea boat.

Your first try at stopping should be done with the boat upright. The paddle blade is placed vertically in the water behind you, at an angle of about 45° to the kayak's hull (Figure 42:1). As the blade bites the water, push it forwards against the pressure of the water then quickly change your stroke over to the other side and do the same again.

The first two strokes should stop you moving forwards. The second two should have you moving in the *opposite direction*. Do not worry if your first attempts send showers of water over your bow as your paddle fails to bite the water. Keep practising until you can stop quickly without looking at the paddle blades and you are able to use your body-weight to press downwards on the flat paddle blade (Figure 42:2).

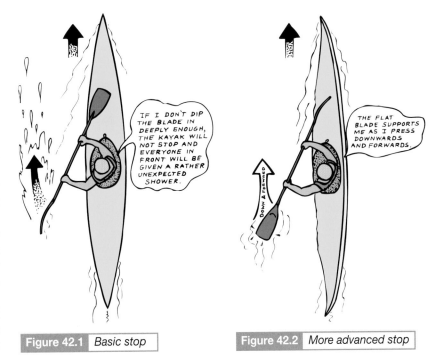

Figure 42.1   *Basic stop*

Figure 42.2   *More advanced stop*

The Forward Sweep Stroke

(Bow Sweep Turn)

FUNCTION

The Forward Sweep Stroke can be used to turn either a stationary kayak or one which is moving forwards. It may be done either to avoid obstacles or as a corrective stroke.

The Forward Sweep is one of the easiest of all kayaking techniques and yet it is perhaps the most

Figure 43.1   *The Forward Sweep Stroke or Bow Sweep Stroke*

Figure 43.2 *Skim the back of the blade across the surface to return the paddle to its starting position*

important. Because it appears to be an uncomplicated stroke, many paddlers tend to perform it in a slip-shod manner. If your technique is bad, you will be wasting energy simply because it will take more separate paddle movements for you to obtain the desired result. Novices usually prefer to sit up straight during their first attempts at the Forward Sweep. In short, rockered kayaks, this is all that is necessary for a good turn. In a sea kayak the stroke cannot be performed successfully unless you tilt the boat over on to its gunwale and thus cancel out the effects of a straight or pronounced keel. To do this your body must lean as well.

METHOD
Lean forwards. The paddle is placed as near to the bow as possible (Figure 43:1). The blade should be positioned so that the top edge is angled slightly outwards. As you start to sweep out, angle the blade even more, *keeping its leading edge high*. At the same time tilt the kayak. Sweep the paddle out and around in a semi-circle towards the stern. *Rotate your body and pull the paddle round with your arm straight*. As you pull with your arm, push forwards with the foot on that side.

It is the angle of the blade that will provide lift and give you support. Your greatest angle of lean, therefore, will be during the first half of the stroke. Once your paddle passes the half-way mark, your body can start to come upright. Finish the stroke when the paddle is at an angle of 45° to the stern.

THE RECOVERY
The method of returning the paddle to its starting position is almost as important as the main stroke. Your most vulnerable time is when your body is twisted round and the paddle is closest to the stern. To prevent any chance of a capsize, do not clear the water completely with the paddle when you remove it. With a forward rotation of the knuckles, flip the paddle over on to its back face and return it to the bow by skimming it along the surface. During the return the blade should hardly touch the water, but the paddle is ready to apply a low brace support at any time. If this return phase is done correctly it is possible to maintain a considerable angle of tilt throughout the whole stroke cycle (Figure 43:2).

EXTENDED PADDLE POSITION
If you are turning a long, straight-keeled kayak in a high wind, you will find you have more success if you take advantage of the extra leverage afforded by the extended paddle position (Figure 32:3).

Correcting course

There may be times when you find it difficult to maintain a straight course due to a side wind causing you to 'weather-cock' (i.e. swing your bow into the wind). To correct this tiresome problem, alternate your forward paddling stroke with a sweep stroke on the windward side. As you push your foot down on the stroke side, remember to *knee-hang* on the other (page 52).

The Reverse Sweep Stroke

FUNCTION
The reverse sweep stroke is used to turn a stationary kayak in a backwards direction. You may find it easier to turn your kayak by means of the reverse sweep than by using a forward sweep stroke. This is especially true where you have a strong wind pushing against your bow.

As a novice, you may be a little reluctant to lean over, however, as with the forward sweep stroke you will again be leaning your straight keeled kayak over on its side. In this way the curved gunwale once more acts as the new keel and thus makes turning easier.

Figure 43.3 *The Reverse Sweep Stroke Combine this stroke with the Forward Sweep Stroke to pivot the kayak in a complete circle.*

METHOD
In figure 43:3 the stroke is illustrated on the right side. This will turn the kayak in a *clockwise* direction.

Twist your body around, edging the kayak slightly. Place the outer paddle blade with the back of the blade downwards, at an angle of 30–45 degrees to the rear of the kayak. The knee on the opposite side of the stroke is hooked under the cockpit coaming (knee-hanging). With the paddle in this position, you should be able to put your weight onto the blade. As you sweep it forwards, the leading edge is slightly angled upwards. Press downwards and increase the angle during the short distance the blade travels forwards. Reach out as far as you can. Think of the stroke as a sweeping outrigger. The pressure on the back of the moving blade will allow you to remain leaning out, and put a considerable amount of weight into the downwards and forward push. Throughout the stroke, you should be pressing hard on the lower footbrace. I describe it to my students as pushing the kayak round with the lower foot. It is important that you are sitting upright again as soon as the paddle starts to draw level with your body i.e. when the paddle gets into a position at right angles to the boat's hull.

Do not be tempted to continue the stroke into a front quadrant as there is no support for the blade in this position.

This is a very powerful stroke but the key to its success in rough conditions is due solely to the support angle of the blade as it is presented to the water.

SUPPORT OR RECOVERY STROKES

The moment beginners realise that a capsize is imminent, they instinctively drop their paddle and clutch the sides of their boat. This is a natural movement, but sadly not the correct one. They think, mistakenly, that the kayak is the only solid thing in a moving, watery, unstable world. It is in fact the *paddle* that would have been their means of support; and it is the area of the paddle blade, pressed on to the water, that would have prevented their capsize.

The Stationary High Brace

Aim: to recover the balance of the kayak from a potential capsize situation.

To gain confidence, the student should first hold the paddle in the extended paddle position, *driving face down*. He then leans over *until he is off balance* (Figure 44.2). Only then should he bring the paddle down smartly on to the surface of the water. As he feels the capsize halted by the paddle blade he can flick the kayak back into the upright position. At the same time, with a motor-cycle throttle-movement forwards, the blade is turned through 90° and is sliced upwards out of the water.

Figure 44.1 *The Stationary High Brace in normal paddle position*

Figure 44.2 *The Stationary High Brace in extended paddle position*

Figure 45.1 *The Sculling Brace (sculling for support)*

Another method of bracing the kayak is merely to lay the extended paddle blade on the surface of the water. I tell my students to make a depth-charge noise by pulling the blade suddenly and violently downwards. The blade hardly sinks at all but the resulting 'plat-oosh' sound and the sudden halt of the paddle's downward motion let them feel the pressure build-up under the blade so they know that they are getting the support that they need from the paddle.

With a small amount of practice you should be able to lean the hull over until about 2 inches of your spray skirt is underwater. Eventually you will be dipping your face in the water but a wet spray skirt is enough to allow you to move on to the next stage.

The paddle is now held in the normal paddling position: *the driving face is still looking downwards.* The upper wrist is tilted backwards with the palm facing upwards. The best results are achieved by starting the downward stroke slightly forwards of centre and then striking downwards and backwards (Figure 44.1).

The Stationary Low Brace

Slight corrections to balance, such as are needed when you are at rest in an unstable boat or bracing into a small wave, can be achieved by presenting the *back of the blade* to the water. This is known as the Low Brace. During the downward push of the stroke the knuckles are facing the water. Once the boat has been steadied, the submerged paddle blade is taken

from the water by rolling the knuckles backwards in the 'throttle' movement.

The Sculling Brace

The aim of the Sculling Brace (also known as 'sculling for support') is to *steady* or *hold the kayak in a controlled lean* at any angle. This means that, no matter what the condition of the sea around you, your kayak can be held in a state of continued support. If the threat is prolonged – as in for example a tide race or in the hurricane blast generated by a nearby helicopter – the defensive angle can be maintained by sculling into the oncoming waves or wind.

If you are knocked or blown over you will find that this brace can bring you upright again.

Figure 45.2 *The Elbow Scull (confidence exercise showing the 'Knee-Hang')*

Figure 45.3 *The Sculling Brace (paddle held in the extended position*

You will see in Figure 45.1 that it is the *power face* which is angled *downwards*. It is the continual *climbing action* that keeps the blade near the surface and thus provides the necessary support. All the supporting power is supplied by the arm and hand on the side of the bracing stroke.

To prove to yourself which is the controlling hand, try resting the paddle shaft in the crook of your elbow – I call this 'Elbow Sculling' (Figure 45.2). You will discover now that during the stroke your upper hand was merely *supporting* the shaft. If you find that the blade begins to sink and your support is lost, it is either because your paddle angle is too steep or you have lost the planing angle on the driving face of the supporting blade.

For greater leverage and support the paddle can be held in the *extended paddle position* (Figure 45.3). With a little practice you will be able to scull with your head laying on the surface of the water. In order to keep their centre of gravity low during the stroke, some paddlers find it helpful to lean back on to the rear deck.

The Paddle Brace

Probably the most important sea kayaking technique, if we exclude an extremely strong forward paddling stroke, is the Paddle Brace. This is simply the ability to sit parallel to a breaking wave and stay upright, i.e. to not capsize. Once it is mastered, one's whole attitude towards bad weather and towards fol-

lowing and breaking seas out in deep water becomes much more controlled and philosophical.

THE LOW BRACE
This stroke is of more use when waves are smaller and less violent. Find yourself a piece of safe, sheltered beach and have a companion near at hand, even if they only sit on the shore and watch.

Paddle out a few yards and sit sideways on to a small breaking wave. Hold the paddle in the Low Brace position on the side of the approaching wave (Figure 46.1). As the wave strikes the side of your

Figure 46.1 *The Low Brace on to a small wave*

hull the sudden jolt will try and knock you sideways in the direction of the shore. To prevent any tendency to capsize, *lean slightly seawards*. Let your weight go over on to the *back* of the paddle blade and allow it to support you as the boat is pushed sideways. If you use the Low Brace to support yourself on a slightly larger wave, the boat may swing round, pointing its bows towards the beach. You will find that this change of direction has now put your paddle in the Low Brace Turn position. You can

Figure 46.2 *The Paddle Brace into a medium wave*

I THROW THE KAYAK AND MY BODY IN THE DIRECTION OF THE ARROW AND OVER INTO THE WAVE. I WILL FEEL THE UPSURGE OF WATER SUPPORTING THE PADDLE — AND ME — AS I AM SWEPT SIDEWAYS TOWARDS THE SHORE.

Figure 46.3 *The Paddle Brace, large wave.*
The paddle is pushed into the heart of the wave. Be prepared for a severe arm wrench!

carry on shorewards, steering by this, or gently convert to a stern rudder (page 69) and then, by pushing outwards, put the kayak back parallel to the wave and into the Low Brace position once again.

To paddle brace on a larger wave, and still within view of your companion, paddle out a little further to where the waves are of medium height – say the height of your shoulder. Gather up your courage and position yourself sideways to an approaching breaker. Extend your paddle in the High Brace position and out towards the oncoming wave. The driving face should be *down*.

As the wave breaks against you (Figure 46.2) it will try to throw you over towards the shore. To prevent this, *lean towards and into the wave*. Place your paddle over the top of the breaker and lean on it. You will find that the blade is supported on the upsurge of power inside the wave. Hang on, keep leaning seawards, and you will find yourself bouncing happily sideways to the shore, still in the upright position. *The larger the wave the further over you must lean.* If you capsize, it will be either because you leant shorewards away from the wave, or because you continued to lean into the wave *after its power was spent.*

With practice, waves of quite gigantic proportions can be braced into successfully. This arm-wrenching business is classed as an 'advanced technique'. To brace into a very large breaker (Figure 46.3) your paddle is pushed *into the face of the wave* as it breaks. As before, the driving face is downwards, while you lean right over into the wave.

You must be prepared for a severe jerk on your arms at the initial impact, after which you will be carried shorewards with great violence, holding your breath while the kayak bucks up and down in a welter of foam, noise and spray. Your paddle will still be extended seawards, supported on the upsurge inside the wave.

THE DRAW STROKE

FUNCTION
Sea kayaking is not merely paddling in a straight line and there will be many instances when you will want to move sideways. Positioning the kayak for rescues must be done quickly as any time spent in cold water can be dangerous. It is the Draw Stroke that will move you sideways faster than anything else.

Speed is especially important when positioning the kayak for an Eskimo rescue. Although the dangers of cold water are less during this particular rescue, it must be remembered that the paddler waiting for rescue will be hanging upside down, trying to hold his breath and perhaps feeling somewhat apprehensive.

The Draw Stroke

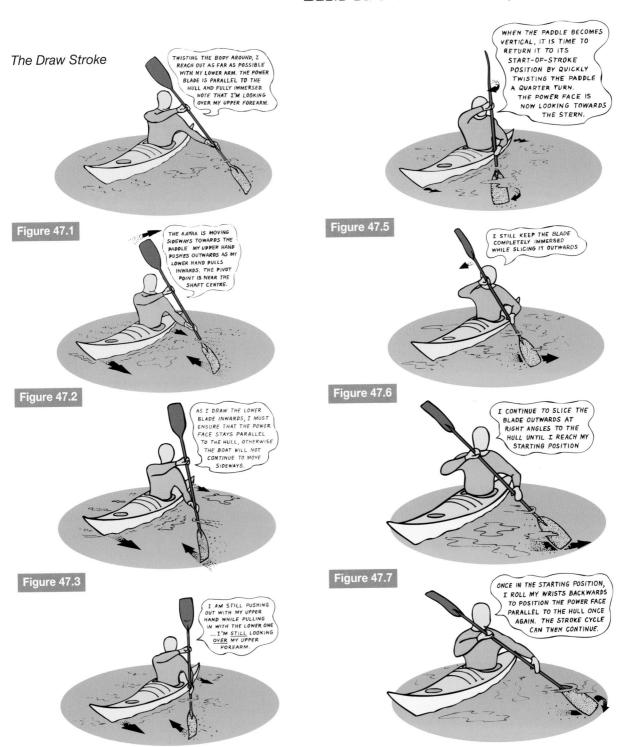

Figure 47.1

Figure 47.2

Figure 47.3

Figure 47.4

Figure 47.5

Figure 47.6

Figure 47.7

Figure 47.8

In Figures 47.1–47.8 on page 67, I talk you through the stroke as I would if I were demonstrating the movements to you on the water. Throughout the stroke the paddle is held in the *normal paddling position*. If you feel unsure and want to make things easy for your first couple of attempts, move your lower hand down the shaft and grip the paddle at the neck, where the shaft joins the lower blade. In this way you will get the 'feel' for what the underwater blade is doing during the stroke. Revert to holding the paddle in the normal position as soon as possible.

Only experience will tell you how far to reach out to begin the stroke (Figure 47.1). With practice, you will be able to extend your reach by leaning the kayak well over on to its side. This will certainly give your stroke more power. However, you will also discover the submerged gunwale digging into the water affects the stroke's efficiency.

As I draw the kayak towards the paddle (Figure 47.2), my knee on the opposite side to the stroke is exerting an upward pressure under the cockpit coaming.

Beware of 'violining'. This is a common mistake that occurs when the upper arm moves upwards rather than being pushed outwards and away from the body. There is no drawing power in 'violining' because the submerged blade merely slices through the water.

Another danger is what I call 'overrunning'. The dynamic part of the stroke is over but the kayak is still moving sideways with its own momentum. There is a need for caution when you twist the paddle. If the hull overruns the blade before you twist it, the paddle could pull you over into a capsize.

The Sculling Draw Stroke

FUNCTION
The Sculling Draw is used to move a kayak sideways. Unlike the Draw Stroke the Sculling Draw has no return or recovery phase. The kayak is pulled sideways by a *continuous*, vertical, underwater sculling action. Because of this, the paddle can be moved into position to begin a different stroke without being taken from the water, and the angle of

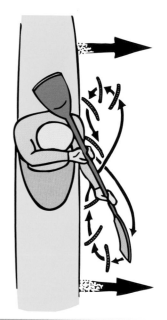

Figure 48.1 *The Sculling Draw Stroke*

the stroke can be altered to support the paddler in bad conditions.

METHOD
Turn the upper part of your body sideways in the direction in which you intend to travel. Hold the paddle as you would for stage 4 of the Draw Stroke (Figure 47.4, page 67). The Sculling Draw combines this paddle position with the sculling configuration of the Sculling for Support Stroke (Figure 45.1). You must knee-hang on the opposite side to the stroke, and your sideways movement can only be maintained by the continuous sculling action of your lower arm, wrist and hand.

If at first you have difficulty in getting the paddle to do what you want, move your lower hand further down the shaft to the neck. Place the palm of your hand on the back of the blade under the water. This will help you to direct the sculling action of the blade near the surface until you get the 'feel' of the stroke.

Another approach is to start off by performing the Sculling for Support Stroke. Without discontinuing this stroke, gradually move the lower blade in towards the kayak. The supporting figure-of-eight

Figure 48.2 *The One-hand Scull*

configuration is now being performed by your *vertically-held paddle* and your kayak is moving sideways.

The One-hand Scull

Sculling with one hand is a pleasurable and rewarding exercise for those *with some experience*. Before starting the scull it is necessary to hold the paddle at or near the blade at the neck. The blade must be submerged and the paddle balanced vertically. Moving the lower blade in order to scull will illustrate to you which hand does the controlling during the stroke. It will also let you see the small area into which the figure-of-eight can be compressed and yet still move the kayak sideways at a considerable speed.

I discovered that the One-hand Scull is ideal for moving sideways away from the proximity of larger seagoing craft, while clutching a glass of whisky or a cup of hot coffee handed to me by some generous skipper (Figure 48.2).

INDOOR DRY-LAND DRILL
Try sitting on a stool or an armless dining chair. Place the book with Figure 47.1 on the floor next to

you. The figure-of-eight diagram applies equally to both right and left sides. Position yourself so that you are directly above the page, and then follow the movement with your paddle – either until you have mastered the movement, or until your concerned friends have taken your struggling body to hospital.

TURNING STROKES ON THE MOVE

The Stern Rudder

Aim: to steer the kayak while moving forwards with the minimum loss of speed. To give the paddler a delicate control over the direction of the boat.

The Stern Rudder is one of the most important strokes in kayak surfing, but it can only be applied when the boat is moving forwards (either by being paddled forwards or carried on the face of a wave).

METHOD
The paddle is placed in the water vertically and trailed at the rear of the boat with the back of the blade facing outwards. For the stroke to be efficient the blade should be completely submerged (Figure 49).

To turn right: push the controlling blade *outwards*, away from the hull. *To turn left:* pull the blade *in*, towards the hull. The steering is limited on this side. *To go straight:* allow the controlling blade to trail with no sideways movement.

When you are running with a following wind out on open water you may find you have difficulty in keeping the boat straight. You can counteract the effect of small waves by incorporating a stern rudder into your forward paddling stroke.

If the following waves are large and green you may have to apply the correcting stroke more powerfully and for a longer period.

If the changes in direction are sudden, and the powerful '*out-push*' part of the ruddering stroke is the only way to correct, you may find yourself continually having to change sides.

Depending on the hull shape, the turn may be easier if the kayak is made to lean slightly *on the opposite side to the ruddering stroke*. You will discover this as you practice in your own boat.

50). The kayak in the illustration should turn to its right, but if its hull shape is one that is likely to skid the paddler may find that the boat is going to the left. With practice, there should be no need to change sides to correct this.

If you are using a white-water kayak in surf or a following sea, you can finish up actually leaning down the face of the wave, the paddle stroke on the outside of the turn. It may sometimes become necessary to change direction quickly, as on the face of a moving wave. Pushing downwards at the beginning of the stroke will lift the stern and jerk it sideways. The kayak can thus be turned sharply to zig-zag on the face of a wave.

Figure 49 *The Stern Rudder (steering stroke). Best results are obtained with the steering blade held completely submerged*

This stroke affords very little support, and the blade cannot be leant upon unless the kayak is moving very fast.

The Low Brace Turn (Low Telemark Turn)

Aim: the Low Brace Turn supports the paddler and turns the forward-moving kayak.

METHOD
Paddle forwards fast, then reach out with your right arm and present the *back* of the right blade to the water *with its leading edge high* (Figure 50). Your arm is almost straight, with the knuckles turned downwards. The angle of the blade is such that it planes on the surface of the water, enabling the paddler to lean right over on to the blade, thus getting plenty of support. The left arm is passed in front of the body. The paddle is held at a low angle to the water (Figure

The High Brace Turn (High Telemark Turn)

FUNCTION
The High Telemark Turn is a high-speed turn performed in the High Brace support position. Once the turn is completed, the paddle can be drawn in towards the bow (Figure 51B) and into a position from which it can move smoothly into the Forward Paddling Stroke.

The High Telemark Turn is both fast and powerful. The stroke's main application, therefore, is in surf or broken water. The turning qualities of short,

Figure 50 *The Low Brace or Low Telemark Turn. The kayak is moving forwards fast. The paddler leans over on the turn and is supported on the back of the blade as it planes on the surface of the water. The greater the speed of the kayak – the farther the lean – the better the turn*

rockered, white-water kayaks are such that, as you perform the stroke, your paddle will remain stationary in the water while your boat executes a tight spin around the blade.

METHOD

Paddle forwards fast. Reach well out and place the paddle into the water with the leading edge high.

The paddle shaft should be at an angle of between 30° and 70° to the water. Lean your body over and tilt the boat so that you are supported on the 'lift' of the blade. As you lean, knee-hang on the high side of the coaming and exert pressure on the water by increasing the angle of the blade, at the same time pushing it towards the bow.

Take note of the correct position of the upper arm in the illustration. The elbow is thrust forwards, the wrist is thrown back and the palm of the hand supporting the blade is facing upwards.

The quality of your turn will depend on how fast the kayak is moving forwards, on the angle of tilt of the kayak's hull, and on the angle of the paddle blade to the water.

The Bow Draw or

Duffek Stroke

The Bow Draw is one of the most commonly used variations of the basic Draw Stroke, and is also the most important. This fast, powerful, tight-radius turn is more often used by white-water paddlers for 'breaking out' into eddies or 'breaking in' to the main stream. The speed of this turn, introduced into slalom racing by Milo Duffek, completely revolutionised the sport. Although its original application was ideal for the narrow confines of the slalom course, the stroke also has a twofold application for the sea kayaker.

The result of applying the Bow Draw will depend to a large extent on the type of kayak you are using.

In a white-water kayak, the response by the boat to the stroke is immediate and the kayak can be spun round through 90° within its own length. As the kayak completes the turn, the blade arrives in a posi-

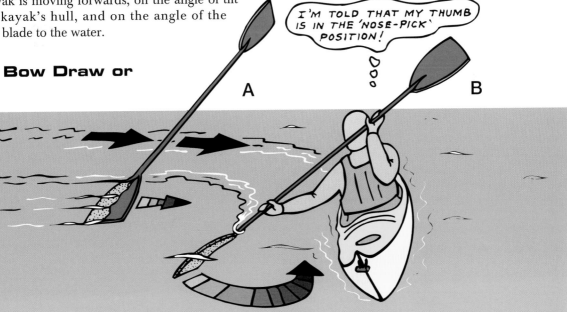

I'M TOLD THAT MY THUMB IS IN THE 'NOSE-PICK' POSITION!

A   B

Figure 51   *The High Brace or High Telemark Turn.*
'A' shows the planing angle of the paddle blade as it skids over the surface of the water. This angle supports the paddler during the high speed lean-over
'B' shows the change in paddle angle as the turn nears its completion as the kayak slows down. Pulling the blade in towards the bow compensates for loss of momentum and leads into the next forward paddle stroke

tion which allows it to continue without pause into the next forward paddling stroke. The speed of the turn and the subsequent follow-through makes it ideal for positioning and manoeuvring in surf or among standing waves when speed is necessary and space is limited.

Sea kayaks do not have the same dramatic turning qualities as shorter boats, although their response can be improved if one is prepared to utilise the pivoting effect of a wave passing beneath the hull.

The Bow Draw can be used effectively when paddling close inshore among rocks. If a rock suddenly appears in front of your bow, you merely apply a bow draw. Although it will not appreciably turn the bow, it will pull your kayak bodily sideways, thus avoiding the rock without any interruption in your forward progress.

METHOD
How far out you place the paddle at the start of the stroke will depend on the speed of the water flowing past the kayak. To put it another way, you will have to contend with the pressure of the water against the paddle blade. When performed, the Bow Draw appears as one smooth movement; it can however be broken down into three phases: the ruddering phase; the drawing phase; and the propulsive phase.

The ruddering phase (Figure 52.1)
As the water moves past the hull, the paddle blade is placed into the water in a position approximately opposite your knee. The driving face is forwards, at an angle of about 45° to the kayak. The ruddering effect of the paddle blade locked into the moving

Figure 52.2

water will turn the kayak.

The drawing phase (Figure 52.3)
Immediately the pressure against the blade begins to ease off, continue the turn by drawing the blade forwards and round in an arc towards the bow. Do this until the driving face is parallel to the hull. By this time you will have stopped turning.

Figure 52.3

The propulsive phase (Figure 52.4)
At the moment when your paddle blade is parallel to the hull and about a foot from it, turn the shaft so that the driving face of the blade is now pointing towards the stern. Without any pause, you can now continue with your forward paddling stroke. (Figure 52.5).

The result of your Bow Draw will be more dramatic if the bow of the kayak is already starting to swing round. This will occur after a forward paddling stroke on the opposite side to the proposed turn.

Figure 52.1

Figure 52.4

Figure 52.5

In the illustrations, the paddler is sitting almost upright. However, by leaning the kayak over during the ruddering and drawing phases, the length and power of the stroke is greatly increased.

Known as the Bow Rudder, the ruddering phase of the Bow Draw is used as a separate stroke in its own right. As with the Bow Draw, sea kayaks do not respond well to this front ruddering action.

Plate 8 *Paul Hutchinson aged 10 being instructed by his grandfather. The water is calm and sheltered and there is a beach nearby in the event of a swim*

(Photograph: Hélène E. Hutchinson)

Advanced strokes and techniques

3

Launching in dumping surf

In a launching of this kind it is better if the most experienced person goes last. When the others are all ready in their kayaks with their spray covers on, he can hold each one steady, time the waves for the lull, then push them out. When his turn comes he holds himself steady on the steeply sloping beach, and, as the last surge comes up the beach from the last big 'set' or group of waves, he pushes himself off, using the water as it runs down the slope. He must beware that it does not twist him sideways, beam on to the next approaching wave. If this does happen it is no time for a heroic paddle brace. He should jump out quickly if he can, get clear of the kayak and leave it. To stay with it may result in an injury.

Landing in dumping surf

Study any surf as it rolls in to the beach. There will be six to eight large waves, then usually a pause with much smaller waves. Sometimes the swell may even die out altogether. Then far out to sea the dark ridge parallel to the horizon can be seen as another big set marches majestically shorewards. (See Chapter 7.) The three men in Figure 53 are all in different stages of negotiating the nasty dumping shore waves on a steeply sloping beach.

Number 1 got as far up the beach as he could on the surge of water from the broken wave. He stopped himself being sucked back into the next wave by holding himself on his paddle and his hand. Then, very quickly, he jumped out, grasped his kayak and paddle and ran up the beach out of the way of the next bone crusher.

Number 2 sat watching the waves. Every time one came up behind him he back-paddled so as not to be hurled forwards on the face of the wave. When a big set died down he paddled forwards very hard on the back of the wave as he is doing in the illustration. This will carry him up the steeply sloping beach.

Number 3 hasn't managed things so well. Although he landed well, he threw his paddle up the beach while the surge was still going up the beach, and then when he was half out of the cockpit the water started to come back down the slope again, taking him with it into the next curling wave.

Figure 53

Seal launching and landing

Many of the areas which provide beautiful scenery and freedom for the sea kayaker also provide rocks, cliffs and a variety of difficulties for landings and launchings. Fortunately or unfortunately, seas have a habit of calming down while one is asleep in a tent. Upon walking down to a large flat slab which was regularly awash the day before, you may discover it many feet above a placid sea.

Depending on the room available on the rocks, it might be necessary to launch sideways. With rudders and skegs, which are awkward in this situation, it might be advisable to launch backwards so that the skeg hangs in space and then hits the water first, rather than catching and hooking on all the rocks while the launch is in progress.

Negotiating mudflats and quicksand

It is as well to be especially careful when exploring low laying, tidal wetlands and estuaries. Although these areas are ideal for studying nature and usually sheltered from the dangers of wind and rough water, they can present us with their own unique problems. When the tide drains from large flat estuaries and inlets, it can often leave large expanses of soft sand or leg sucking mud of *unknown depth*. Whether you are landing. launching or for some reason you have been cut off from solid land, and have now been forced to make a crossing, *keep together and always stay with your boat*. In other words, if you have to move – *take the kayak with you*. Of course, the really sensible thing to do is to sit in your boat and wait until the tide comes

Figure 54   *Crossing mud or quicksand flats can be at best unpleasant, and at worst quite frightening and fatal. The thing to do is to stay together and keep calm. Some of the areas in Britain where these low tide problems exist are The Wash, Holy Island and the Solway Firth. In North America, I can think of San Francisco's East Bay, The Everglades and the Knik Arm of Alaska's Cook Inlet as posing similar problems.*

Figure 55 | *The Seal Landing*

back in again. But that is not always possible.

Let us suppose that you have to make way over this kind of surface. Pull the kayak behind you so that you can use it for support if necessary. If the mud is too deep for you to walk across safely, sit astride your boat and slide it forward over the mud, making sure you stop sliding it while there is still plenty of the hull's buoyancy underneath. Then you'll have to extricate your legs and hitch forward along the kayak, before sliding it forwards underneath you once again.

This can be a slow business, but you will be quite safe so long as there is some part of the kayak underneath you.

If you do find yourself alone and sinking into mud or sand, you should lie across the surface and attempt to move forward by swimming as if you were doing the breast stroke.

Wind Techniques

In a beam gale, wriggle down as far as you can in your cockpit; doing this will give the wind less to grab. Lean over into the wind. Keep the paddle blade on the windward side low. If things get really bad, at the end of each forward stroke let the back of the blade skim the water. The wind will tend to push the blade on to the water or cut across it altogether, rather than catch it underneath and tear it (and you) up and over (Figure 56). A strong gust could take the paddle out of your hands altogether or if you managed to hang on tightly, capsize you by whipping the paddle over in an arc. If a gust comes from the right, say, and the right-hand blade has been caught by the full force of a violent gust and is about to take off, do not hold on. Relax the grip with your right hand and let the paddle flip over on to your left side, allowing your left wrist to twist over with the loom. This way you will keep your paddle and you won't finish up underwater.

If you are battling into a head wind, remember that although you may think you are making no headway you'll be going forwards a little at a time.

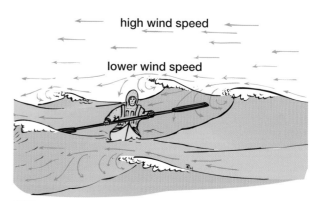

Figure 56 | *Wind eddies behind waves.*
The paddler keeps his arms low while paddling forwards, especially on the windward side. He is sheltered to some extent by the wind eddying behind each wave. The danger of having the paddle snatched by the wind is greatest when he reaches the crest. He must keep his left hand blade as low as possible as he travels forwards; he does this by making the forward stroke on the right side so low as to be almost a sweep stroke

Figure 57 *Localised downdraughts are sudden and violent and usually of a greater velocity than the wind that caused them*

lean into wind

Hunch up and keep your head down to stop the salt spray lashing at your face and eyes. Try to shut your mind off from the flying spray and the white tops breaking all around you. Get a nice rhythm going and punch your way through, always forwards. Your body can do it; if anything lets you down it will be your will-power. When crossing the entrance to a bay, remember that any strong offshore wind will produce large waves once the protection of the land is left behind. A safer, though much longer, course will therefore be to hug the shore, leaving open crossings for calmer days.

A gap in high protective cliffs or hills (Figure 57) can cause any strong winds to accelerate due to a funnelling effect, and therefore much stronger gusts can be expected and must be allowed for.

Figure 58.1 *Paddling straight in a beam wind – correcting course. You are moving forwards with a strong wind blowing onto your left side. The waves are close together. Just before the wave hits you the paddle is angled as it would be for a sweep turn. As you sweep the paddle back with your left hand, you will realise that the stroke is more of a propulsive paddle brace than a forward paddling stroke. In order to keep the kayak on a straight course, you must lean over into the wind and knee-hang on your right side*

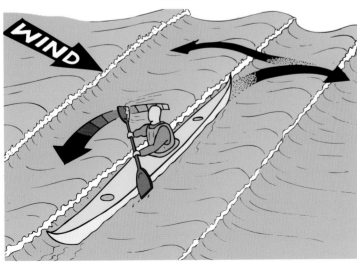

Figure 58.2 *Turning a kayak in a high wind. The kayak will not respond to a Forward Sweep on the left side so the paddler must lean into the wind and perform a Reverse Sweep on the right side. As the kayak moves backwards, the 'weathercocking' action of the wind will help turn the kayak into the wind. The paddle may be held in the extended position but care will be needed to avoid breaking he paddle under the tremendous strain*

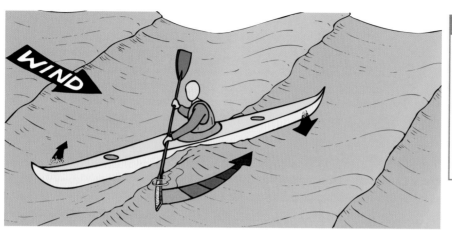

The Ferry Glide

When any boat is held at an angle to fast-moving water, or in the case of much sea kayaking, at an angle to the wind, it will move sideways across the main flow. In river kayaking this is called the Ferry Glide because of its associations with flying ferries on fast-moving rivers. At sea, the manoeuvre is still loosely referred to as the Ferry Glide, although it would be more technically correct to call it 'making an allowance for set and drift'. This manoeuvre on open water can be a very prolonged affair, and using it to travel across several miles is a very different matter from using it to cross a narrow river or even the narrows between two islands (Figure 59).

This is when the use of transit bearings (see Chapter 9 on navigation) really proves a blessing.

A compass is almost useless in this situation, as the paddler has no means of calculating even the approximate speed of the wind when he is moving forwards. The only way to ensure a straight ferry glide across the wind is by selecting transit markers.

When the paddler looks across a channel, the fastest flowing water is always marked by a white-topped broken wave. If the strong current is opposed by even a moderate wind

it will produce a short, steep chop. This is because the waves are foreshortened or compressed by the wind, causing them to break. So beware when the tide changes against the wind during the crossing of a wide channel. It could produce conditions that might prove a nightmare, if not a complete disaster, for normal proficiency-standard paddlers. In windy weather be sure to make a specific note of what time the tide will be turning.

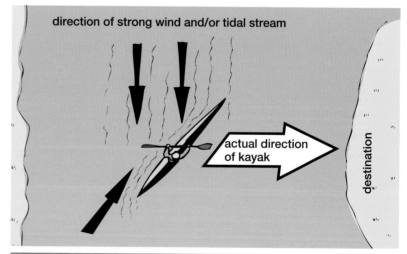

direction of strong wind and/or tidal stream

actual direction of kayak

destination

Figure 59 *The Ferry Glide.*
Kayaker paddles in direction shown by black arrow. If it is windy he leans over to his left onto it. With luck the paddler may find landmarks which will serve as transits thereby making him aware of any drift off course

THE ESKIMO ROLL

The Eskimo Roll is the skill of righting the kayak after it has capsized. It is hardly surprising that the Eskimos invented this system of self-rescue. The water in the Arctic being as cold as it is, any swim may well be the last. During the winter in some areas the Eskimo actually laced his sealskin anorak tightly on to the manhole rim, making an exit from the kayak impossible and a roll the only way of ensuring survival.

During extreme conditions out in the open sea a bail-out could prove hazardous, not only for the man in the water but also for his companions, who might be stretched to the limit themselves in dealing with the situation. Furthermore, any rescue would be virtually impossible in very rough seas or high winds, or inshore near cliffs during a heavy swell or over reefs at sea. A coaching colleague once had the rather horrifying experience of being swept along sideways, upside-down in the blackness of a sea cave, and having to roll up with the broken ends of his kayak jammed against the rock sides. In circumstances such as this, any other type of rescue would obviously be almost impossible.

A good deal of sea kayaking has been done by people who cannot, and have no desire to, perform an Eskimo roll. However, having the ability will increase your confidence and improve your whole attitude towards the sea and rough-water kayaking.

There are also much happier uses for a good

A window into a new world...

rolling technique. It is necessary for any high degree of competence in surf work. And when you are armed with a face mask on a warm summer's day, it gives you a window into a world which is denied to everyone else except divers.

The best way to learn to roll is to get a properly qualified instructor to teach you personally. Go to a

Plate 9 *The author performing an Eskimo roll. 'I thought the water in San Francisco Bay would be warmer than that in the North Sea – but I was wrong'*

pool course organised by a qualified instructor or coach. The water will be nice and warm, and there is the comfort of having someone standing next to you while you are underwater. Wearing a face mask or a nose clip makes the experience even less unpleasant by giving you a clear view while upside-down and preventing water from shooting up your nose.

The Hip Flick

1 Hold on to the side of the pool or anything else which will give you a firm handhold.

2 Lean over and dip your head into the water. As you lean, remember to 'knee-hang' (see 'Basic Strokes', Figure 33). Hook your upper knee under the cockpit coaming and then pull the kayak over onto its gunwale with a flick of your outer hip.

3 Bring the kayak upright again with another flick of your outer hip. Your head should leave the water about the time the hip movement is finishing.

An efficient hip flick (Figure 60) brings the kayak upright due to the fast twisting action of the lower trunk. At the end of the flick, enough momentum is gained to pull the body out of the water and help return it to its upright position.

Capsizing the kayak and swimming to the other side of the pool without getting out of the boat is another good exercise in confidence. To extend your swimming distance it is possible to push down with your hands and get a quick gulp of air as your head comes out of the water. Swimming with the kayak means that if you lose your paddle during a roll you can always retrieve it and then continue the roll.

Before starting to roll, make sure that you and the kayak are as one. A tight, snug-fitting moulded seat, thigh grips, knee supports or bars, and a well-adjusted footrest are needed to make sure you 'wear' the boat, rather than just sit in it loosely.

For sea kayaking it is not necessary to be able to roll on both sides. If, for instance, you capsize on your good side, do a normal roll. If you capsize on your wrong side in a broken wave, the wave will force you round and bring you up into the Paddle Brace or Support position. If you capsize in turbu-

lence, hang upside-down until the turbulence stops and then roll up in the normal way.

The roll which my associates used to teach first at one time was the 'Put-across Roll', in which the paddle was pushed out from the side. At one stage it was not under full control because the hand grip was rather loose, so that if the water was at all lively the paddle tended to be swept away. This particular roll, therefore, does not merit inclusion in a sea kayaking book because of this possible danger.

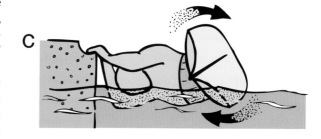

Figure 60 *The Hip Flick*

So you want to roll. Well, are you sitting comfortably? Good. the paddle is on your left side. Hold the nearest blade at the top corner, thumb downwards, fingers inside. Don't reach too far forwards with the right hand; the knuckles should be uppermost looking away from the kayak. The outward edge of the forward paddle blade can be tilted slightly towards the water. Are you ready? Right, take a deep breath and capsize. Turn the page round now, and keep holding your breath!

Fish Eye View

angle of sweeping blade

Wait, open your eyes, study the picture. Try to orientate yourself – good, don't panic; it's only water. Bend your body and push your face towards upwards the surface. Push your hands upwards towards the surface. Swing out with your right hand blade, the outward edge tilted upwards as it planes out in an arc along the surface. Keep that right arm almost straight. The left hand pushes up out of the water and forwards

Figure 61.1 | *The Pawlata Roll*

The Pawlata Roll

In my opinion the Pawlata (Figure 61:1) is the best roll to teach a beginner. Many of my coaching colleagues would support this view because the Screw Roll, the most important roll of all, is a direct progression from the Pawlata. But as long as you can roll first time every time, then the particular technique used is irrelevant.

If you have difficulty with the Pawlata, think about the following.

1 The angle of the blade as it moves from the kayak must be such that it planes out and along the surface.
2 You must lean forwards.
3 The roll should be executed with great vigour.
4 Don't try to roll before you are upside-down.
5 The forward arm is swept out to the side in an arc by the straight arm, not pulled downwards.
6 Don't forget to push the left arm forwards and to the surface; otherwise the blade will hit the side of your hull and you will not be able to sweep the forward blades outwards.
7 After the sweep outwards with the right hand, the upper part of the right arm should brush past the nose and over the head as you break the surface. Failing to do this is the most common reason for an unsuccessful roll.

The Screw Roll

The Screw Roll (Figure 62) is probably the most important roll of all, because the basic position of the hands on the paddle loom remains unaltered. Sometimes the paddler becomes unsure of his hand position in relation to the angle of the paddle blades. This is no problem with looms which are slightly oval in the area of the hand position. Aluminium looms can be shaped by squeezing them in a vice. If in doubt, the paddler can move the nearest hand quickly along the loom until it reassuringly touches the blade in a recognisable position, and then put it back in place for the commencement of the roll. With practice it will not be necessary to move the hands from the normal paddling position. Because the leverage is shorter, a higher degree of skill is required for this than for any other roll.

It is during the performance of this roll that we discover another advantage of using the longer, narrower sea paddle. The roll is made easier because the upper blade does not have to be pushed up as high to clear the bottom of the kayak. The blade which, in the meantime, is sweeping outwards on the

You should be in the position shown as your head breaks the surface. Your right bicep should have just brushed past your nose. Push down hard – you have just completed your first Pawlata Roll

Figure 61.2 *The Pawlata Roll – human's eye view*

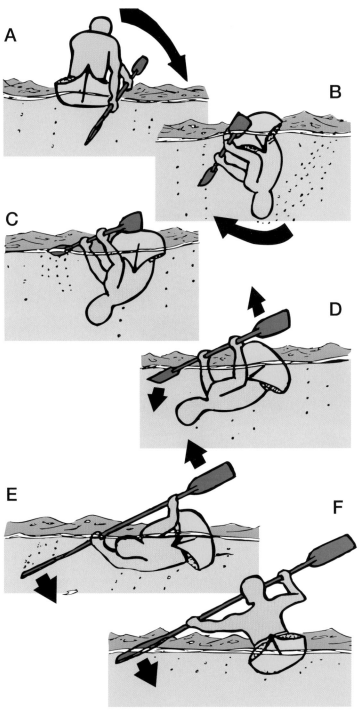

surface of the water is also at a better angle for the downward stroke of the roll proper.

The King Island Roll

An Alaskan roll or King Island is shown in Figure 65. This is done with a single paddle blade. Note that when the paddler is in the inverted position, the paddle is held at arm's length downwards. Because of its angle, the blade takes a rising path towards the surface during the sweep round and finishes up in a position behind the man. The remaining forward sweep, bringing the man upright, reminds one of the European Steyr Roll illustrated in Figure 63.

While hunting in the rough waters of the Bering Sea, a man could be caught by a sudden capsize. If unable to roll up with his paddle, he could withdraw himself up into the roomy body of his kayak and wait until his comrade paddled to his assistance and turned him upright again. It has not been unknown for a hunter who has lost his paddle to attempt a roll using his throwing-stick, and sometimes in desperation even attempting to use the blade of his knife.

Other rolls include the Eskimo Storm Roll (Figure 65), the Vertical Storm Roll (Figure 66) and the Greenland Roll (Figure 67). The ultimate in kayak rolling is the No-Paddle Roll, otherwise known as the Hand Roll.

| **Figure 62** | *The Screw Roll* |

The paddler sits in the middle of the large manhole with his back unsupported. He hooks his knees under the first thwart forward of the cockpit. This roll is a good one for a tired paddler; it is a gradual roll, spreading the righting action over a longer period. The paddle is held out in front of the body horizontally. The paddle blade sticks out to the left. The kayaker is now in the position for the capsize

Fish Eye View

The arms can be extended during the capsize or immediately afterwards. To roll up, the paddle is swept forwards as indicated; the leading edge of the blade planes towards the surface during its sweep round. This must be done with some speed to gain lift towards the surface. The change of direction for the forward sweep must also be executed quickly, so as not to lose the momentum of the rising sweep round. This roll can be done successfully with a double-bladed paddle

| Figure 63 | *The King Island Roll* |

Hold the paddle as if for the Pawlata. Then lie back along the rear deck, with the right arm either above the head as in (A) or across the face as in (B). This is a most uncomfortable position, especially for the left hand. You will also feel unstable. Twist the top half of your body to the left, then capsize on that size

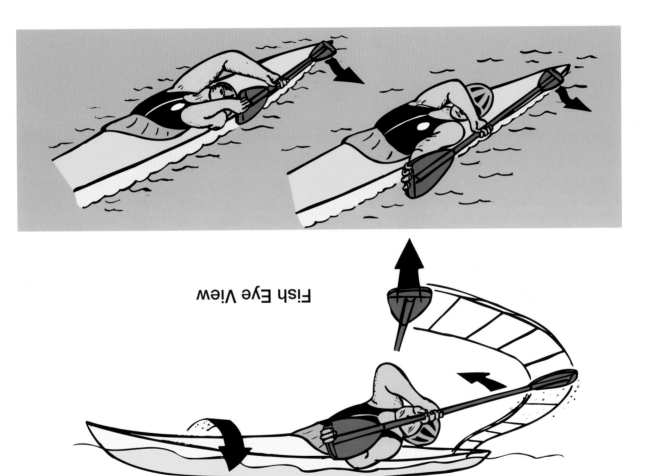

Fish Eye View

Wait until you are hanging upside down and your head is twisted back looking at the rear of the kayak. Push the right hand and arm across your face and out to the side. Push down as the paddle sweeps out and you will rise to the surface. Much less effort is needed for this than is needed for other rolls, but it lacks popularity because the preparatory position or 'wind up' is a difficult one to adopt under water

Figure 64 | *The Steyr Roll*

This is a true Eskimo roll as used by the Eskimos of the Angmassalik area of Greenland. The starting position or 'wind up' is rather like the Pawlata, except that the forward paddle blade is at an angle of 30° from the side of the kayak

Fish Eye View

Lean well forwards and push upwards with the right hand, so that the forward paddle blade is about a foot above the surface. Now pull down violently. You will rise very quickly. The paddle goes down vertically for about one foot, then starts to plane outwards as the roll nears completion

Figure 65 *The Eskimo Storm Roll*

Use the same 'wind up' position as for the Storm Roll

Fish Eye View

The blade when pushed above the surface is in a vertical position. The edge of the blade nearest the water is angled slightly outwards from the kayak, so that although the blade bites down very deeply – 2 to 3ft, it will eventually slice outwards and down for maximum support

| Figure 66 | *The Vertical Storm Roll* |

It has been thought, quite wrongly, that because a kayak is very unstable when the right way up, it is easy to roll when upside down. It is obvious that the bottom hull shape, apart from its narrowness, exerts very little influence on the kayak when it is being rolled. However, if the deck has a 'banana' shape lengthwise, when the boat is upside down it will try to turn on its side, upon which it will normally readily float. This action is assisted by the buoyancy of the kayaker's body. Boat and man finish up at an angle of about 45° to the surface of the water (B), the kayak in many cases showing an almost flat bottom to the sky. In this position the man is ready to start the roll

A

B

The paddle is held alongside the kayak with the blade in a vertical position. The blade angle is altered as it leaves the side of the kayak. It is then planed outwards. This can bring the man to the surface, or the roll may be finished off by a quick forwards scull, the paddle blade finishing on or near the surface of the water

| Figure 67 | *The Greenland Roll* |

The Hand Roll

1 An assistant is needed at first. The stand on your right-hand side.

2 Lean well back in the cockpit to touch the back of your head on the rear deck.

3 Place the knuckles of your right hand well behind your left ear, palm outwards.

4 Capsize on your left side. Keep your head touching the back deck.

5 Your partner will put his upward-facing palm in a position where it touches your downward-facing palm. Hook your fingers into his.

6 Sweep your arm violently in a wide arc towards the bottom of the pool and follow through until your right arm is fully extended sideways.

7 As you break the surface, fling the left arm forcibly over sideways; this will assist the momentum.

This exercise will give you confidence. Next try the same with a table tennis bat or a polystyrene float. You can assist the first part of the roll by dog-paddling to the surface first on the right-hand side. With your head on the back deck, quickly fling your right arm downwards and round with great force, throwing your left hand out as a counterbalance to help the last part of the roll.

Once you have learned to roll, by any of the methods described, practise at every opportunity, especially in rough conditions; surf is ideal because a failure means only a short swim.

Always keep calm when you are upside-down. Worry makes your heart beat faster; this takes more oxygen, which is unobtainable. So keep cool and think about something else. You will be surprised at just how long you can happily hold your breath: you should be able to do so for about 30 seconds, if not a little longer. The time will depend on many factors: some physical, some psychological, some environmental (the temperature of the water is a major factor).

Some people have taught that one's time under water can be lengthened by *hyperventilation*. 'Over-breathing increases the endurance time by removing carbon dioxide from the body and delaying the time at which its concentration builds up again to the point at which it produces an irresistible stimulus to breathe. The overbreathing does not appreciably increase the amount of oxygen stored in the body, as the haemoglobin of arterial blood is almost saturated with oxygen even during normal breathing.'

If you exclude carbon dioxide from your body for too long you will lose the desire to breathe, and after doing the longest underwater hang on record you will quite painlessly lose consciousness and subsequently drown. In all rolling practice it is vital to have qualified instructors near at hand in case anyone unwittingly induces hyperventilation.

Assistant hooks student's fingers from underneath

The capsize: student and assistant's fingers are locked together; the assistant supports their wrist with other hand

The student rolls using hand support

Figure 67A   *The Hand Roll. Instructor Assistance.*

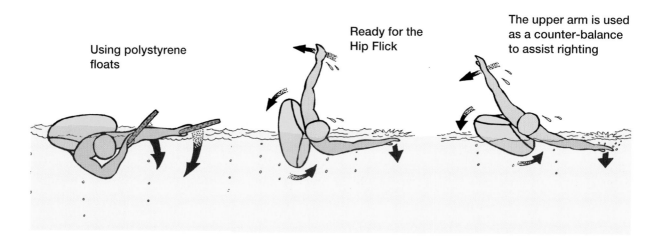

Using polystyrene floats

Ready for the Hip Flick

The upper arm is used as a counter-balance to assist righting

Figure 67B | *Hand roll practicee using floats. The floats are gradually reduced in size until only the hands are used.*

Plate 10 *The author allows a wave to pass underneath before heading in to the beach*

EQUIPMENT

The power of surf is tremendous. In big waves I have seen a number of glassfibre kayaks snap in half with the occupants still sitting in them, and once I even saw a kayak 'pop out' of the water quite empty, while the man, complete with spray cover attached to the cockpit rim and seat, struggled to swim ashore still in his ejection seat! Buy the best and strongest equipment you can.

Types of boat

Any kayak will surf. But if the keel is straight, as in a long touring kayak, manoeuvring on the waves is out of the question. Well-rockered glassfibre white-water kayaks are most widely used, reinforced with extra layers of glassfibre, Diolen or carbon-fibre strips which can be incorporated in the 'lay up' during manufacture. Another type is the specialised surf kayak described at the end of this chapter.

My glassfibre white-water kayak weighs about 45 lb., but even 10 lb. less than this would still be fine. Added strength comes from the kayak's buoyancy. Air bags tailored to the kayak's shape can be blown up in position, preventing any flexing of the hull and deck. Polystyrene blocks touching the top of the deck and bottom of the hull can also be used to give support, although they are not sufficient on their own. Every available spare inch of the boat's interior should be filled with some sort of flotation material that cannot leave the kayak in the event of a capsize.

Spray covers

Advanced surfers have traditionally worn two spray covers of the nylon neoprene or nylon PVC type. Spray covers of neoprene wet-suit material lined with nylon are the more popular, as they are extremely watertight and flex with the movements of the paddler's body. All spray covers should have a quick-release strap or toggle, especially the rubber

wet-suit material type, which can be fitted tighter than those made of less stretchy material. Spray covers should be tight, but when they have to come off they must come off quickly.

The funnel or sleeve which fits around the body should be higher on a surfing spray cover than on those used for normal paddling. This is so that it can be worn tucked up under the lifejacket waist strap, thus preventing the apron being forced downwards by the weight of the water pressing upon it. Some spray covers are fitted with shoulder straps to stop this.

Lifejackets and buoyancy aids

Any spectator at a kayak surfing or rodeo championship will notice that most of the competitors wear buoyancy aids rather than lifejackets. The competitors justify this on several grounds. As noted in Chapter 1, a lifejacket must be inflated in order to float the wearer face upwards and provide maximum buoyancy. However, it should not be worn inflated, and when deflated it provides less buoyancy than one of the better buoyancy aids. Bearing in mind that surfing accidents happen suddenly, and that they frequently involve lung or head injuries resulting in loss of consciousness, one must ask who supplies the air to blow up the lifejacket and convert it from an inefficient buoyancy aid to a lifesaving device.

On the other hand, buoyancy aids provide reasonably effective body armour and seem to give greater freedom around the neck. A lifejacket has to be tied tight around the body, and since surfing is often done without the buffering effect of a wet-suit jacket the straps can cut uncomfortably into the paddler's sides and back. The added buoyancy of wet-suit trousers also seems to inhibit the true lifejacket from doing its job properly. Capsizes in surf do not always result in injury but frequently make necessary very long swims to shore, with or without a kayak; such swims are much easier with a buoyancy aid than with a life jacket.

Whatever you decide to use, *make sure you do wear it*, tied, buckled or zipped-up securely. To surf wearing no personal buoyancy at all is absolute madness and can endanger not only your life but also the lives of those who will have to rescue you.

Crash helmets

These are a must. It is not so much that, wearing one, one's head will bounce more easily off the sea bottom; but rather that it bounces more safely off other people's kayaks, with or without occupants, or off airborne surfboards without riders. Bailing out on the inshore side of your own boat without a crash helmet, when a wave is about to break, will soon give you a large lump on your head.

There are plenty of strong, lightweight, good-quality helmets on the market. Choose one that is brightly coloured so that you can be seen when swimming to shore. Your helmet should also float.

Toggles

I have dealt with toggles elsewhere in this book in the context of touring. For hanging on to a kayak in surf, toggles at the bow and stern are essential. Without them you will not be able to maintain your hold on a twisting kayak. Rope loops tend to twist round and trap your fingers. Unfortunately, most plastic kayaks are only fitted with tape straps for carrying. If this is the case, thread your own toggle, on a short piece of cord, through the existing loop.

Footrest

The strain on your footrest when you are surfing can be considerable. When I surfed a fibreglass kayak, my footrest was a very strong piece of oval wall-bar from a gymnasium, glassed solidly in position. Some manufacturers fit a fail-safe model, so that if by some misfortune a paddler's feet are forced past and behind his footrest he can withdraw them by swinging it out and round. With this method, please be careful in your choice of footwear. Laces and loops have been known to catch on the bolts or wing-nuts, causing concern.

Bulkhead footrests are not fitted in all plastic white-water kayaks, because they are expensive to incorporate. But they make unnecessary any fail-safe consideration, since your feet cannot slide past and around

Figure 68 *A typical surfing situation. Note the man rolling to protect himself, whilst the capsized man hangs on to his paddle as well as his kayak*

them thereby causing entrapment. I have opted for a bulkhead footrest, with adjustable fastenings in the cockpit area, in my polythene kayak. This seems to be the best system on the market at the moment.

Any system that will not allow your feet to slip past, or that will not break when the sudden weight of the body hits it during a pole vault off the bottom, will do fine. But remember that bolts can sheer through; and that if the deck and hull of the boat compress, the sides will move outwards, springing the footrest free and causing your feet to fall past and perhaps become stuck into the front of the kayak.

TECHNIQUES

Surfing – the ability to handle violent breaking waves, to run with them, battle out against them and take them on the beam – is probably the best training anyone can have for tackling rough water out at sea. However, surfing is not sea kayaking. There are many men and women who love the sea and paddle on it to a very high standard, but who prefer not to enter the world of surf acrobatics; just as surely as there are some virtuosos in surf acrobatics who wouldn't dream of rolling a kayak way out at sea, and who certainly haven't got the stamina or mature outlook for prolonged sea expedition work in rough water. Doubly happy are they who can both surf and indulge in sea touring.

Kayak surfing and rodeo, which can soon draw a crowd, appeal to the exhibitionist in all of us. They are also rather like a drug: every loop is going to be the last before lunch, and the last...and the last, till the aching, happy, hungry paddlers drag themselves from the water like so many worn-out selkies.[4]

Surf is the white water of the sea. It is exhilarating and exciting but it can be dangerous if not treated with respect. Surfing utilises the basic sea kayaking skills – the Stern Rudder, Low Telemark and Paddle Brace. With just these basic skills, quite a high standard of skill can be yours; although for big surf and acrobatics an ability to roll is essential.

[4]A mythical sea creature – half man, half seal – of the Scottish outer islands.

To embark on your surfing career, first choose a companion – you never surf alone – and a day when the waves are not too large. Start by sitting in the 'soup'; this is the broken wave as it tumbles to shore. Let yourself become used to the feeling of paddling about and paddle bracing if need be.

Forward running

Paddle out a few yards, turn and point your bow shorewards. When a small broken wave is a few feet behind you, paddle forwards. The wave will catch you up, and you will feel yourself seemingly hurtle forwards. Try to keep your balance and steer with a stern rudder. The boat is bound to turn either left or right, so let your rudder convert into a low brace and lean on it – not too much, just enough for support – and you'll move sideways, upright, having just surfed your first small wave. Keep practising, and when you feel confident go out to the green waves beyond the break.

Wait until a fairly steep humping wave is about 5 or 6 yds. behind you, then paddle forwards fast, leaning forwards, As the wave catches up, your stern will be lifted and you will be carried in, more or less planing on the face of the wave depending on its angle and speed. Steady and control your run with a stern rudder. You might have to change sides quickly to keep running straight. Eventually the boat will swing to one side or the other. If it keeps running straight you must choose a side on which to turn. Then, as the wave towers steeply over you and you are parallel to it, either do a vigorous stern rudder, which will take you back over the top of the wave just before it starts to break, or, if it starts to break and you are still on its face as your paddle is trailing down, flip over into the High Paddle Brace position and hang on as your paddle is supported on the upsurge inside the wave as it breaks and sweeps you to the beach.

If you see someone paddling out and you think you are on an eventual collision course with him, capsize. The weight of your body upside-down will stop the forward momentum of the kayak. Then if you can roll up, do so. If not, bail out and tow your boat and paddle to shore, pulling them in by a lively backstroke. If a large wave looms up, don't look along your upturned hull at it; otherwise when it picks up your boat and stands it on end it will harpoon you. Instead, move to one side slightly, hold on tight and let the kayak be thrown shorewards (Figure 68). You'll be glad you're holding a toggle and not a loop as the kayak twists round and round.

A word of warning! Do not capsize if you are on top of a breaking wave and someone is paddling out immediately to one side of you and inshore. You will be skewered upside-down on his bow. Sit tight and paddle brace. He must capsize and allow you to pass over his upturned hull. He will then either roll up or bail out, depending on his skill.

During the slow tow to the beach, keep the boat upside-down, even if it is full of buoyancy; otherwise breaking waves will fill what space there is, and the surge will then float your aquarium up on to the sand, there to stand immovable because of the weight of water, slowly splitting and cracking at the seams.

If your swamped kayak is in danger of being beached the right way up, quickly drag it back into about 2 ft. of water and either turn it upside-down (so that at least it will drain itself out when beached – it tends to get full of sand this way) or get someone to help you empty it in thigh-deep water. While you do this, don't get parallel to inshore 'soup', as it will either knock the boat out of your hands or keep filling it up again as fast as you empty it.

Reverse running

Face the green oncoming waves. When one is a few yards away, lean backwards and start back-paddling fast. The kayak will be picked up and will move backwards quickly. Lean forwards up the wave as the angle steepens. The kayak will change direction quicker than it does when forward running, so be ready to place the paddle in near the bow and do a ruddering stroke.

If, say, the kayak swings violently to your right, allow the ruddering blade to trail and swing out and over the wave into the paddle brace position, supporting you as you lean on to the paddle and into the wave.

Paddling out through large surf

It is best to paddle out fast in the lull between sets, helped if possible by a rip current from the beach. Watch out you don't mistime things; otherwise you could find yourself a hundred yards out from the shore with a huge set bearing down upon you. If this happens you must employ techniques such as the following.

Paddle fast towards the oncoming wave. As it looms up in front of you, if you think you can lean back without the boat being hurled backwards into an unwelcome reverse loop, do so; the shock of its hitting you will be lessened. Otherwise lean well forwards, keep paddling and punch your way through (watch the wave doesn't remove your crash helmet). The difficulty is trying to judge whether it is possible to slacken off your forward paddling to minimise the impact with the wave, or whether this would again send you backwards. Doing this I once had my own paddle loom smashed against my forehead – before crash hats were as popular as they are now – producing a lump the size of an egg above one eye.

Perhaps the best way of coping with the whole situation is to roll over as the wave is a few yards away, so that when it strikes you will be hanging upside-down, nice and safe. The kayak may move about quite vigorously so that you will get that washing machine feeling around the head. When all goes still again, roll up quickly. Keep paddling out fast, and hope you can beat the next wave before it breaks.

Before you start your run, look behind on the side to which you are likely to turn and make sure that no one is in your way. Remember where everyone is and in what direction they are paddling in relation to your proposed run. Then look behind on the other side in case the wave alters your plans.

Tracking or cutting back

If the wave is a very large one, the kayak will run down the face into the trough in front of it. It will lose speed dramatically as the planing speed is lost. The breaking wave will then overtake you in a welter of spray and foam, leaving you to paddle brace and mourn the loss of a superb wave which further along its length has not even broken yet.

To avoid this, look quickly along the wave in both directions as you surf in, and determine on which side the wave will start to break. Do a sharp stern rudder on the opposite side to the curling wave. The kayak will then travel almost parallel to the sloping wave, moving sideways and climbing towards the crest again. Then lean down the wave slope into a low telemark, converting into a stern rudder as the kayak once again faces down the wave, but this time much higher up its face. Keep cutting back like this, using all the wave has to offer. If you wish to leave the wave, track close to the crest; a sharp stern rudder jerked outwards on the side of the crest will cause the kayak to flip over the back of the wave.

Although you had a clear run to the beach when you started, you may now have moved 80 to 100 yds. sideways into an overpopulated area full of bathers. Don't allow your kayak to hurtle sideways as the wave breaks, scything a path 15 ft. wide through small children and nervous swimmers. Either pull off the wave in the normal manner or capsize and

hope that the weight of your body will slow you down. Once you are paddle bracing on a large wave, all the capsizing in the world won't stop you if you are parallel. Only by capsizing at a slight angle to the break will you have any chance of slowing down.

SURF ACROBATICS

The Loop or 'Endo'

If you surf for long enough, the day is bound to arrive when, quite accidentally, the nose of your kayak digs in and before you realise it the whole thing goes end over end. You have just done your first loop. At the end of the day you'll tell your admiring friends all about it and how easy it was.

What makes the kayak do this? Well, when a wave is critical it is in a state where its steepness does not allow a normal white-water kayak to plane in a controlled manner down its slope. Instead it will plunge down to the bottom of the wave, burying

Figure 69 *'The Loop' or 'Endo'. Lean well forwards and wind up into a roll position. You will be over and up before you know what has happened*

Figure 70 *The Loop and Flick – pirouette*

its bow deep. You will not have to paddle forwards to make it do this. Thus at an angle of about 60° all forward movement is arrested at the bow, while the moving wave still pushes the rest of the kayak into an upright position called the loop position. The bow of your kayak may touch the bottom – a pole vault – or it may stand on end and uses its own buoyancy for support. The rest of the kayak then falls over, completing the loop. Although it all looks quite horrific to the uninitiated, it is the stern of the kayak which performs the large arc through the air, not your body. Your head travels perhaps only in an arc of 3 or 4 ft while the loop is in progress, because when the boat stands on its end the wave carries on, giving you a soft bed to fall upon. Thus you will not finish your loop way down below in the distant trough, but on the back of the wave.

If you lean forwards, as you will if you prepare yourself for a roll, your head will hardly travel any distance at all (Figure 69).

A loop can be done as a finale to a run when the wave is about to break; or else the paddler can wait at the break-line, catching the waves when they are too steep for a run and allowing the bow to plunge into a loop.

The Flick and the Pirouette

The upright loop position can also be the start of other exciting manoeuvres. By reaching down onto the water with the paddle blade and performing a quick push and hip flick, you can turn the kayak so that as it falls back down it will be facing out to sea again and you won't even get wet (Figure 70). This is a spectacular trick, and it can be improved upon.

With the kayak standing upright on its bow, stand on the footrest, your body at right angles and the paddle held slightly to the left side. Straighten your body quickly, your head travelling in the direction of the back deck. As you do so, fling round both arms, holding the paddle across to the right and violently twisting around to the right from the thighs. With practice the boat will spin round and round in a pirouette.

This is an extremely difficult trick, requiring a lot of practice. A friend of mine in Bristol, a winner of many surfing prizes, can do this without a paddle, having dispensed with it at the beginning of his run down the wave. If necessary he can do the Loop, Pirouette and Roll, all without a paddle.

The Reverse Loop

This is the Forward Loop in reverse, quite simple and requiring perhaps less courage than the Forward Loop because your body tends to be nearer the water during the actual loop and it is your back which is presented to the water, not your face and front.

Watch out for a reverse pole vault. This can cause you to jerk backwards, leaving the footrest and jarring your spine against the coaming. A back-strap is handy there, although I prefer to have inflated buoyancy protruding into the rear of the cockpit with a polystyrene bath float jammed between it and the seat to absorb any shock.

The Eskimo Loop or Reverse Loop and Flick

This is probably the most graceful trick in surf acrobatics (Figure 71).

As the kayak is running backwards down the wave, the stern will begin to dig in. Just before it reaches the vertical position, the paddler winds up into the Screw Roll position. He then rolls into the wave, rotating the kayak vertically on its point through 180°. As the front end of the kayak continues in its arc through the air, the paddler will be completing his roll and, hopefully, will find himself continuing his run on the same wave, this time forwards.

The Pop-out

This is sometimes called a *sky-rocket* (Figure 72). With practice it is possible to manoeuvre the kayak to the crest of a large wave. The boat will drop down the steep face and, with great force, will bury itself and you down inside the wave. Like a ping-pong ball in a bucket of water the kayak is forced skywards, with any luck completely out of the water. While in this airborne condition you can execute a flick or pirouette, shout in exuberance or perhaps just admire the wonderful view.

SURF KAYAKS

At first glance, the shape of the early surf kayaks belied their performance. Generally fairly narrow with rather squared-off ends, they resembled ungainly surf boards which had grown a top shell. Recent surf kayaks have shown a more graceful line, and in the almost flat hull, the tapered flat stern, the upswept front or kick-up and the pronounced rail (bottom side edge) they closely resemble Malibu surfboards, whose manoeuvres they can so nearly emulate. As a particular type of craft, surf kayaks, regardless of shape or size, can all make manoeuvres in surf which cannot be achieved in other kayaks, sea or white-water kayak.

Figure 71 *The Eskimo Loop or Reverse Loop and Flick*

Figure 72 *The Pop-out or Sky-rocket*

Figure 73.1 *Surf kayak designed by the author.*

Typical features: Dimensions seem to vary between 7–9 ft in length and 22–24 ins wide. Note the 'hard rail' (bottom edge), sharp 'kick-up' (front) and flat bottom. The seat is near the centre of the cockpit and has a back strap

Perhaps the biggest difference between the surf kayak and the white-water kayak is the ability of the surf kayak, in very large, intimidating surf, to provide one with an escape route. Many times in my slalom kayak, low down on the face of really big waves and with no hope of climbing to the crest and off, I have wished for some magic way out – perhaps an ejector seat – rather than face the alternative of a shoulder-tearing, lung-bursting paddle brace or a particularly violent, uncontrolled somersault. The surf kayak provides this magic way out with its extreme manoeuvrability, both on the face of the wave and in the 'soup'.

The surf kayak requires a steep take-off slope, so to start the run the wave should be getting near to its critical pitch. This is because the craft cannot be paddled fast to catch the more gently sloping green waves. You might think that starting on a steep slope is putting you in a loop position, but the surf kayak rarely loops forwards. Once away, it has the speed to cut across to where the wave is at a less acute angle.

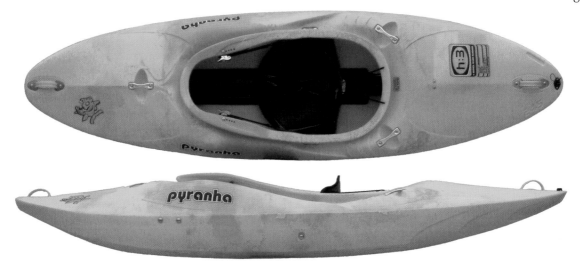

Figure 73.2 *A modern rodeo play boat has a flat bottom similar to the surf kayaks, but the rodeo boats tend to be much wider and easier to control. Convex indentations run fore and aft along both sides underneath the hull, and this rail, together with the increased volume and kick-up at the stern, give these tiny craft a straight running quality which is quite surprising.*

The h:3 kayak illustrated, has ratchets on either side immediately above the thigh brace. These allow the backrest to be moved forwards or backwards whilst in the sitting position. The tiny drain plug at the stern makes emptying an easy matter and one wonders why all boats do not have this facility. Rodeo boats are always roto-moulded in polyethylene – surf kayaks on the other hand are usually made of fibreglass

If you are caught in the Paddle Brace position, don't wonder why the boat will not lean over into the wave. It won't lean: it has a flat bottom. Place the paddle out into the usual position, try to transfer some of your weight on to it, and you will probably find that the boat is still upright as the wave breaks. Then with a little practice, instead of paddle bracing all the way to shore, you can lift your paddle above your head in bravado as the flat bottom of the surf kayak planes and gives you all the support you need.

In a surf kayak you can run forwards in front of the piled-up 'soup' of huge waves, a feat impossible in a white-water kayak. Its responsive shape makes it easy to cut back and away from that vulnerable position at the base of a wave and makes possible other sudden changes of direction. Its great speed is such that when tracking it can be made to zigzag up and down the wave by rapidly changing from a stern rudder on one side to one on the other, a movement known as a *roller coaster*. Although it is exciting to perform a roller coaster, travelling at speed along the wave with the breaking curl following behind, the cut-back proper is even more exciting. This is cutting back the opposite way, under the breaking curl. The kayak is swiftly and deliberately swung round on to the steepest, most critical part of the wave, to pick up even more speed, before being swung back round again for another roller coaster. This, to me, has always seemed the nearest thing to flying that kayak

surfing can offer.

The shape and size of the surf kayak make it possible for a skilled handler to perform 360° spins on the face of a wave while still progressing down the wave – an experience which some find even more exhilarating than the cut-back. A number of consecutive spins can be performed on the same wave. For a spin, the surf kayak must be travelling at its fastest, usually when dropping down the face of the wave just after the cut back or during the drop of a roller coaster. As the hull skims and planes down the wave, the paddler must do a violent reverse sweep with the paddle, moving rapidly from a stern rudder position while pushing hard with the appropriate foot on the footrest to give more power to the paddle stroke. The paddler must not lean the boat, but must sit upright, thus keeping the hull flat on the sloping face of the wave. Even when broadside on to the wave, the kayak will still be sliding downwards while it is spinning.

The surf kayak must be travelling fast before trying the 360° spin. If by chance the kayak has descended to the lower part of the wave and lost some of its momentum, it will do only a half spin (180°), leaving you looking up the face of a breaking wave while still moving backwards. In this position just resign yourself to a graceful reverse loop. Surf kayaks don't do this violently but seem to stand on their tails for a considerable time before flipping over.

People evolve their own combinations of manoeu-

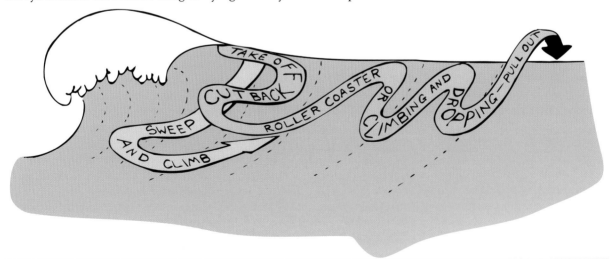

| Figure 74 | *Surf kayak and rodeo manoeuvres* |

Plate 11 *This is a good example of a planing hull. Note that the kayak is not leaning over despite the leaning action of the paddler, Rusty Sage who is performing a vigorous stern rudder.* (Photograph: Jenning Steger, SL Productions)

vres that they enjoy performing. My own favourite is a spin, then a roller coaster followed by a cut-back, and then a drop down into another spin until I run out of wave.

Like the surf kayak (figure 73.1), Rodeo playboats are also flat bottomed and therefore have the ability to plane on the face of a wave. But that is where the similarity ends. With its stern under water, paddling out through the oncoming waves in my surf kayak was always hard work. The boat was slow and it would often take all my efforts to prevent an unintentional back loop. The short Playboats boats on the other hand, are designed to perform all the basic white water manoeuvres and fortunately, this also includes paddling forwards. The hulls of these boats are flat but their width and volume give them comfort and stability making them equally at home

on white water rapids or in surf. The joy of these missiles is that, while on the face of a moving wave, they can be held, or directed and controlled and made to move in just about any direction.

If you are caught sideways to a breaking wave in a round-hull white water boat, your only choice is *to lean into the wave* and hold what can often be an arm wrenching paddle brace, while you are hurled to shore in a welter of unbreathable froth.

The joy of the rodeo playboat on the other hand, is that it can be directionally controlled even directly in front of the soup of a breaking wave.

When paddling 'round hulls', our directional strokes are controlled by *leaning the kayak over*. It is the supporting position of the paddle that keeps us from tipping over, while at the same time allowing us to place the hull in the best position to respond to

Plate 12 *Clive Kerswell working hard to stay 'in the slot' at the Northern Surfing Championships 1993*

(Photograph: Eric Chacksfield)

Plate 13 *The author performing a pirouette at the Northern Surfing championships during one of his energetic periods*

(Photograph: Derek Holmes)

Plate 14 *During the Bitches Rodeo Competition, Andy Middleton shows that you don't have to sit down all the time. The spring tide is running from left to right*
(Photograph: Sonas McWilliam)

Plate 15 *A fast tidal stream rushes over the Bitches Rocks (from right to left) forming an impressive overfall. These tumbling, standing waves form the setting for the Bitches Rodeo. the judges are perched on the nearby rock*
(Photograph: Kevin Danforth)

our paddle strokes.

The Rodeo playboat is totally different. When paddling these flat bottomed craft, we must concentrate on keeping our weight *over the boat*. We normally brace because we are intentionally reaching out beyond the cockpit to place our hull in the best position to respond to our paddle strokes. However, in order to perform any fancy manoeuvres in our playboat, we must sit *upright* and allow the hull to do its job properly. Any leaning or sideways movement of the body should be avoided.

Rodeos

White-water kayakers on inland rivers have always played in 'stoppers' and 'holes'. One of the joys of river waves is that they don't move, they just stay where they are. This is the opposite to surf waves on the sea which roll in towards shore and break on the beach.

Overfalls are the white-water, stationary waves of the sea. One of the most famous overfalls in Britain is known as The Bitches, in Pembrokeshire. The large smooth waves created by this overfall would bring tears of delight to any river white-water enthusiast.

In May 1988, the first rodeo competition in the United Kingdom was held on this overfall formed by the Bitches Rocks. The aim of the competitors in these events is to attract the judge's attention with an imaginative display of white-water skills. Paddlers perform pop-outs, paddle-spins while wave riding, pirouettes and 360s. Because these are sea waves, and therefore the paddlers are staying in one place, some extraordinary aquabatics are made possible. Some paddlers do aerial spins and even stand up while surfing the wave. I have heard that at least one top-level performer was seen to whip out his juggling balls and keep them aloft during part of his performance. For someone like myself, who could just about manage enough co-ordination to spin a paddle while surfing down the face of a wave, I find these advanced stunts quite breathtaking.

Any short white-water boats of either plastic or

Plate 16 *This is the earliest picture I know of depicting a kayak being handled in surf. ('Eskimo Life' by Fridtjof Nansen, from a picture by A. Bloch)*

fibreglass can be used, but plastic has an advantage because the bows tend to hit the bottom. Make sure you wear a good quality crash helmet and buoyancy aid, and that the kayak has adequate flotation.

If you wish to try this particular activity, make sure that you can execute an efficient Eskimo roll. Then find a quiet green wave on some not-too-severe overfall. With a companion present, practice on different parts of the wave. Try running the wave forwards then backwards. *Never practise alone.*

B.C.U. Life Guards

With his knowledge of surf techniques and skills, the kayaker offers a relatively fast method of reaching anyone in distress in open water. He can travel much faster than a swimmer and arrive far less exhausted. The use of a kayak also enables any lifeguard to patrol beyond the surf line or within it if necessary. In this way he can be a welcome addition to any existing rescue facilities, such as inshore rescue boats and rocket lines, and he augments the reel and line team while in no way replacing it.

The B.C.U. Life Guards was originally founded to operate in times of flood and natural disaster. It has now moved away from its original concept and sets a high standard in the field of beach and estuary rescue, life-saving and patrolling techniques.

One of the main purposes of the B.C.U.L.G. is to train young people in kayak handling skills so that they in turn will be able to go to the assistance of anyone in, on or under the water. The training is rigorous, as the risks involved are not inconsiderable, and it covers a wide and varied programme and is constantly changing as a result of experience, changing conditions, new equipment and more advanced techniques.

All lifeguards are trained in the following.

1 A high standard of kayaking ability, i.e. B.C.U. proficiency tests and coaching awards.

2 Royal Life Saving Society and Surf Life Saving Association methods and awards.

3 First Aid.

4 Signalling.

5 B.C.U. Life Guards methods of rescue using a combination of kayaking and life-saving techniques varying from unit to unit depending upon local conditions.

6 Patrolling methods, which also vary from unit to unit depending on local conditions.

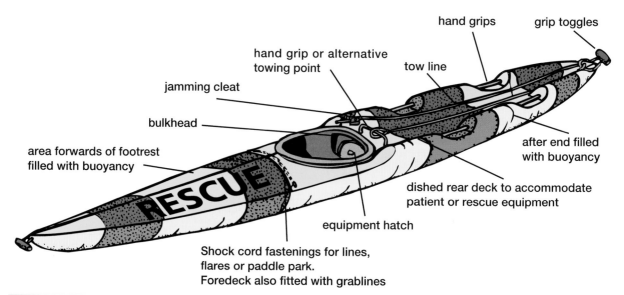

hand grips   grip toggles

hand grip or alternative
towing point   tow line

jamming cleat

bulkhead

area forwards of footrest
filled with buoyancy

after end filled
with buoyancy

dished rear deck to accommodate
patient or rescue equipment

equipment hatch

Shock cord fastenings for lines,
flares or paddle park.
Foredeck also fitted with grablines

Figure 75 *A Rescue kayak*

Plate 17 *When launching from a flat beach, remember to time the waves so that you paddle through the smallest of the set. Here Brian Henry paddles out from the shores of Vancouver Island. any equipment carried on deck must be well secured* (Photograph: Current Designs)

I suppose our attitude to physical activities is always the same. At first we just want to be able to do something. Then, once we feel we are becoming reasonably competent at something, we want to see just how good we really are compared with everyone else. In the early stages we naturally tend to match ourselves, almost unconsciously at first, against our immediate paddling partners. I should give you a word of caution here. You may find that your tendency to always want to be out in front does not particularly endear you to your friends; indeed you may soon discover that your desire to constantly keep that tiny bit ahead of your companions renders you totally friendless. Fortunately for your social life, and for the general safety of the group, the time will come (the sooner the better) when you will look further afield for these challenges.

This is when you will discover racing. I'm not talking about the International Olympic stuff here. I'm referring to the type of fun races put on by clubs, stores and organisations, who offer prizes of various kinds, ranging from small amounts of cash, to items of equipment that have been donated by sponsors (you might even pick up a free kayak).

Racing has a lot going for it. It's obviously very physical and the training you need to dedicate yourself to is aerobic and utilises your whole body mechanism, right down to the tips of your toes. But it has other attractive components such as glamour, colour and excitement. Sometimes there is even an element of danger, although organisers try to keep this to a minimum.

For me personally, it's not merely the actual race that appeals. The whole circus is a delightful thrill, right from driving my car into the race car park to fastening the kayak back onto the roof at the end of the day. As I look for a place to park, I can see all manner of different craft being unloaded. Nowadays you would see quite a number of narrow racing skis adding to the colourful scene.

All competitors have to register and while standing in the line, you will notice that everyone seems to know everyone else. There is excited banter as sticking on numbers or perhaps brightly coloured numbered vests are collected. It is this lively atmosphere which starts to kick in the adrenaline. There is no shortage of humour as there is always someone who makes the startling discovery that the white numbered circle they have been allocated refuses to stick to the deck of their boat. Long forgotten holes are discovered and the cry for duct tape is heard. Others, meanwhile, are searching their tool kits for pliers in order to string together wayward rudders. One race I have entered on several occasions demands that all competitors carry certain items of safety equipment before they are allowed to enter. These items include two hand flares, a repair kit, a first aid kit, a tow line and a large plastic exposure bag. Under the eagle eye of the scrutineers, most competitors discover they lack some item or other. Fortunately, the trade anticipates this and is on hand to supply the need – at a price.

The joy of these informal, fun races for sea kayaks is that people can turn up with just about any kind of kayak or ski. So long as there is a class for your type of kayak, and it passes the eye of the scrutineers, all you have to do is put your name down to gain your position on the starting line. The paddles and buoyancy aids that competitors use are the normal everyday touring kind, and the skills required to win are simply being able to maintain your normal touring stroke faster and longer than anyone else.

Starting can be hilarious. Trying to get fifty or a hundred competitors to stay in position for a 'straight' line start, can try the patience of any organiser. Personally, I prefer the Le Mans type start. In this, the kayaks are lined up on the sand at the water's edge. At the sound of the gun, horn or whistle (sometimes even a distant dog bark!), everyone sprints down the beach. Kayaks are then snatched up and dragged twenty yards or so to the water's edge. Depending upon the rules, spray skirts will have to be fitted before pushing off from the beach.

I remember one memorable massed start I took part in. Our kayaks were all lined up right at the waters edge. I was number 13 and I had my strategy all planned. With water lapping against the hull, I placed my kayak as near to the water's edge as possible. All I had to do was jump in and push off from the sand. That was the plan!

As I stood, leaning forwards into the start position, adrenaline coursing through my veins, the starter/organiser took the opportunity to launch into an infuriatingly lengthy preamble, running over the details of our island hopping course and the marker buoys that had been placed at strategic points to help us find our way around. He went on to outline the duty of the numerous rescue craft. There was even a moment when I thought he would mention them all by name. He droned on and continued to enlighten us on the morning's weather forecast, the wind speed and the temperature of the water. I never actually heard him finish. All I could think of was run down, jump in and push off!

Suddenly the gun went off and I was away like a startled greyhound. I sprinted down the beach and jumped into my boat well ahead of everyone else. Just as I reached to put on my spray cover, I realised that everyone on both sides of me had picked up their boats and were running past me and on into the water, which had now receded some 20 yards. Unfortunately, I had not noticed that the tide had been going out and the boats had been left high and dry! Thankfully, things did improve after that and I gained first place.

Time moves on and although we can still race our touring sea kayaks, the fast narrow, racing skis have introduced the Olympic Rotary stroke to the sea kayaking scene.

THE RACING STROKE

The racing stroke I am about to describe, is performed with what is known as a 'Wing' paddle. The cross section of a Wing blade echoes the cross section of an aeroplane wing. It has broad leading edge, while the top curves away to a fine trailing edge. If

the Wing blade is presented vertically to the water at the commencement of the stroke and then moved outwards, the dihedral angle will cause the blade to 'fly' forwards with no slip towards the rear and therefore no loss of power. (Fig. 76.4). Let us look at this new stroke in stages. I have drawn in an imaginary floating marker, positioned exactly where the paddle enters the water for the catch. This will help you appreciate the position of the immersed paddle blade throughout the stroke.

Phase one

Fig. 76.1 shows the position of my body just before my upper arm is thrown forwards and I present the paddle to the water in the 'catch' position. In reality, I fall onto the paddle blade as it enters the water. This is also known in racing circles as the Bent Shaft Position, (BSP) and it was first described to me by Barney

My right arm is almost at a right angle and is well out from, but almost level with, my right ear.

My right wrist is low and my left arm is straight

My right leg is starting to straighten in anticipation of its forward push against the footrest.

During the stroke cycle, this is the position of my body immediately prior to the 'catch' or Bent Shaft Position. It is also the body position a split second after the right blade has been clipped from the water at the end of the stroke on that side.

Figure 76.1 Phase 1

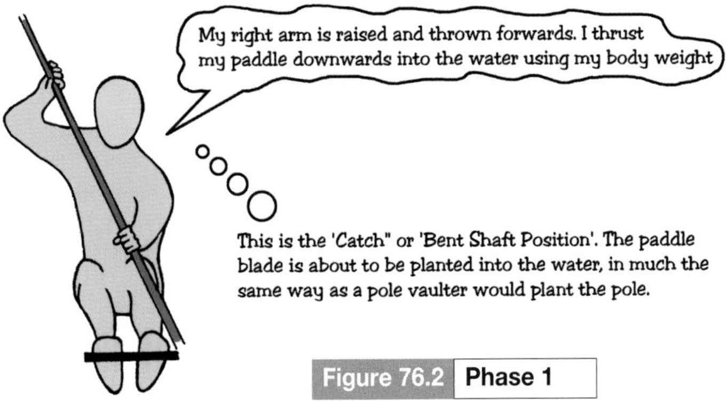

My right arm is raised and thrown forwards. I thrust my paddle downwards into the water using my body weight

This is the 'Catch" or 'Bent Shaft Position'. The paddle blade is about to be planted into the water, in much the same way as a pole vaulter would plant the pole.

Figure 76.2 Phase 1

Wainwright, the BCU's Sports Science Officer.

'The Bent Shaft is when the paddle is bent due to the stress put on it during the "catch". This is almost impossible to see except in some photographs and only during high, forceful efforts. It is akin to a pole vault when the pole is locked into position and the athlete is driven up and forwards. In the same way, your blade is locked into the water and you are driven up and forwards, thereby reducing drag. This is a conceptional model to visualise during paddling and really only applies to racing.'

What you are trying to achieve therefore, is to bend the paddle shaft by the combined tension of the pulling and pushing arm. It is the blade's com-

pression against the water that triggers the locking tension in the shoulder on the stroke side.

Fig. 76.3 Anyone looking at you from the side should see your back in full view.

Just as walking forwards on land can be described as a continuous falling action arrested by alternate feet, in a similar manner, consider the *forward racing stroke as a series of capsizes arrested by alternate 'catches'.*

Fig. 76.4 Viewed from above, the apparent and actual path of the paddle becomes clear. The stroke can only start when the paddle blade is vertical in the water i.e. the when the paddle shaft is as vertical as it is possible to get it.

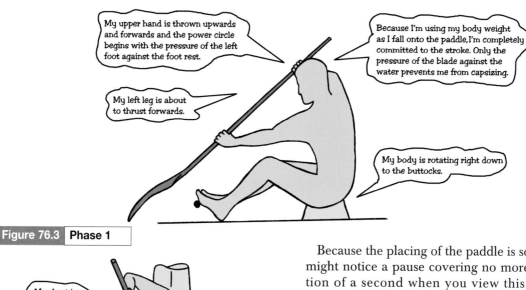

My upper hand is thrown upwards and forwards and the power circle begins with the pressure of the left foot against the foot rest.

Because I'm using my body weight as I fall onto the paddle, I'm completely committed to the stroke. Only the pressure of the blade against the water prevents me from capsizing.

My left leg is about to thrust forwards.

My body is rotating right down to the buttocks.

Figure 76.3 | **Phase 1**

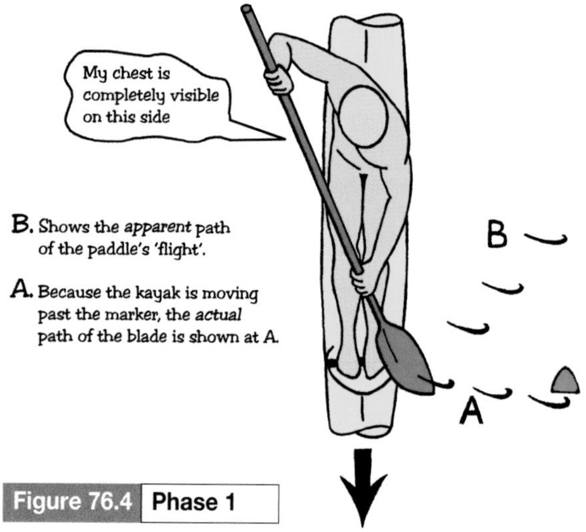

My chest is completely visible on this side

B. Shows the *apparent* path of the paddle's 'flight'.

A. Because the kayak is moving past the marker, the *actual* path of the blade is shown at A.

B

A

Figure 76.4 | **Phase 1**

Because the placing of the paddle is so critical, you might notice a pause covering no more than a fraction of a second when you view this stage in the stroke cycle.

Phase two

Fantastic though this may sound, your aim is to pull the weight of your buttocks off the seat. If you are paddling correctly at this stage of the stroke, you should feel that your body, together with the boat, are being lifted out of the water. Concentrate on rotating your body vigorously forward. In this way, the line of power down from the pulling side shoulder to the opposite hip will maintain the tension. You should try and imagine that your shoulders and the *paddle* are hanging on strings like a wooden

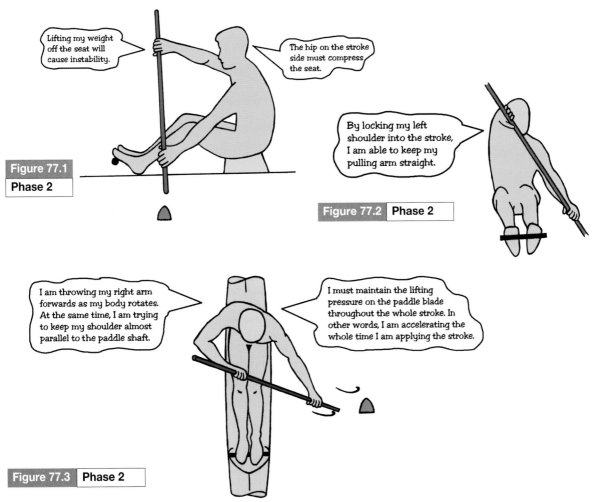

Figure 77.1
Phase 2

Figure 77.2 Phase 2

Figure 77.3 Phase 2

puppet. This is only possible if you maintain the pressure against the paddle blade *and keep the kayak accelerating all the way throughout the stroke.* The tension from the pressure applied to the footrest, is transferred to the stroke shoulder. At the same time the lower hand pulls against the paddle as it 'flies' outwards. Remember that powerful legwork is vital for the structure of the whole stroke (Fig 77.1).

If you present the paddle to the water efficiently and maintain a constant pull on the paddle blade during phases 1 and 2, your bodyweight will be transferred from the kayak to the paddle. In this way you will lighten your boat as it moves forward. The more powerful the swing forwards, the greater is the force which locks the blade in the water. Remember

to keep your pulling arm almost straight throughout the stroke (Fig 77.2).

Looked at from above, it can be seen that the paddle shaft is kept parallel to the line of the shoulders. Notice that, during the stroke, there has been no slip backwards on the part of the paddle blade in relation to the marker buoy (Fig 77.3).

Phase three

This is the final stage of the stroke cycle.

The kayak has been pulled forwards, towards the locked blade and then moved past it.

It is vital that the kayak is kept straight and level, so you must avoid any *bouncing, snaking or rocking*

Figure 78.1 | Phase 3

Figure 78.3 | Phase 3

Figure 78.2 | Phase 3

Figure 78.4 | Phase 3

from side to side.

You must rotate your lower body towards the pulling blade; in order too counteract any turning effect that your pull on the paddle may have.

You must recover quickly between the strokes so that there is no time for your body to sink backwards and downwards and thus allow the kayak to settle back into the water.

Mastering the Racing Stroke will not be immediate but with practice you will come to appreciate how all your body movements interact with the kayak.

It is because a high speed cyclic motion has to be maintained, that racing paddles should weigh as little as possible.

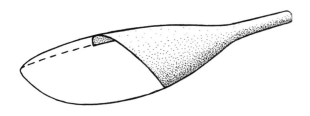

Figure 78.5 *Wing paddle blade – cut away cross section of a right hand wing paddle blade:*
The original wing paddle blade was developed by Stephen Lindeberg of Sweden in 1985–6. Extensive testing was carried out using both conventional blades and wings, and it was found that though it was slightly slower off the start, overall the wing was more efficient if the correct technique was used.

The Swedish team used the wing before anyone else, and had exceptionally good results. British paddler Jeremy West realised the potential very quickly – winning the 500m and 1000m at the Montreal World Championships.

A few years after the wing was introduced, a Norwegian called Rasmussen improved the design by adding a slight twist to the blade. This reduced vortexing, improving its efficiency. Now there are hybrids of this design produced all around the world, and all sprint and most marathon paddlers use the wing shape.

CONCLUSION

In this chapter I have tried to present to the everyday touring paddler, the Racing Stroke as used by international competitors. First let me warn you that racing kayaks or the equally fast racing skis have an unstable cross section that is designed for speed and speed alone. Unfortunately, for you as a touring paddler, stability is an important consideration, so if you jump into (or onto) one of these missiles in an attempt to impress your friends by rocketing over the horizon, be prepared for a wetting. First, you will have to spend some time getting used to the racing boats tippyness. Then you'll have to go out, purchase a wing paddle and come to terms with its peculiar handling characteristics. As I previously explained, the 'Wing' is designed for travelling in the 'flying' direction through the water. However, the minute you try to perform any of the basic strokes which include draws, sculls or braces, you will have only limited success and you could well finish up swimming. The problem is that by attempting some of these strokes, you will be forced to put the Wing into a position where you are actually trying to make it fly backwards. This could make for a very unhappy day and make you wish you had worn your immersion clothing.

If you want to try for a little extra speed, it is quite acceptable to use a Wing paddle with your touring kayak. Remember however, that because your touring boat is wider than the racing boat, your forward stroke will start much farther out from the centre line of the boat. Therefore, the length of your outward 'flight' will be shorter. Because stability is not a problem, as you plant you blade for the 'catch' in your touring boat, you will not have the advantage of capsizing your bodyweight onto the paddle blade.

CAUTION. When you finally buy your wing paddle, please do not be tempted to immediately thrash off into the middle distance at high speed. Athletes train for this kind of thing and they build up their speeds and distances gradually. In this way, their heart beat and respiration keeps pace with their performance. Any untrained paddler, who sprints off at high speed and who attempts to maintain this for as long as possible, will soon begin to pant for breath. This means that they will be sucking in an excessive amount of oxygen to the detriment of Carbon Dioxide. Now it is the Carbon Dioxide in the air that you inhale, which triggers your involuntary breathing mechanism. So, if no Carbon Dioxide goes into your lungs, then you will not want to breathe. It is called hyperventilation and it's very dangerous. The result of this strenuous effort is that you will very probably black out. It once happened

to me many years ago when I was training for a cycle Road Race. I'd been peddling furiously and then suddenly I woke up with a very sore head and my nose buried in the tarmac amidst and a good deal of blood. The good news is that in a kayak, your landing will be softer. The bad news is that the results could be more permanent.

REMEMBER A life vest may prevent you from sinking but it won't prevent you from drowning.

Plate 18 *This picture, taken at the Marathon World Racing Championships in Nova Scotia 2000, bears close scrutiny. The front group of paddlers from left to right: Ivan Lawler (GBR), Greg Barton (USA), Tomas Jezek (CZE), Conor Holmes (GBR), Dolph Te Linde (NED), Manuel Busto (ESP), Istvan Salga (HUN). The race had only 16 km to go and to ensure a good result, a good position at this stage is vital. In this race the competitors have chosen not to wear spray skirts. In rougher conditions this may not be the case.*

This is a good photograph to show the lateral movement of the wing paddle. However, note that by the time the paddle has reached this point, the face of the blade is angled well back, meaning that there is little propulsion in the forward direction available. By this stage of the race, fatigue will have set in and the paddling technique will not be at its most efficient. Top arms will have dropped quite low and the paddle will stay in the water a little too long.

(Photo & Caption Barney Wainwright)

Plate 19 *Anna Hemmings pictured at the Marathon Racing World Championshps, Stockton-on-Tees, UK, 2001. She had a good position in the boat, sitting upright but leaning slightly forward which enables more body weight to be put on the blade at the next catch. Good rotated position after finishing one stroke will enable a lot of rotation during the next stroke. As can be seen, the line of the shoulders is virtually parallel with the paddle shaft. The right leg has already fully extended and now the left leg is ready to push against the footrest just before the left blade enters the water.*

Anna Hemmings is using a drinks system in which the fluid reservoir is fixed to the boat. Even in these moderate conditions in the UK (19°C), fluid intake is important and is taken on early, as can be seen here, 8 km into the race. For races over one hour, the consumption of fluids is essential, to both avoid dehydration and offset the depletion of carbohydrate stores in the muscles and liver, both of which will decrease sustainable work rate and performance. If the environmental conditions are very hot and humid, fluids may be needed for events shorter than one hour. A beverage should contain between 4% and 8% carbohydrate depending on whether the preventing dehydration or providing energy is more important. Fluid intakes of 0.5 to 1.0 litres per hour may be required depending upon the environmental conditions and the intensity of work. For races or activities of longer duration it may be necessary to use a carbohydrate-electrolyte solution containing sodium. This will help to replace sodium lost in sweat and increase the thirst drive, making the paddler drink more frequently.

(Photo & Caption: Barney Wainwright)

Plate 20 *Greg Barton was a four time Olympic Gold medal winner. In the stroke cycle, viewed from the left side, he is a fraction of a second ahead of Anna Hemmings, (Plate 19). He is about to present the left blade into the catch position. His back is fully visible and he is still pressing down hard with his right foot.*   (Photograph: Barney Wainwright)

Plate 21 *A kayak race by the Port Burwell Eskimos during HBC Governor P. A. Cooper's visit, 1934.*

(Photograph: H. Bassett)

Rescues

6

Capsizing is part of the sport of kayaking. It is what happens after the capsize that is most important. The Eskimo Roll is the first line of defence. Of course, rolls can go wrong, paddles can break, strange and weird things can happen to technique on cold windy days when the hands are numb. So the next line of defence is the Eskimo Rescue. There comes a time, however, in steep breaking seas following close on top of each other, that Eskimo rescues, if indeed possible, should be attempted only with the greatest caution for fear of injury to arms, head and boat. All rescues, needless to say, must be practised first, preferably in a swimming pool or sheltered water.

The Eskimo Bow Rescue

The Bow Rescue by the Eskimo method is the easiest rescue to teach as well as to do, and hence it is the most common.

When you capsize, bang quickly and hard on the bottom of your kayak to attract attention – it really does! Then slowly move the hands fore and aft in an arc (Figure 76:1A), covering about a yard during the sweep. This gives you more chance of contacting the bow of the kayak which is presented to you, saving your rescuer unnecessary manoeuvring – and, of course, time. You may feel toggles or the round ending of some Eskimo kayaks. They are very comforting to grasp and give you something to hold on to. Then pull yourself up, as in Figure 79.1B. In the illustration the patient is in such a position that he will now have to turn his left hand round to continue his upward push. It sometimes helps if the rescuer can paddle in towards the patient as he pulls himself upwards. The rescuer must lose no time in getting over to his patient, but the last yard must be careful and controlled. When practising this in a pool, it is as well to wear a crash helmet, just in case someone is over enthusiastic.

A

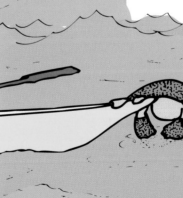

B

Figure 79.1 *The Eskimo Bow Rescue*

Figure 79.2 | *The Eskimo Side Rescue – the approach*

The Eskimo Side Rescue

The Side Rescue is by far the more useful Eskimo method. If someone capsizes in front of you, paddle fast; as you come alongside the upturned boat, without slowing down grasp the nearest wrist of the patient tightly. Then, as your kayak loses momentum with the drag of the other, place his hand on your paddle loom (Figure 79.3). Your man brings his other hand round underneath to hold your loom and pulls himself to the surface (Figure 79.4). The man in the illustration will have to change the grip with his right hand to finish off his push into the upright position. It is important that the rescuer place the nearest hand on the paddle loom; otherwise the capsized man may well grab the loom on the wrong side. An hysterical little scene is then enacted as our hero tries to pull himself up on the wrong side, usually to no avail, while the rescuer tries as calmly as possible to inform the man, still underwater of course, that he wants to be up on the other side. The man being rescued must have sufficient control and air not to clutch in desperation the first thing his hand touches. Grasping the rescuer's wrist in a vice-like death clutch doesn't help anybody. The joy of the Side Rescue is that it can be done quickly. Even if the rescuer is approaching from a position at right angles to the upturned boat, he can always turn at the last minute and execute a side rescue rather than a bow rescue, thus minimising the chance of putting a hole in the boat.

Figure 79.3 | *Guiding the hand*

Figure 79.4

DEEP-WATER RESCUES

A man in the water with an upturned kayak beside him presents an entirely different rescue situation. Over the years, various methods of deep-water rescues involving emptying and re-entering a capsized kayak have been devised, tried and tested. Some have been rejected out of hand as being far too complicated, while others have failed in rough conditions.

Figure 80.1 | *HI Deep Water Rescue – 3 persons. Positioning the upturned kayak*

Figure 80.2 | *Emptying the kayak*

Figure 80.3 | *Rear deck method of re-entry. This view of the rescue is from the opposite direction in order to show the method of re-entry more clearly*

One, called the 'H' Rescue, was popular for many years. The upturned kayak was lifted and emptied while being held at either end by the rescuers, their kayaks being parallel to each other and the boat to be emptied at right angles to them. In choppy or windy conditions, paddles went astray, the rescuers were unsupported, and the boats drifted together, putting the men in a very unstable position while they were still holding the kayak in the air. I have not included this rescue as its use is so limited.

The HI Rescue

The most successful rescue in really rough conditions is the 'HI' (so called because of the position of the kayaks), also known as the Ipswich. During the rescue the paddles are under control; the kayaks form a close raft giving stability, and the man in the water, besides being able to help considerably with the rescue, need never lose contact with the rescue kayaks. The rescuing paddlers position themselves at either side of the upturned bow about a yard apart, facing into the swell. The three paddles forming a bridge across the boats, the bow of the upturned boat is lifted high so that the cockpit clears the water (Figure 80:1).

Helped by the man in the water, the kayak is then fed backwards over the paddles and rested on its cockpit coaming, where it can be see-sawed by the rescuers. They are assisted by the man in the water, who supports himself on one of the bows while pushing upwards and then pulling down, all in time with the swell, thus emptying the kayak (Figure 80.2).

The boat is turned the right way up, put on to the water, pushed forwards, then back under the paddles into the re-entry raft position. To execute a rear deck re-entry, the paddles can be kept across the boats or pushed out of the way. The positions of the rescuers' arms are also variable. They can be as in Figure80.3 or they can be crossed over each other, one hand of each man grasping the opposite side of the cockpit coaming, thus making a stronger link. Practice will help the individual decide which is best.

The patient comes between his own kayak and one of the rescuing boats, places his hands on the apex of both decks – his afterdeck and the other's foredeck – the head is thrown back level with the water, the legs are hooked into the cockpit, the behind is raised up and entry is accomplished by an ungainly forward wiggle. The rescuers keep support-ing the raft until the spray cover is firmly secured.

From the positioning of the kayaks to the finish of the rescue should take about one minute during prac-tice on calm water. I practise this in a swimming pool, creating artificial waves by tossing a boat up and down in the shallow end, while helpers splash with paddles all around the deep end and the odd sadist throws buckets of water over the participants for added realism.

Some points to remember on open water:

1 Be quick! The man in the water may freeze.

2 It is better to lift the bow first, because there should be more buoyancy in the back half of the kayak. For all methods of rescue the boat must be full of buoyancy. I was going to go on to say that if you did have inadequate buoyancy, you deserve all you get, but unfortunately someone else gets it. You won't have the job of lifting your own waterlogged kayak, although you will have to spend much longer freezing to death in the water while someone else does the struggling.

3 The man in the water must at no time lose contact with the rescue group if conditions are windy. His kayak and those of the two rescuers can be blown away faster than he can swim after them. So hang on to at least one boat at all times.

4 Re-entry can sometimes be a problem.

The man in the water must remember to tuck his spray cover out of the way before hoisting himself up on to his rear deck. A rear deck carrying equipment, together with all the attendant elastics, ropes and hooks, can present a man whose legs are straddled across a flat Eskimo deck with untold problems as he tries to hitch himself forwards towards the cockpit.

Considerable strain is sometimes placed on the rescuers' arms when the patient raises himself from the water on to the back deck.

The 'T' or 'X' Rescue

The 'T' Rescue is a rescue whereby a capsized kayak is emptied and the rescue completed by only one paddler. Because of this, it is ideal for instructors and leaders who wish to get people out of the water quickly. This rescue is also of practical use for those who paddle with only one companion.

1 Prevent both pairs of paddles from floating away. This can be done with a paddle leash, or the person in the water can tuck the paddles between his legs. The swimmer's hands are now free to hold on firmly to the rescuer's cockpit coaming and give stability during the initial lift.

2 The rescuer grasps the bow of the upturned kayak and lifts quickly in order to prevent any further water from entering through the cockpit opening (Figure 81.1). The upturned boat is then pulled across until its cockpit is resting on the foredeck of the rescue craft. Beware – this rescue is a spray-skirt shredder.

3 The rescuer see-saws the upturned boat until all the water has drained out. Assistance may be given by the person in the water who can pull down on the bow toggle (Figure 81.2). To reach that position, the swimmer should move hand-over-hand along the foredeck of the upturned

Figure 81.1

Figure 81.2 | *The 'T' or 'X' Rescue*

boat, holding on to the deck lines. In strong winds, even losing a grip on the boats for a second can allow them to be blown away faster than anyone can swim after them. In the event of this unpleasant situation, the kayak would have to be emptied by the rescuer alone and then towed in the upright position back to the swimmer. This is assuming that the rescuer had maintained visual contact with the person in the water.

If there is too much water in the capsized boat, its excessive weight could crack one or both of the decks during the see-saw operation. It would be more prudent to remove the worst of the water by the Curl (Figure 90) before attempting the 'T' Rescue.

T-Quick Rescue

This is possibly the quickest and the easiest of all the deep water rescues, but to be successful, your kayak needs to have the modern safety feature of watertight compartments and bulkheads.

In practical terms, it means that rescues can now be performed without the ever present fear of swamping – with its attendant horrors. It also means that with very little practice you can put your partner back into their boat in less than a minute.

Because of the position that boats take up on the water, this rescue is still virtually a 'T' Rescue but due to the speed and safety by which it can be performed, I have called it the T-Quick.

Figure 82.1 *The T-Quick Rescue: Position yourself at the BOW of the upturned boat. When boats are floating upside down, it can be difficult to distinguish the front from the back. Look for the two screws that hold the footrest – that's the front. The swimmer holds onto the stern and, with your help, lifts and twists the bow of the kayak so that it turns right side up. Some water will be scooped into the cockpit but that is to be expected*

Figure 82.2 *The T-Quick Rescue: Grasp the bow toggle and get your capsized friend to press gently down on the stern. Use the wedge-shape angle of the bow to help you to lift and pull the front end of the boat over onto your deck. Your friend can help with a push*

Figure 82.3 *The T-Quick Rescue: Pull the top of the bow over towards you so that the boat is now resting over on the flat side of its bow. The act of turning the boat over should begin to drain the cockpit and with the cockpit facing you, you'll be in the position to see this happen*

Figure 82.4 *The T-Quick Rescue: If you are fussy and you wish to remove that extra drop of water, haul the kayak farther over your deck, twist it completely upside down and lift it slightly*

Figure 82.5 *The T-Quick Rescue: Now that the kayak is empty, turn it over onto its right side and slide it back into the water. It is now time to get your friend back into the boat. The emptied kayak is now alongside. Make sure it is facing in the same direction. Help your partner climb back in by using the side re-entry as described in Fig. 83*

The All-in Rescue

This is when things begin to look grim even to the most optimistic. You are in the water with an upturned kayak; all your companions are swimming beside you, also with their boats upside-down. There is no one upright to perform a rescue. Don't underestimate the panic factor, especially if there is only you and one other. The situation is not an unlikely one: in fact, all this can happen very easily in a sudden unexpected squall.

Keep calm. All is not lost. I devised the following system some years ago and you will find it works well even in rough conditions.

First of all, collect your wits, then the paddles. Tow two of the kayaks together, keeping them upside-down. The following procedure can be performed simultaneously by other pairs in the capsized group. If they are all novices, they simply wait, holding on to their paddles and kayaks until you are back in your kayak ready to rescue them.

Secure the paddles into the parks or deck elastics so you don't lose them. In the absence of either, tuck the paddles between your legs.

The delicate part of the whole operation is emptying the first kayak without losing the air trapped inside – this will be used as a pivot. The two swimmers position themselves to face opposite ways, on either side of the kayak that we shall call the 'pivot boat'. Underneath the water they each hold the cockpit coaming with one hand. This prevents the boat from tipping sideways and losing the supporting air trapped inside. We shall suppose that you are on the right side, so your kayak will be the first one to be emptied.

As shown in Figure 83.1 you lift the bow of your kayak as high as possible into the air. Retaining your grip on the coaming of the pivot boat with your right hand, you feed or throw the upturned kayak across to your partner (Figure 83.2). Then, with the pivot boat underneath kept as steady and as level as possible, the top kayak can be see-sawed carefully and emptied (Figure 83.3).

Once your kayak is emptied you are faced with the problem of getting back into it without filling the pivot boat. You must form a bridge with the paddles across the two kayaks (Figure 83.4). The swimmer in

Figure 83.1 *Positioning the first boat for emptying. The paddles are secured either by paddle leashes or between the legs of the paddler of the pivot boat*

Figure 83.2 *The pivot boat is held firmly from below while the kayak to be emptied is lifted and pulled across into the see-saw position*

Figure 83.3 *Emptying the first kayak across the pivot boat using a see-sawing movement*

Figure 83.4 *Entering the cockpit is easier if the paddles are placed behind the cockpit forming a bridge as shown*

the water on the far side acts as a counter-balance by putting weight on the paddles. This means that you can put your weight on the paddles at your side. To re-enter the cockpit you will need to kick your legs outwards and haul yourself up so that the weight of your chest is across the paddles. You then direct your legs into the cockpit. This re-entry is not graceful, and in poor conditions it will require much energy and determination. However, any pressure you may put on the pivot boat while you are making your re-entry can be counteracted by your partner. The pivot kayak can now be emptied by means of a 'T' rescue.

Most of the tests I have done have been with kayaks with no buoyancy. This meant that any tilting of the pivot boat caused it to fill and sink. With kayaks even moderately full of buoyancy, the rescues can be completed quickly and efficiently.

There are two points worth mentioning here. During the rescue there will be an upturned kayak between you and your partner. Because of this you may be out of sight of one another. Therefore, in order to communicate, direct and encourage one another, you will have to shout. The result of the following experiment will depend very much upon the shape of your kayak's deck and the position of its rear bulkhead. Swim to the stern of your upturned boat and haul your weight up on to it. With any luck this will bring the kayak's bow out of the water far enough for most of the water to drain out. Then, without letting the boat fall back into the water, flip it over on to its right side.

The Stirrup Re-entry

You have finally emptied the kayak and all you have to do is put the paddler back into the cockpit. Suddenly, you are faced with problems you never anticipated.

Some people simply do not have the necessary strength in their upper body or arms to haul themselves back into the cockpit from a swimming position at water level. If your patient has this difficulty, then the Stirrup Re-entry should solve the problem.

Whether you go for the long or the short stirrup depends entirely upon you. Try both methods in practice sessions. The simplest systems work best.

For the long stirrup make a loop out of, say, 20 ft. of 3/4-inch or 1-inch rope. Adjust the size of the loop to suit your needs. The rope should be the non-floating kind otherwise you'll never get your foot into the stirrup! To make the foothold easy to find, thread a piece of hose-pipe about 8 in. long on to the rope and make a small secondary loop by tying a knot just above it (Figure 84.1). To assist in the re-entry simply pull the loop over your head to around your waist. The other, long, end of the loop lies across the empty kayak with the stirrup hanging about two feet under the water. The weight and athletic prowess of your patient will govern how and where you hold the kayak, the paddles and the paddler!

Some rescuers prefer to loop one end of the stirrup on to the middle of a paddle shaft. This paddle is then placed beneath and at right angles to the two kayaks.

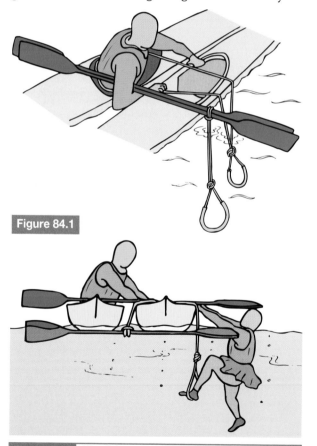

Figure 84.1

Figure 84.2 *The Stirrup-assisted Rescue*

The stirrup end of the loop is brought up between the kayaks, over the empty boat and allowed to hang down on the outside ready for the re-entry (Figure 84.2). All the stress is exerted upwards on the underside of the hulls and not on your rib-cage. But I find this method too time consuming and not something I would wish to do when it's very rough.

For the short stirrup, you want a loop made from a piece of rope about 8 ft. long. Do not forget the hose-pipe, nor to knot the loop. When you perform the normal two-person re-entry, loop the stirrup round the part of the paddle that projects out over the water on the patient's side. Any downward strain is then taken by the paddle shaft pressing upwards under your armpit.

Many years ago, one of my pupils found it very difficult to re-enter from deep water, but found instant success using a stirrup with three little aluminium rungs – rather like a rope ladder.

If, and I repeat, if a rescue must be done within the surf line, 'rafted' rescues are not a good proposition because escape from paddles, partner and a patient's boat is a slow process. With the 'T' Rescue, however, if the rescuer sees a large breaking wave approaching he can throw the upturned kayak off his foredeck quickly and look after himself. Rafted rescues done within the surf line, although providing endless entertainment for onlookers on the beach, rarely have more than a 50% chance of success (Figure 85). At best the rescuers will have many tense moments, at worst, damaged boats and serious injury.

If a capsize occurs within the surf line, entailing a long and dangerous swim ashore, it is best to tow man and upturned kayak farther out to sea and perform a rescue away from the breakers.

Any person who leads or guides groups on open water should be able to take charge of any of the rescues described, if necessary from a position actu-

Figure 85   *Things can go sadly wrong when rescues are attempted inside the surf line*

ally in the water. They should also be able to empty a boat unassisted, something they may have to do more than once when leading novice expeditions.

Over the years, I have been obliged to encourage students to experiment with many types of re-entry to meet the needs of various circumstances and differing abilities. In doing so I have been forced to listen to chaotic crashes and thuds, screams of agony and plaintive pleas, especially from fragile young misses, that arms were simply not strong enough. Finally, in desperation, I developed a method of a side re-entry needing so little effort on the part of the rescuer that a third kayak is unnecessary. The man in Figure 86 could easily let go of the cockpit coaming with his right hand and grasp the seat of the patient's pants or the bottom of his buoyancy aid and assist him into the cockpit if necessary. All the weight is on the paddle loom where it touches the deck, not on the rescuer's arm. The rescuer may feel simply an upward pressure under his armpit.

The person in the water hoists himself up by placing his left hand at the centre rear of the cockpit coaming, the other hand on the paddle loom. He then pulls himself upwards, placing his behind squarely over the cockpit, after executing a neat half turn to the right.

Just before the flare

Paddling a kayak alone on the sea is a dangerous business, but with the high level of expertise which can be reached and the provision of hatches, bulkheads and pumps, more people are going it alone. To condemn the adventurous is pointless; it is more important to develop rescue techniques which enable them to pursue their own particular road to Valhalla with at least some margin of safety.

Various methods of solo deep water re-entry have been experimented with and the results have ranged from the humorous to the horrifying. Any sea condition which is going to eject an experienced man from his kayak is going to be too rough for rear deck 'hitching' even if the paddle can be fastened to the deck in the form of an outrigger. The only system which works every time for me in rough breaking seas is the R & R, that is, re-entry and roll. It requires

KICK YOUR LEGS TO THE SURFACE ~ THEN LIFT YOUR BODY UP AND OVER SO THAT YOUR CHEST IS LAID ACROSS THE PADDLES. KEEP YOUR WEIGHT ON THE PADDLES WHILE YOU ARE GETTING YOUR LEGS INSIDE THE COCKPIT.

Figure 86 *Side method of re-entry*

skill and nerve and on no account should it be practised on the open sea alone.

See Figure 87. Face the rear of the kayak, one arm stretched out underneath the cockpit coaming at the far side. Hold the paddle in the correct hand ready for a roll on the side of your choice. With both hands holding the coaming, steady the boat, take a deep breath and submerge. Still grasping the coaming and paddle, curl up your legs, drop your head back and let your legs enter the cockpit as part of a reverse somersault (Figures 87.2 and 87.3). If you have already practised this in your local swimming baths you should now be able to roll up.

While you are in the throes of this rather drastic manoeuvre you may find that your body is never completely submerged due to the buoyancy of your life jacket. Once in the upright position again, get the spray cover on as soon as possible to prevent any waves breaking into the boat. Start pumping and, with some practice the boat will be dry in 3–4 minutes. This is one occasion on which a hand-held pump is really useful.

If you are unfortunate enough not to have a pump, steady the kayak in the following manner. Rest one end of the paddle across your shoulder and skull for support with one hand, leaving the other hand free to bale or sponge the water out. If you capsize in an overfall it may be necessary to swim clear with the boat or wait until you drift into calmer water before attempting a re-entry.

| Figure 87.1 | *Re-entry and roll method of self-rescue* |

| Figure 87.2 | *Re-entry and roll – fish-eye view* |

| Figure 87.3 | *Re-entry and roll – surface view* |

The Paddle Float Rescue

The Paddle Float is not really a rough-water rescue, although I have seen it done successfully in high winds and a steep unpleasant sea. The person I watched, however, was an experienced man who had no fear of the water conditions. The place was San Francisco Bay and the demonstration made me realise the potential of this comparatively uncomplicated means of solo re-entry.

Any experienced lone paddler who finds himself in the water will probably revert to the re-entry and roll. The novice, however, who finds himself alone and friendless while swimming next to his boat – whether by foolishness or force of circumstance – will have to think of some other method of getting back in again. Even though weather conditions may be calm, a gust of wind or some other unforeseen circumstance may catch a paddler unawares and cause a capsize. It is for just such a situation that I have included this method of unassisted re-entry. The rescue was originally described by Peter Dyer in 1970, in the September issue of Canoeing in Britain.

By utilising the paddle as a fixed outrigger and fastening some means of flotation to the extended blade it was found to be possible for a lone paddler to re-enter his kayak again, after it had been turned the right way up. Unfortunately, the original guidelines for this manoeuvre called upon the capsized paddler to remove his lifejacket in the water, so that it could then be tied on to the end of the paddle. Because there were obvious dangers in this somewhat bizarre advice, the 'Dyer Outrigger Method' was not given serious consideration by the majority of sea paddlers.

Under the name 'Paddle Wing', it was revived in the United States by a kayak designer who gave sanity to the system. He recommended that a water container be tied on to the end of the paddle, and suggested the soft plastic kind that has a carrying handle and a drain tap through which it could be inflated. An ingenious part of his idea was to fill the container a quarter full of water. The added weight would thus minimise the risk of a capsize on the opposite side.

The method was effective but clumsy. However, the whole idea was to be simplified even further by Will Nordby of California, who experimented with various air pillows and bags after he had been involved in a capsize which he felt could easily have proved fatal. His friend Bob Licht of the Seatrek Ocean Kayaking Centre helped with the tests and experiments, and the two men eventually presented their ideas to a manufacturer. The 'Paddle Float' which resulted from their joint efforts is best likened to an inflatable sleeve, consisting of a soft, strong plastic bag with double walls. A valve permits the walls of the bag to be inflated. Once the paddle float

A

B

C

D

E

Figure 88 | *The Paddle Float Rescue*

is slipped over the paddle blade, it cannot be removed until the air is let out again.

If you intend to use this method of rescue, ensure that your kayak is fitted with the necessary straps or shock cord elastics. To hold the outrigger paddle firm, these should be positioned immediately behind the cockpit, on both sides parallel to the gunwale. A double length of shock cord is the least that will hold the paddle in position. The best anchor is the specialised deck rigging, made of non-stretch webbing, which is provided by some manufacturers.

METHOD

1 Keep your paddle float secured under the elastics on the rear deck of your kayak. Do not store the float inside any sealed compartment. Taking a hatch cover off during a rescue could cause your boat to swamp.

2 After the capsize, position yourself on the downwind side of your upturned boat. This is in case the wind blows it away faster than you can swim after it.

3 Right the kayak as quickly as possible. Try to lift upwards as you flip the boat over, otherwise you'll add to your problems by swamping the boat.

4 Slip the float over a paddle blade. Inflate the paddle float slowly (Figure 88A). Blowing quickly could cause you to hyperventilate and black out.

5 If you have any pre-positioned elastics or fasteners, use them now and secure your paddle to act as an outrigger. If not, move on to stage 6.

6 Position your body close to the side of the kayak, aft of the cockpit. Hold the rear of the coaming and the paddle together in the same hand. Hoist your body upwards and hook your legs on to the paddle blade (Figure 88B). Bring one leg into the cockpit (Figure 88C), carefully followed by the other leg (Figure 88D). Keep your weight on the float side as you do this. This is not as easy as it may sound.

7 Sit on the paddle and balance yourself. Do this by maintaining a slight lean on the float side. Then slide forwards into the cockpit.

8 Use the paddle float to help you stabilise the kayak during the time you are bailing out.

It is a good idea to try all these movements in the correct sequence on dry land. Yes, I know you'll look silly – and feel even sillier – but believe me, it is time and effort well spent. Then, as with all other deep-water rescues, the Paddle Float Rescue should be practised in controlled conditions on calm water, in the company of others.

Paddle floats are now also made from a solid, oblong block of closed-cell, polystyrene foam. This means we no longer have to gasp and choke whilst inflating the thing in choppy water. There are also other advantages. You can sit on it while you have a beach lunch or you can stand on it and keep your feet dry whilst changing. The biggest advantage however, is that the solid foam float can be fitted with a reliable and easy to manage counterbalance.

Which ever way you look at it, once you've pulled your body out of the water, what remains of the paddle float rescue is nothing more than an awkward, tiring and nerve-wracking balancing act. Even in calm water, your centre of gravity must be kept low and on the side of the outrigger. This is easier said than done and it only takes a slight change of weight away from the outrigger side, for the float to go flying through the air, and putting you back into the drink once again. The sad news is that now you are worse off than you were before because you will now be even more tired, certainly demoralised and fear may have even started to rear its ugly head.

The joy of the solid Paddle Float is that it is possible to fit a successful counterbalance as an added extra. One firm has already done this and tests have proved it a total success. The under side of their float has a pleated bag attached to it by a strap and buckle. When the neck of the bag is left open, water floods in and expands the bag. A stiff fabric flap at the mouth of the bag stops this water flowing out again. The added weight of 10 to 12 lbs to the end of the extended paddle, makes it very unlikely that any bungling on your part will lift the float back out of the water. Once you are back in the cockpit, all you have to do to remove the water is to merely twist the paddle float over and the water will drain out. You can then re-stow the float under your rear deck elastics. When the float is not in use, a strap positioned at the mouth of the counterbalance bag

Figure 89 *A bad day.*

The lifejacket comes into its own in conditions such as this, as once it is inflated the man can keep still, perhaps even sleep. Even when unconscious he has a chance of not drowning. However, unless adequately clothed, he will not survive the cold for long. His orange exposure bag, filled with wind, his orange paddle blades, perhaps even his orange spray cover tied to the end of his paddle, will all help him to be seen by rescuers. This might be a good time to try your VHF transmitter/wet flares/prayer/EPIRB – not necessarily in that order. Before setting out you should have notifed someone of your destination and your ETA. Help should then be on the way if you are greatly overdue. The inside of your kayak should be marked with your name, address and phone number.

can be tightened so that no water can re-enter.

I would like to offer a cautionary word here to the solo paddler, whose plans for any kind of a future are based on the successful outcome of a paddle float rescue. Although the rescue itself may work fine, it is merely putting you back into the conditions which capsized you in the first place. If you capsize when you are part of a group and you are rescued by your companions, there are several options open to them – even in the roughest conditions – for ensuring your safety. These options are not available if you are paddling alone.

If you can't get back into your boat by any method, keep contact with the upturned kayak at all costs. If you swim to shore, take it with you, because your chances of being seen in rough white-topped seas are very slim. Your orange spray cover and most of your colourful lifejacket or buoyancy aid are underwater and out of sight and unless you happen to be wearing a vivid crash helmet your white face will never be spotted. Fasten your orange paddles into the paddle park, undo one of the deck lines and tie it round your waist. You can send up a star shell – this is what you carry them for – and, if need be, attract attention by waving the paddle to and fro in the air or by taking your large orange polythene exposure bag out of its case and allowing the wind to fill it. This bag can be seen on the water at a considerable distance. The fluorescent orange skull-caps worn by beach lifeguards could well be an added item in anyone's survival kit.

If you expect a long period of immersion and you are not wearing a wet-suit or dry-suit, you might climb inside the exposure bag. Obviously water will get into it, but the top of the bag can be pulled well up around your neck or even up over your head, while one hand still holds on to the kayak. Curl up and lie back on your lifejacket. Any water that enters the bag will become still. You may be surprised how much warmer you will be inside the wet bag than in water that is continually changing round your body!

While carrying out any of the methods of attracting attention, don't thrash about. Keep your arms near your sides if you can and cross your legs, thus preventing loss of vital body-heat from your armpits and crutch. Above all, keep calm. You will live longer: fear can accelerate and intensify hypothermia and shock.

The Curl Rescue

The situation shown in the first picture opposite, known as a Cleopatra's Needle, will of course never happen to you or those with you. Being the prudent person you are, your kayak and the kayaks of those who accompany you will always be filled with some form of flotation. Not everyone will be so circumspect, however, and it is as well that you are able to cope with this highly dangerous situation. It will

probably fall to the rescuer to shout the instructions out to the person in the water.

1 The patient will have to stretch his leg down and hook his foot under the cockpit coaming of the sunken kayak. He will then raise it level with the surface.

2 With the cockpit coaming level with the surface of the water, the swamped boat must be manoeuvred so that it lies parallel to the rescue kayak.

3 The rescuer must hold the swamped boat level and in position while the patient swims round to

Figure 90.1

Figure 90.2

Figure 90.3 *The Curl Rescue*

the other side. He then throws himself across the foredeck of the rescuer's kayak.

4 The patient reaches across and grasps the part of the cockpit coaming that is furthest away from him, with his palms upwards (Figure 90.2).

5 The patient allows his body to slide back off the deck a little, while still retaining hold of the swamped boat. His elbows must come to rest on the foredeck, jammed tightly in place by the weight they are supporting.

6 All the patient has to do now is to *hold the kayak level.* All the weight is taken by his elbows – *he should not try to lift.*

7 The kayak is emptied by the rescuer, who regulates the angle of the cockpit – as it drains – by sculling for support on the opposite side. This can be done in the normal or extended paddle position (Figure 90.3).

8 Once most of the water has been emptied out, the kayak can be flipped over into its upright position and any remaining water removed by reverting to a 'T' rescue or by bailing and sponging out.

I devised this system of emptying a fully swamped boat some years ago, after having the problem thrust upon me in the middle of Lake Windermere.

A word of caution though – the Curl is not easy and the strain on the foredeck of the rescuer's kayak is considerable.

Anchoring a rescue

During deep-water rescues, those involved in emptying boats have little control over their amount of drift. Any accompanying paddler must therefore be prepared to help by either towing the rescuers out of trouble or by acting as an anchor, holding everybody steady in one place while the rescue continues without interruption.

Under normal circumstances any drifting can be ignored; lost ground can always be made up later. However, I can think of a number of situations which would benefit from some towing assistance, for example rescues attempted near busy shipping lanes, surf, rocks or dangerous overfalls. In strong offshore winds, rescue kayaks can be 'anchored' to prevent them being blown further out to sea, or towed in towards the shore to gain more protection.

The planned use of rescue or accompanying boats for kayak expeditions is alien to the dedicated ocean paddler. Sea kayaking with a safety boat is rather like climbing a rock face with a large rope net strung a few yards underneath: suddenly any climb becomes possible. Two situations, however, come to mind in which safety boats are possibly acceptable: crossings of the English Channel, where the volume of shipping traffic is such that the safety factor is taken completely out of the hands of the paddler; and outdoor centre expeditions, where young novices are given a feeling of adventure by being taken on short sea trips and a feeling of safety in the knowledge that help is within hailing distance if needed in a hurry. It must also be borne in mind that all rescue boats are not reliable. I have known more than one accompanied trip where the rescue craft either broke down or was unable to cope with the prevailing sea conditions, thus endangering not only the lives of their crew but also the lives of the paddlers they were supposed to protect.

Towing

It was a cold, dark night. The place was Alaska and it was raining. My back had seized up with cramp and I couldn't move a muscle. My friends looked after me and towed me for six rain-drenched, moonlit miles. I had never been towed before and it was only then that I realised that nobody's perfect.

Whether you are leading groups or merely paddling with friends, you will soon discover that giving assistance by towing is a fact of life on the sea. It is never easy, and over many miles it can be gruelling, heartbreaking work, especially when you feel that your stamina cannot keep pace with the urgency of the situation. People rarely need towing in good conditions, so because towing in wind and spray is physically demanding, whatever towing system you use must be comfortable and efficient right from the start. Once you are in the towing situation is not the time to decide such matters as the length of the line or the position of the anchoring point.

Figure 91 | *A rescue being towed out of danger whilst in progress*

The following might make towing necessary:

1 Exhaustion when weather conditions become adverse.

2 Any illness, injury or severe cramp.

3 Instability caused by fear. In such a situation there should ideally be a second helper. This person will bring their own kayak alongside and steady the frightened paddler with both hands. The paddler offering assistance must then tow the two linked kayaks to safety.

4 A rescue raft drifting into danger while a rescue is in progress. A paddler can fasten a tow line to one of the rescuers and act as an anchor.

5 Other small craft in difficulties. It is in your power to prevent small motorised craft and other small boats from being blown on to rocks in high winds, or inflated boats from being blown out to sea.

TOWING METHODS

The Single Tow Fasten your tow line to the bow toggle of the victim. The single tow is hard work: towing in this manner your speed will drop by about half. If you are with a group you will find it difficult to keep up with the main party. If there are only the two of you, there is no other option.

The Tandem Tow This arrangement has three paddlers in line, with the victim positioned last. In other words, the tower is being towed. This is a good, powerful system with the danger of collision kept to a minimum. Towing by this method you should be able to maintain the cruising speed of the main group.

The Fan-trace or Husky Tow This method is favoured by some leaders and so I have included it here. As the name implies, the paddlers who do the towing are arranged in front of the victim rather like the husky dogs in front of a sledge. I once tried this in a rough sea. The tow certainly had power, but the whole affair almost finished in calamity with kayaks colliding and paddles clacking together. I confess to not having tried this method in calm weather.

LEADERS

It can all go wrong when conditions are bad or you have a following sea. Be prepared for a towed kayak becoming swamped or even sinking. In such a case, do not try to perform a rescue with the tow line still fastened.

During a tow, the kayak can either override your back deck and jab you in the rib-cage or it can harpoon your hull. Think of some of the worst scenarios, then work out how you might cope with them – for example, try towing six people against the wind! As a leader, your towing capabilities should be beyond question. However, once you are linked up to another kayak in a towing situation you cease to be an effectual leader with full control over the group. Routine towing jobs should therefore be delegated to skilled assistants.

DEEP WATER REPAIRS

It has been discovered that a kayak is leaking. The two experienced paddlers are well out to sea. The man from the damaged boat sits tandem on the other kayak, sculling the paddle backwards and forwards to steady the rescue boat. The leaking boat is hoisted across the the rescue boat, cockpit uppermost. If the leak is only small or very gradual, the boat can be righted and the trip continued. However, if necessary a repair kit can be taken from the damaged boat by the rescuer, or from behind his cockpit by the man sitting tandem. The repair can then be carried out by drying the boat and sealing it with broad tape. The rescuer's paddle is trapped against his hull by the patient's leg or placed in a paddle park. If two kayaks participate in this rescue the patient will only get the bottom of his legs wet. If there are more boats involved he can lie across the decks and keep completely dry. I have seen this operation performed successfully by an experienced coach, repairing his own boat whilst sitting on the foredeck of the rescue craft facing a very inexperienced rescuer, who did the support sculling. The emptying with the rear deck tandem can be done in very rough conditions and in high winds.

PLAY TIME IN THE POOL

Some of the training exercises on the open sea, can, to say the least, be a little traumatic and moans can come thick and fast, especially in climates where the sky is grey and the water is cold and rough. Indeed there are some parts of the world where kayaking on the sea is actually considered to be a seasonal sport. Who would have thought it!

The joy of a swimming pool is that it gives us a comparatively safe environment where students can be instructed and at the same time be under the constant, watchful eye of the coach. This is certainly desirable when they might be experimenting with awkward or tricky rescue procedures. For example, it is only in a swimming pool that the Curl Rescue can be practiced in complete safety without the very real danger of loosing a kayak. Another nightmare is the thought of someone practising donning their life vest while treading water out on the open sea.

I started using a pool for sea kayak training way back in the early '60s. Unfortunately, once my students reached a fairly high standard of proficiency – rolling by the same method over and over again appeared to be the main preoccupation – the warm, swimming pool soon lulled them into thinking that it was OK if their time degenerated into a go-as-you-please-do-as-you-like session. Bearing this in mind, I thought it best to describe a few ways in which I

| Figure 92.1 | *Positioning the damaged kayak* |

| Figure 92.2 | *Deep water repairs* |

Figure 93.1 *Some activities which can make pool time fun. However, it is advisable not to try all these exercises at the same time*

managed to inject a little variety and vitality into my pool sessions, and also utilise the limited space and time that I had at my disposal. The '*props*', you will need, such as brooms, chairs, long poles and such like, are usually readily available around the pool. You will need some long lengths of knot-free rope but shock cord might present a problem. I managed to acquire mine from an ancient trampoline and it really is fantastic stuff.

You will see that many exercises can be carried on at the same time but a quick glance at Figure 93 should make it obvious that the *law of common sense must prevail.*

Polo kayaks, fitted with front and rear toggles or loops, are the best boats to use in a pool because they have rounded ends which should protect the pool sides from damage. Their slight lack of stability will also give paddlers a more realistic, rough water feeling. Rodeo play boats are a good second best, but their fine extremities are not kind to head or pool sides. As an instructor, if it's your intention have someone practicing in a full size kayak, make sure it is just for stationary rolling practice only. If

you allow your students to paddle around the confines of a pool in 17 ft sea kayaks, you will soon become familiar with the Emergency Services. (Forcing a kayak up someone's left nostril is not easy nor is it painless!)

Launching

You'll find that even launching in a pool is fun and it is also good training for when you find yourself having to launch from docks of varying heights. Depending on the configuration of the lip around the side of the pool, most people will become quite blasé about launching and merely climb into their boat while it's high and dry and then allow themselves to slide forwards and downwards into the water.

A good launching method to practice in the pool is the SIDE DROP. I have used this launching technique many times and its allowed me to launch from the decks of small boats and numerous high docks. The method is simple; although on your first 'drop' I'm sure you might feel a little apprehensive. The first thing to do is position your kayak right on the edge of the pool and parallel to it. Make sure your spray skirt is on and then inch the boat sideways, a little at a time, until half your hull is hanging in space and you are almost at the point of balance (Figure 93.2). You should be positioned so that your 'good' side, (for strokes), is on the side of the water. This is because you will have to brace on that side when you hit the water. (In the illustration, the paddler happens to be left handed.)

The general idea is not merely to drop into the water, but to *lift* and launch your self *out* into space and get well clear of the pool side. To do this you will need some momentum. Remembering that you are at the point of balance, twist your body round and bring the blade which is over the water, through approximately 100 degrees so that it's now well over the 'land' side. Try to imagine that your body is a spring and you are tightening it by swinging the paddle round. Go through the 'one – two – three' routine, and on the third outward swing force the paddle to sweep *upwards* as well as *outwards*. At the same time and with the help of the paddle, you alter the point of balance by giving your body a violent hitch upwards and outwards. With any luck, you will

land hull first and slightly over towards your 'good' side. The second you hit the water you will need to perform an instantaneous high brace (Figure 93.2). If you happen to feel a little nervous about the success of your High Brace, you can always hold your paddle in the extended position.

THE LEMON GAME (A in Figure 93.1)
The student's kayak is fastened to the side of the pool by a length of shock cord about 10 ft long and about 6 ft in from one corner. They paddle up the pool taking up the slack. When tension is felt a marker is then moved into position hanging on a string (I use a small plastic lemon but a tennis ball will do nicely). This is hung about a foot above the water and around 4 ft in front of the paddlers bow – the distance depends on the strength of the class *and the strength of the shock cord*. The position of the hanging ball should be noted in relation to pool tiles and marking, so that any competition held will be fair to everyone. A circle can be drawn on the fore-deck; the paddler than moves forward against the tension of the shock cord until the deck circle is directly under the suspended ball. A partner can sit on the pool side holding a stop watch and steadying the chair which holds the pole and ball. This partner then times the paddler to see how long they can hold their boat under the dangling ball. To add a little touch or realism, the paddlers can be asked to roll when they finally give up exhausted, and as the elastic shoots them backwards.

ACCELERATING AND FORWARD
PADDLING (B in figure 93.1)
This is rather like the fairground game of hitting the peg and ringing the bell. One end of approximately 20 ft of double or heavy duty shock cord is fastened to something *solid* at one end of the pool. The other end is secured firmly to the stern of a kayak.

Paddlers race off up the pool and as the slack is taken up they see how far they can force their kayak up the length of the pool against the inevitable jerking resistance of the shock cord. The competition is to see who can force their kayak farthest up the pool, taking the best out of three attempts. Rolling on the final rebound can also give an unusual feeling as they are drawn violently backwards, upside down.

Figure 93.2 | *Launching by means of a side-drop is best practised in a swimming pool*

An assistant should mark the distance up the pool by means of a broom.

PADDLE BRACE (C in figure 93.1)

After being taught the principles of the paddle brace (Figure 48:1–48:2), students can practice this while being pulled up the pool, gently at first, by two assistants who walk along opposite sides of the pool. One has a rope attached to the bow of the kayak, the other pulls a rope fastened to the stern. Capsizes and rolls can all be done without any pause in the pulling along. Even wet exits should be done while the boat is kept moving.

STERN RUDDER (D in figure 93.1)

The idea is to see how many zigzags can be done by each paddler, as the kayak shoots diagonally across the pool, being pulled by a rope that has been passed round a pool rail of something similar. This is pulled at high speed by two assistants who have the robe tied to the broom that is pulled between them. Both forward and reverse rudders can be practiced. If the paddler capsizes, the boat should be kept moving during any attempts to roll.

Storm rescues

All types of deep water rescues and re-entries can be practiced in simulated rough conditions. These rough seas can be simulated in the pool and provide amusement to more than 90% of the class! You will soon discover that it is advisable to wear crash helmets while doing this. The method is for the rescue boats and the rescuee to position themselves at the deep end of the pool. Half way along from the shallow end of the pool, two assistants stand and hold onto the bow and stern of a full size kayak. They then bounce the boat up and down in the water, (not see-saw), this creates large storm waves down at the deep end and these rebound off the sides to make even steeper waves. The rest of the class now position themselves round the side of the pool overlooking the rescue, splashing and generally creating mayhem with their paddles. Meanwhile, two well chosen sadists, each with a bucket, can make things even more realistic (miserable) for those in the water.

Someone once remarked to me that throwing buckets of water and splashing people with paddles fulfils a basic need in us all; so perhaps rescues done in this manner do us all a bit of good. It's a good idea for those in the water to wear life vests during this exercise. It adds realism to the proceedings and re-entry techniques are made less easy by wearing any kind of buoyancy aid.

All rescues gain benefit from experimenting in this controlled rough water. The difficulties of the Paddle Float can soon be appreciated as well as the use of stirrups for heavier paddlers. The re-entry and roll can be explored whilst standing on the bottom in the shallow end and then practiced in one of the 'storms'.

LOOPING FROM THE POOL SIDE

The kayak is balanced on the edge of the pool with half the boat hanging out above the water. A friend then lifts the stern up from the pool side. As the kayak slides into the water the stern is lifted even more until the boat is vertical. It is then pushed over and away to complete the loop.

LOOPING FROM A 3-METRE SPRING BOARD

For this trick it is safer if you use a normal white water kayak. I do not recommend that kayaks should always be dropping from the skies near those practicing beneath but as stunts go it is quite exhilarating and you should be able to do this without having to spend the rest of your life in a wheel-chair provided you are properly cautious. The water at the deep end should be no less than 10 ft deep. Before you try this, the pool should be cleared. Probably the worst part of this stunt is anticipating the first drop rather than actually doing it. However, the success of this stunt depends largely on the assistant who controls the *launching* – they should know exactly what they are doing.

With a certain amount of wriggling and some gentle pushing by the helper, your kayak should be positioned on the end tip of the springboard at the boats point of balance. With the assistant holding the stern you are now in a position where any forward lean on your part will cause the boat to plummet to the water.

The stern of the kayak is held by the assistant and lifted up just past the 45 degree angle. Remember that it is this take off angle which is important for a pain free landing. As the kayak starts to slide off the board *and down*, your helper should push the stern gently outwards. The kayaks downward fall should not be vertical but at a slight angle to the water. A good angle would be that shown by the kayak on the board in (E in Figure 93.1). As you fall, you should be leaning slightly backwards. It is possible to control the angle before you hit the water by throwing your weight forward or leaning back so that your body is in line with the rear deck. The kayak will bury its bows in the water up to the cockpit and perhaps even past it. It will then pop out or loop forwards. The correct angle of entry is vital because if, during the resulting pop out, the kayak jumps sideways or backwards, it could damage the pool tiles or you could finish up hanging in amongst the iron work of the springboard supports. I can tell you this is painful on the elbows. Care should be taken not to hold your paddle shaft anywhere near your face when you hit the water. The water will stop the shaft and you will hit it with your nose or teeth, no doubt ruining a perfectly good paddle.

Some years ago I performed this free fall trick a one of L.L. Bean's Sea Kayak Symposiums. Sadly my assistant was new to the game and he launched me with an overly enthusiastic lift of the stern. The memory of that drop lives with me still. Even though I threw my weight backwards, my face hit the water only a fraction of a second after the bow. The kayak continued on it's journey, under the water and inverted upside down. I waited until I was near to the surface before rolling up with my now bleeding nose. As my head cleared the water, the body of my assistant hit the water like a depth charge, not far from my ear, on his way down. He had realised his mistake and jumped in to help me. Strange, but Bean's have never let me do that trick again.

Rolling

The swimming pool is an ideal location for teaching the various types of Eskimo rolls. In many cases the group can work in pairs, with one person acting as a helper standing next to the one trying to roll.

I would advise any instructors who teach rolling to work at the shallow end and position themselves so that, even as they work, they face down the length of the pool. In this way, even as they teach, they can keep a safe eye on the proceedings.

The scope for activities, games and experimentation in the safe confines of a pool are endless. At the end of a session, say the last 15 minutes, the class can always be rewarded with a game of polo. Another good way to finish is to have a Chariot race. With two kayaks side by side you merely stand with a foot in each boat and get pulled along by a third.

Points to remember

Just because it is indoors **you cannot consider the pool as a 'safe' area** and caution must be exercised at all times:

- There should be no pushing people into the pool and definitely no horse play of any kind (the most unruly group I ever taught were Police Cadets!).
- People should not swim when there are kayaks in the pool.
- Anyone who has to run during the rope pulling exercises should wear some kind of non-slip footwear.
- It's often a good idea to wear crash helmets during 'storm rescues'.
- All kayaks should be hosed out and cleaned before they are placed in the pool. Leaves and dirt can clog filters.
- **Never chew gum in a pool** – gum it is difficult to inhale and an emergency tracheotomy is not something you want to practise.

Plate 7 *The Author, Alaska, loading ciné film.*

Waves

7

During all your happy years of sea kayaking, waves of one kind or another will be your constant companion, so that every paddler should know something about the waves he is likely to meet (or which are likely to meet him). By looking at a map or chart and equating certain coastal features, such as depth and shape of the sea bottom, with certain weather conditions it is possible to anticipate roughly the type and character of the wave you will meet, even if you cannot foretell its size and ferocity. Looking at a chart and noting the various submarine gradients makes it possible to know whether a certain beach will be suitable for different kinds of kayak activities – that is, will you be able to surf, will you be able to land at all, will the surf be dangerous?

Waves are caused by the wind. All waves have two things in common: a *crest*, the highest part; and a *trough*, the lowest part. 'Soup' is the name given to the wave after it breaks.

Wind moving across still water immediately produces ripples, which are the smallest waves, with only a split second between one crest and another. Wind blowing across water flowing at the same speed will produce no waves, and wind blowing against the tidal stream produces steep standing waves. The expanse of water the wind blows over, the amount of time it blows and the speed with which it blows all influence the size of the wave. The unobstructed distance over which the wind travels creating waves is *fetch* (Figure 95), and the greater the distance of fetch, the more opportunity the wind has to create larger, more powerful waves. Some waves travel faster than others, and as they move along across the oceans for hundreds, sometimes thousands, of miles, other wave patterns join them on their journey. It is little wonder that the sea often looks confused.

Storms hundred of miles away will create a swell, and it is this undulating movement of the sea which, when it reaches our coasts, causes surf to break on our beaches and pound on our rocks. Although the swell or wave moves a stationary kayak up and down, the relative position of the boat on the surface of the water alters very little (Figure 96.1).

Notice the orbital movement of the water particles. When the kayak is paddled and moves forwards, the surface movement of the water particles has a definite influence on its progress (Figure 97). Long undulating swells hold no danger for a kayak, but if the wind blows strongly enough and the height of the waves increases to more than one-sixth of their wavelength,

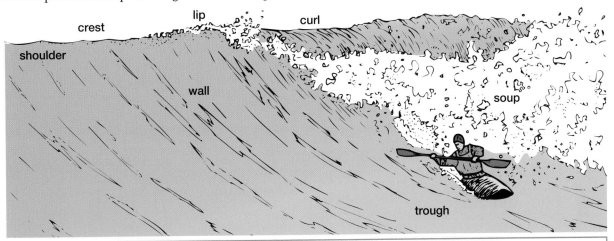

Figure 94 *A surfing wave. As the water breaks, it tumbles over from the top and tumbles down the slope. For the whole of its life-cycle this is the finest form of surfing wave. Both the breaking wave and the 'soup' it creates lack the violence of the dumper or the storm waves. if the wall of this water was steeper, the 'curl' would topple over and form a 'tube'*

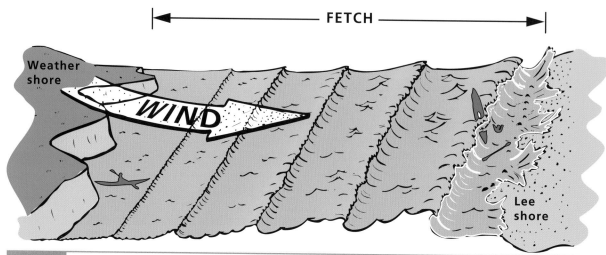

FETCH

Weather shore

WIND

Lee shore

| Figure 95 | Sheltering in the lee of the cliffs on the weather shore, wind and water conditions appear suitable for the trip to the island. However, conditions in the open sea are quite different and a landing may be impossible |

the tops fall over themselves, forming whitecaps. The kayaker who is out at sea in a swell, and perhaps in a high state of tension, may find it difficult to judge the height of the waves. Remember that when you are on top of one crest, another crest, the height of which you are trying to estimate, may be on its way down again. Waves tend to look much larger and more menacing when viewed from the trough (Figure 98).

As I have mentioned, water particles move with a circular motion. As a wave reaches shallow water it slows down, and when it gets into water 1½ times its height (called its *critical depth*), the frictional resistance caused by the bottom makes the crest topple over, producing a broken wave (Figure 97).
Figure 99 shows how the swell rolling in parallel to itself is slowed down near the shore, while the outside of the swell marches on at its original speed,

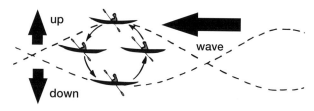

up

wave

down

| Figure 96.1 | Track of a stationary kayak. |
After returning to the crest from the trough the kayak is almost in the same position

producing what is called a *refraction curve*. This refraction gives kayakers and board surfers the graduated surf suitable for experts and beginners alike, and also the breaking 'shoulder' which is the delight of surf kayak paddlers. When you paddle out from a piered harbour, remember that the swell which does not affect you whilst you are in the sheltered area between the piers is quite a different matter when you reach exposed water around the piers and beyond. This is because waves are reflected from piers and cliffs, and as will be apparent from Figures 100.1 and 100.2, the crashing together of two wave patterns can produce the haystack effect of *clapotis*. Clapotis can also be produced by waves being refracted around an island (Figure 101).

A dumping wave, depicted in Figure 102, is caused by a steeply shelving bottom. The wave reaches its critical depth quickly, peaks up and breaks suddenly, dragging with it sand and small stones which rise up inside the curl. Then wave and stones crash down with tremendous impact, smashing craft, filling eyes and ears and sand-blasting the battered paddler. The breaking of the wave is almost explosive, because the air trapped and compressed inside the breaking curl exerts tremendous pressure. This is undoubtedly a most dangerous type of wave. Landings and departures through such waters should be made with extreme caution.

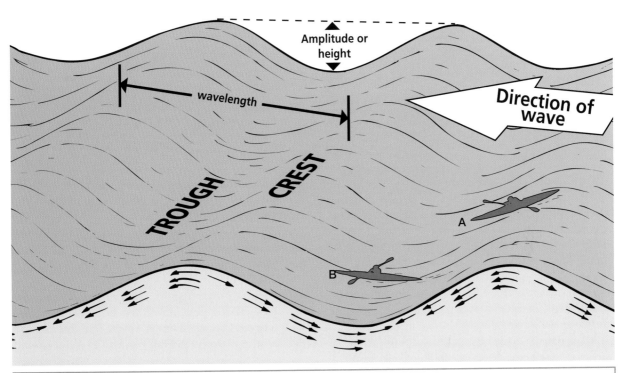

Figure 96.2 *Formation of unbroken sea waves.*
Paddler A is almost surfing down the face of a wave while paddler B is retarded in the trough. This is the dreaded 'following sea' of the novice. The wave will catch up to B and throw him forwards. This type of following sea is a godsend for the experienced paddler on a long sea trip, although surfing experience may be needed at the end of the journey

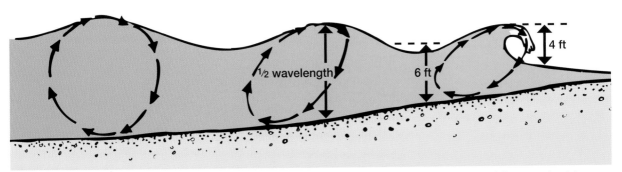

Normal circular orbital movement of wave particles before wave reaches shallow water

Orbital movement begins to become elliptical as the wave approaches shallow water. This is caused by the frictional resistance or bottom drag, and usually occurs when the depth is half the wavelength

When the depth is approximately one-and-a-half times the wave height, the wave begins to break

Figure 97 *Orbital movement of wave particles*

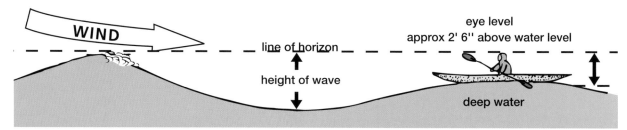

WIND

line of horizon

eye level
approx 2' 6" above water level

height of wave

deep water

Figure 98 | *Paddler judging height of wave. If the waves are higher than one-sixth of their wavelength and the wind is blowing, the tops will fall over in whitecaps*

More deadly than shore dumping waves are the waves of storm water shown in Figure 103. These are huge, pounding, crashing waves whose area of breaking extends far out to sea. Occasionally some parallel order of approach can be noticed in the waves, but mainly the pattern is confused. Close inshore at C the surf may look manageable for kayaking. I shall call this the *secondary break area*. But even the inshore 'soup' here generates power tremendous enough to capsize and inhibit rolling. The man and his boat can be forced backwards as he tries to paddle out, his

kayak stabbing viciously into the sand with a backbreaking jerk. A paddler may roll up and find he is under water. Viewed from the level of the beach, the primary break at A and B may be hardly visible as the picture has a foreshortened look with the waves appearing to pile one on top of the other. Only by climbing higher up the beach can one obtain a better view of the whole situation. The primary break is the area of the fearsome, dumping, deep-water waves which because of their great height now break over depths which would normally have no influence on

swell

deep

shallow

Figure 99 | *Refraction curve off a headland. As the parallel swell appproaches the shallow water of the point, the wave lines are slowed down inshore, while in the deep water the swell tries to continue as before, producing what is called a 'refraction curve'*

Figure 100.1 *Waves strike the pier and are reflected back; these superimpose themselves on the original wave pattern. The trough of one may be cancelled out by the crest of another; or, if a crest meets a crest, the wave height may be higher*

Figure 100.2 *The crashing together of the two wave patterns producing a high, vertical, broken wave is called clapotis. This type of area offers an exciting and challenging playground for experienced and skillful paddlers*

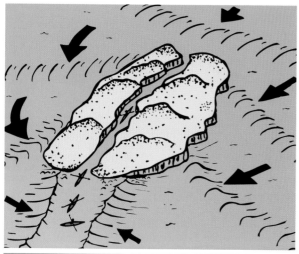

Figure 101 *Wave refraction round an island*

the surface swell.

Each of these deep-water dumping waves forms its own dreadful undertow. Rescue in this area is very difficult, if not impossible. Storm water is not for recreational kayaking and should be avoided, and even the secondary break should be treated with great caution.

The type of wave which surf kayakers travel many miles to use is shown in Figure 94. These waves can

be very large, but because of their shape and because the break topples gently over from the top they are quite manageable. Found on beaches which have a long, even, gradual slope, these surfing waves do not usually have an undertow.

A *rip* is a phenomenon consisting of water moving at a different speed from that of the water adjacent to it. Water which has come ashore as surf is taken back out to sea by rips as shown in Figure 104.2. On the beach at low tide, deep channels may be seen (Figure 104.1). At high tide these channels form rips taking water back out to sea in large volumes at 1 or 2 knots, faster than you can tow a kayak back to shore if you capsize one. Rip channels, which provide a swift means of getting out through surf, can also be found at the sides of bays (Figure 104.3).

If you are swimming, it is almost impossible from your position at water-level to know that you are in a rip. If you are in a kayak you will have to inform any swimmers as to the correct direction in which to swim clear.

Figure 102 *Dumping wave. Air is trapped at A as wave breaks. Note the water draining back out to sea at B. This is the undertow*

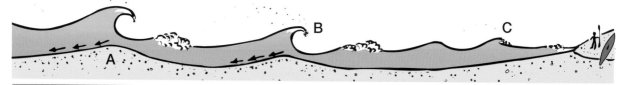

Figure 103 *In the area of primary break at A and B, the waves are breaking a quarter to a half mile out to sea, creating a powerful undertow more associated with inshore 'dumpers'. In normal conditions the presence of the shallower water at A and B would remain unknown. C marks the area of secondary break and provides a dangerous playground for paddlers*

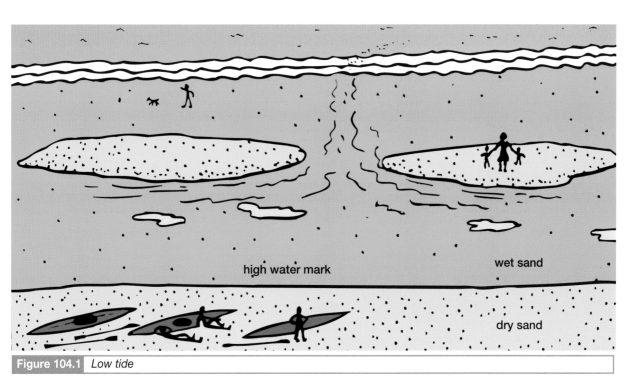

Figure 104.1 *Low tide*

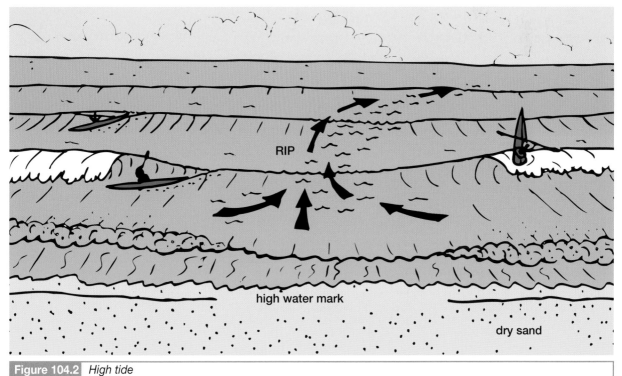

Figure 104.2 *High tide*

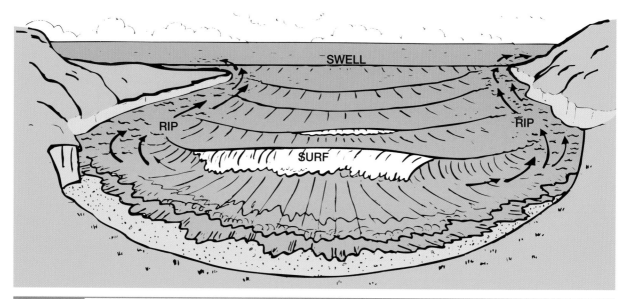

Figure 104.3 *Wave refraction and rips in a bay. When surfing in a bay use the surf in the centre; then use the rip as a quick and easy way out again. The swell refraction is caused by the sides of the bay*

As far as the sea kayaker is concerned, for weather read *wind*. Rain, sleet, hail, fog – all these are water off a paddler's back, but wind is a different matter. It is the whistling, tearing, shrieking wind that grasps at the fluttering, jerking paddle blades. Flying spray fills smarting eyes and lashes the face. It drains the strength gradually at first; then, as realisation comes that progress forwards is almost nil, demoralisation and the seeming futility of the fight take away the will to go on. Arms that are still physically strong suddenly feel weak. The kayak becomes almost impossible to turn. The discovery is made that the constant crashing of the sea over the bow and along the deck, is gradually filling the boat, finding its way through the spray cover, which is impossible to remove in these conditions to mop out. Body-heat just seems to be snatched away. If ever paddling on the sea had an enemy, the wind is it.

Winds do not arrive from nowhere, and we can be reasonably prepared. The following are useful aids.

1 A radio weather forecast.
2 A knowledge of clouds and weather lore.
3 A check of the barometer.
4 Bad-weather cones outside the coastguard station.
5 A phone call to the local weather centre or coastguard station.
6 A knowledge of previous weather conditions for the time of year.
7 Intuition.

CLOUDS

Cirrus

Fibrous and feather-like, these are the highest clouds of all. They herald the approach of a Frontal Weather System and are sometimes called 'Mares' Tails'. If they are arranged in a haphazard manner or if they start to dissolve, fine weather is indicated. However, if in parallel streaks feathering up at the ends, this probably means high winds, blowing in the direction of the streaks.

Cirro cumulus

Cirro cumulus are spread over the sky like the ripples in wet sand on the beach. They cast no shadows and are usually an indication of fine weather, but the wind could be strong. This type of cloud, nicknamed the 'Mackerel Sky', is associated with the cirrus cloud in that both are very high and both indicate the approach of a Front.

Cirro stratus

This is a milky white sheet covering the whole sky. The sun shines through very weakly, while the moon will have a halo.

Alto cumulus

These appear in isolated formations of waves or lines and are rather like the 'Mackerel Sky' in appearance, although lower. They are a light or medium grey colour depending on the direction of the sun. When the cloud is castellated, i.e. piled upwards in a castle-like structure, this could mean thunder.

Alto stratus

Forming an even grey cloud sheet covering the sky, these tend to give the sun a dilute watery appearance.

Strato cumulus

These big, soft, grey clouds give an overcast effect. The weather should be dry and settled.

Stratus

This is an even layer of cloud, really a high fog. The weather will be mild, warm and damp.

Nimbus

These are big, black rain clouds, ominous in appearance. As nimbo stratus they form a heavy layer of rain cloud.

Cumulus

These huge white clouds are like giant balls of cotton wool. Fracto cumulus, small broken clouds, mean fair summer weather.

Cumulo nimbus

These are very high mountainous clouds. The summit of the towering mass often forms itself into an anvil top, which is the classic shape for a bad-weather thunder cloud.

These should not be confused with the Thunderhead Cloud (figure 105). These monstrous clouds have a considerable vertical development, sometimes as high as 6 miles. The updraughts inside these clouds rise rapidly, often reaching over a 100 mph (160 km/h). This large volume of condensing water vapour causes more of the droplets to collide. This gives us those large raindrops which are so characteristic to thunderstorms. However, if the darkening of the sky, the torrential rain and the thunder and lightening are not enough, there is worse to come. Those powerful updraughts inside the cloud are also the cause of vicious, explosive downdraughts called *microbursts*. These microbursts cause even larger rain drops to fall and when this blast hits the surface of the sea, it can create winds of up to 100 mph (160 km/h). I think this is one of the most frightening things that can happen on the water.

A microburst can knock down large sailing vessels level with the surface of the sea with disastrous results; it has also caused very large aircraft to crash onto airport runways while landing. As far as a kayaker is concerned, it can blast you and your

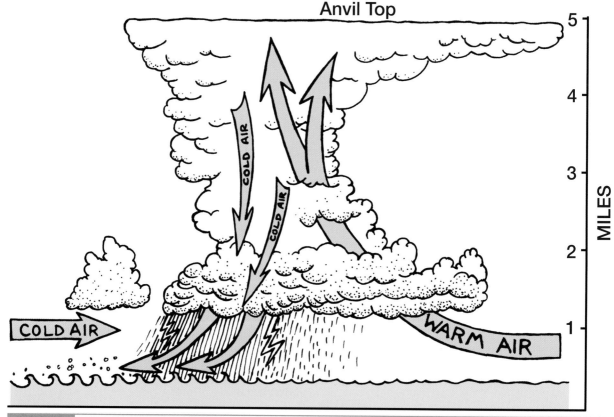

Figure 105 *An anvil top thunder cloud is formed as warm air is forced upwards by a cold front. The downdraught or windsheer can cause winds of over 100 mph*

group out to sea, even if you are paddling only a few yards from shore. On open water, it can also capsize a whole group of unsuspecting paddlers and render any kind of rescue almost impossible.

I remember once off the coast of Maine being hit by one of these horrific downdraughts. Luckily, I had seen the storm coming and I had already got most of my group to shelter; unfortunately, somebody capsized and I then had to talk my frightened and inexperienced companions through a deep water rescue. To prevent them from being blown to oblivion, I fastened my towline onto the rescue group and paddled backwards into the wind and towards the shore, all the time shouting out the necessary instructions.

Here are some more visual signs in the sky.

1 If clouds start and get lower, it means bad weather is coming.

2 If you see the rising sun breaking above a bank of clouds, beware of wind.

3 If the clouds at sunrise have a nasty purple look, it is going to be stormy and windy.

4 When the sun sets in a copper sky (bright yellow) look out for wind.

5 A halo around the moon or sun after a fine spell means wind.

If the clouds high up are moving in a different direction from those lower down, or in a different direction from the wind at ground-level, the wind is going to change in their direction.

SQUALLS

Wind speeds given in weather forecasts refer to the average sustained wind speed, not to gusts, which can take the form of squalls. A squall is a brief, violent windstorm, usually with rain, hail or snow. When a squall is stretched across the sky, heralding the approach of a cold front, it is called a *line squall*, which should not be confused with the isolated squall cloud. To give a violent downdraught these clouds must have a considerable vertical development. If the squall cloud is above you, the heavy cold air can rush out of the cloud in one almighty initial blast, which

can capsize a whole group of unprepared paddlers. This is the squall front.

On another occasion, I remember being about a mile off Holy Island, Northumberland, watching a squall approaching. The breeze was soon livened by a few outriding gusts. The sea seemed to be tumbling and falling towards us. Then suddenly there was a howling, streaming wind and white-tops all around. The raindrops were so close together that sea and sky seemed to be one. The paddler in front of me was outlined by the spray bouncing off his head, shoulders and kayak. We seemed to be beaten down as we leaned on what appeared to be a solid wall of wind, sea-spray and rain. Suddenly it started to ease, the drops of rain seemed smaller. I could lift my head up and see again. In a matter of minutes it had gone as swiftly as it came and we watched the ominous wall of rain retreat into the distance. If you can brace yourself and warn your group to prepare themselves, once the violent blast is over the rest is almost an anti-climax. Continuous squalls can however upset a planned journey.

WARNING

The lightening that is associated with thunderstorms is dangerous so get off the water and seek shelter as soon as possible. In the USA on average 100 people are killed by lightening every year. In Britain the average is only 4. In order to find out how far away the thunder storm is from your position, wait until you see a flash of lightening. You then count the number of seconds between the flash and the thunder clap. Then divide by five to get the distance in miles and three for the distance in kilometers.

RESEARCH YOUR OWN WEATHER CHART

Over the years a number of readers have commented to me that they feel that my weather overview in this book is too narrow, and that even though this is an interntional book, I give only the weather scenarios for the British Isles. Of course, what I have given you is merely an example of what you should all be doing for yourselves. That is, doing a breakdown month by month of your local weather patterns.

I can think of many examples. Let us say you want to go paddling in Baja, Mexico. You will find that winter is the best time, but even that has its problems. During the day, the hot air of the desert inland rises up, leaving low pressure near to the ground. This sucks in the air from the sea, causing fierce on shore winds. Unfortunately, these start to blow predictably every morning around 10.00 am. Because of this, the only sensible time to paddle is during the first four hours of the day. This means getting up at around 4.00 am, packing dew soaked gear in total darkness, and then paddling off at 6.00 am.

In the bay area of San Francisco something similar happens during the summer months. The sun heats up the inland valleys causing westerly on shore 30–40 knot winds to blow every afternoon under the Golden Gate Bridge. The winter months therefore give more settled weather for paddling. Remember that the fogs in the Bay Area are notorious. During the summer months in the Chesapeake Bay area and the states adjoining it, you will hear a Hot Weather Advisories broadcast (it is interesting to note that more people in the United States die from heat than from any other natural disaster, including earthquakes, floods and tornadoes). The sudden thunderstorms in these areas are as severe as any I've seen anywhere.

So dear reader, there you have it. Everywhere is different. I once paddled on Pyramid Lake in the Nevada Desert. It was July and we had SNOW! Next time there is a lull in your paddling programme, do some reserach and produce a month by month weather breakdown similar to this one of mine. Choose either your local area, or the area in which you intend to paddle.

The weather chart below is based on monthly surveys over a period of 100 years. It could be called the Historic System of Weather Prediction. There are variations in the weather, but on average certain weather conditions occur again and again. Reading this chart may well give some indication of what you might expect when planning trips and expeditions months in advance.

Wherever you are in the world, make a point of drawing up your own weather chart for the year.

Jan.	Violent storms. Low pressure with high winds can often build up huge seas. Good boat-building weather.
Feb.	Very bad weather. Hail and snow. Varnish some paddles. Visit the National Canoe and Kayak Exhibition.
Mar. 1–10	'Many weathers'. Storms and gales. This is the stormiest period in Britain. Kayakers in the North and in Scotland face much stronger winds than those in the South.
11–20	Much less stormy. Sometimes very fine with settled conditions.
21–31	Storms and gales. Low temperatures. Possibility of snow, so try the ski slopes.
Apr. 1–15	Unsettled weather. Moderate storms and gales. Prevailing winds are W/NW.
16–22	Season of the 'anvil top' thunder cloud, although it can be bright and sunny.
23–30	Unsettled weather again, perhaps snow, sometimes the odd gale.
May 1–10	Slightly higher temperatures. There can be some cold winds, usually from the N/W, and the occasional night frost. So into the loft and check the camping gear.
11–22	Usually a cold period. Winds can be strong from the north.
23–31	A little warmer. The winds have dropped, but this time of May has produced some heavy thunder-storms with flooding. Good for white-water kayakers.
June 1–10	Changeable and cool, but the weather starts to improve towards the 10th.
11–30	Usually fine and warm, sometimes very hot. Don't forget the dark glasses and sun cream. Watch out for thunderstorms, and perhaps a squall.
July 1–7	Rather unsettled showers and thunderstorms.

8–21   Good chance of hot weather. Watch out for sea fogs during humid spells. Light or moderate southerly winds. Odd thunderstorms.

22–31   Unsettled.

Aug. 1–7   Still unsettled and a little cooler.

8–15   Warmer again and more settled. About this time we get the most sunshine and the highest temperatures, especially in the south-east. Sunburn and fog are both dangers.

16–31   Still warm but there can be thunderstorms.

Sept. 1–14   Dry settled weather conditions (now that we are back at work).

15–30   Can be stormy with strong winds from the N/W. Enrol now for that course in Eskimo rolling at the local pool.

Oct. 1–7   Campers, this is the wettest month of the year. It can be very stormy. Low- pressure systems keep travelling across the country from the west. Temperatures start to fall noticeably.

8–21   Unsettled conditions can prevail this time of year as we know to our cost from various N/E Kayak Surfing Championships.

22–31   Long periods of storms.

Nov. 1–7   ...And more storms: one depression after another. Plenty of rain.

8–12   Settled weather but it's cold now. In the morning you'll have to jump on your buoyancy aid to soften the ice before putting it on. Watch out for that cold sea fog.

22–30   Storms and winds (these can almost be guaranteed for your advanced sea course) usually come from the N/W or N, with of course the odd N/E gale.

Dec.   Usually gets a little warmer at the beginning of the month, but gets colder and stormier as the month goes on.

THE BAROMETER

Make a habit of checking your barometer. I was brought up in a home where the barometer was tapped every morning and evening. It gives an instant indication of air pressure, so let us see what happens when you observe it.

Starts to rise. If it starts to rise after being well below its normal for the time of year, the first part of the rise may well bring very strong winds or severe gales from the north. If it keeps on rising it will bring fair weather.

A quick rise means the good weather may not last and the wind may come from the north.

A steady rise means good weather is on its way. High pressure brings an anti-cyclone, which means good weather is here and is going to continue. Light winds blow in a clockwise direction. During the summer months the anti-cyclone brings hot fine weather with very little cloud. In winter, the still air brings fog and frost.

A quick fall means a storm is on its way, so don't go far offshore.

A steady fall means bad weather is on its way but taking its time.

A fall while a southerly wind is freshening and backing to the south-east means the wind could veer and produce a westerly gale.

A fall while south-easterly winds are blowing could bring a gale. However, south-easterly gales do not last long.

A fall during south-easterly winds while the temperature starts to increase could make the wind veer to the south and south-west.

A fall while the wind is backing to the south and south-west is a sure sign of bad weather.

Constant low pressure brings unstable and changeable weather with thick, heavy clouds, gales and storms, and big swells. This is a depression, which we in Britain know and love so well. Low pressure systems travel very quickly.

THE BEAUFORT WIND SCALE

When we left the world of Fahrenheit and started measuring temperature by Centigrade, it was all very confusing. Tell me the temperature is going to be 40°F, and I know what I'm going to take when I go kayaking. But if told I'm going to experience 20°C, I know not whether I am going to sweat or shiver. In the same way, I am one of those people who were brought up on the Beaufort Wind Scale. If I hear that a Force 6 is due, I know exactly what the wind will feel like on my face, and what it will do to the water and the boat. But if I am told that the wind will be blowing at 30 m.p.h., I honestly don't know what it means until I convert it to Beaufort. So for poor mortals like me, here is the Beaufort Wind Scale, modified somewhat for the kayak paddler.

The question of whether it is safe to venture out to sea does not entirely depend on wind speed, since the degree of danger or risk inherent in any wind speed can be heightened or lessened by the particular circumstances. The area being exposed, a large existing swell, the wind against the tide – all are factors that can increase the risk, which means that in some circumstances a force 5 or 6 could be a foolhardy gamble for a paddler with little advanced experience, whereas with a sheltered area, a flat sea roughened only by the high wind, and the wind blowing with the tide, even a Force 7 or 8 could be quite a reasonable proposition.

THE BEAUFORT WIND SCALE

Beaufort No.	Speed (mph)	Term	Grading	Conditions (these will depend on whether wind is on- or offshore or sheltered)
0	0	Calm		A nice quiet paddle is indicated. Do some fishing; spear a few flat fish. Long trips by coracle possible.
1	1–3	Light air	Very easy	A few ripples. Still good for fishing. Take the open Canadian out.
2	4–6	Light breeze	Easy	Feel wind on face; little wavelets. Take the open Canadian back in.
3	7–11	Gentle breeze	Fairly easy	A few scattered white-tops. Flag flutters straight out on coastguard station.
4	12–16	Moderate breeze	Moderate	Proficiency standard should start for sheltered water unless an onshore breeze.
5	17–21	Fresh breeze	Moderately difficult	Lots of white-tops. It's hard work into the wind for the inexperienced. Proficiency standard tackle this only in sheltered water or near shore.
6	22–28	Strong breeze	Difficult	Rescues will be difficult. Warnings issued to small craft. Seas getting big; white-tops and spray. Proficiency man will be in trouble.
7	29–35	Moderate	Very difficult	You *must* be strong and experienced; your equipment should be good. Seas are big. Kayaks difficult to turn. Very difficult to make headway. Wind catches at paddle blades.

Beaufort No.	Speed (mph)	Term	Grading	Conditions (these will depend on whether wind is on- or offshore or sheltered)
				Foam is blown off in long white streaks, lots of spray. Communication very difficult.
8	36–43	Gale	Dangerous	Experienced man may handle this in sheltered water. In the open sea, paddlers are extended almost to the limit. Seas are piling up and breaking continuously. Wind catches the kayak on the crests. It's a fight all the time. Communication almost impossible unless *very* experienced. Each paddler must look out for himself. Rescues impractical.
9	44–51	Strong gale	Extremely dangerous	Fight for survival in open sea. Huge, breaking spume-swept waves, close together. No rescues. Communication – hand signals (if you can spare the hand). Try a prayer. I find these work.

Note: Winds of almost hurricane force can be coped with if the waters are sheltered, the fetch and therefore the waves are small. In the open sea or on unprotected water even winds of Force 3 can create problems for the inexperienced paddler.

WEATHER FORECASTS

The late-night weather forecast on television is always worth watching. Radio, on the other hand, still provides the most widely used forecasts, because it keeps the listener informed at frequent intervals throughout the day. The times of shipping forecasts can be obtained from the Radio Times or from most newspapers.

These forecasts open with a short summary of general weather conditions. A forecast is given for each of the sea areas for the next 24 hours, including the direction and strength of the wind, visibility and general weather. After the forecast for the larger sea areas comes a similar one for the coastal areas (Figure 106), and the barometer pressure is given in addition to information as to whether it is rising or falling. When the wind reaches over 40 knots, a gale warning is broadcast. The BBC helps us by interrupting its programmes as soon as the information is received. If a gale is:

Imminent	it will arrive in 6 hours
Soon	it will arrive in 6 to 12 hours
Later	it will arrive in over 12 hours

In North America, continuous V.H.F. weather forecasts are transmitted by the N.O.A.A. in the U.S.A., and by the coastguard in Canada.

When a wind is said to be *veering*, it is changing direction in a clockwise manner. When it is said to be backing, it is changing direction in an anti-clockwise manner.

In the UK certain newspapers such as *The Times, The Daily Telegraph, The Guardian* and *The Scotsman* give detailed forecasts, but these are obviously not as immediate as the radio. However, it might well be that while off the west coast of Scotland you find a battered but up-to-date copy of *The Scotsman*, when all you can get on your transistor are noises from outer space and the sound of an unidentified radio beacon, harmonising with high-speed morse.

COASTAL AREAS

1 *Wick*

2 *Bell Rock*

3 *Dowsing*

4 *Galloper*

5 *Royal Sovereign*

6 *Portland*

7 *Scilly Isles*

8 *Ronaldsway*

9 *Prestwick*

10 *Tiree*

11 *Valentia*

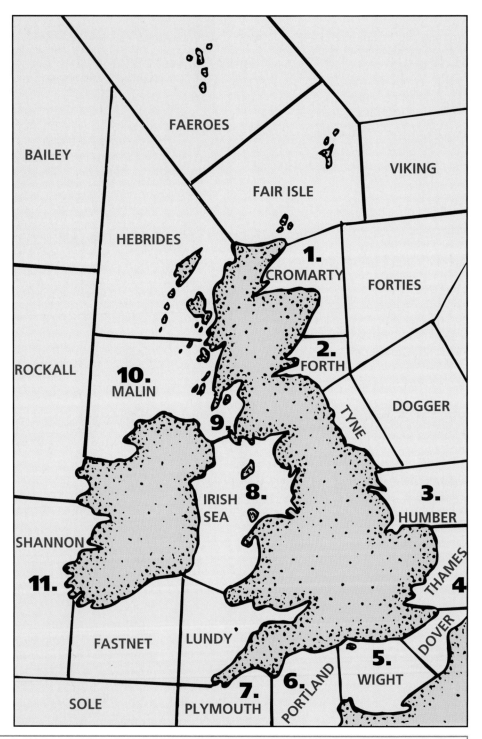

Figure 106 *Named areas used in weather forecasting*

LOCAL WEATHER CENTRES

Set up by the Meteorological Office, these centres are extremely helpful in giving local weather information, and they are usually conveniently located so that members of the public can read there at their leisure. In some areas the weather forecasts are pre-recorded, and by dialling the appropriate number, which can be found in the pages of the telephone book, the kayaker can get an accurate, but rather impersonal, forecast.

THE COASTGUARD

The coastguard are always very co-operative and will give information over the telephone. Apart from the local weather and wind speed, they can also be relied upon to give the height of the swell, which often proves useful.

Do not forget that although the coastguard may tell you that your trip is ill advised when the weather is bad, they are not allowed officially to advise you that conditions are suitable for your trip. Thus if things go wrong – and they often do – the onus rests firmly on your shoulders, not theirs. Even the shoulders of the coastguard are not that broad.

When the coastguard advise against a particular trip because of prevailing weather conditions, they base this advice on a wealth of experience.

Unfortunately they have no idea of the potential of a kayak in rough seas handled by a good kayak man. So while proficiency level paddlers would do well to take their advice and find a piece of sheltered water somewhere, advanced kayakers must fall back on their considerable personal experience, considering all factors, together with the coastguard's advice, and make their own decisions accordingly.

Remember that the advice given by the coastguard is designed to keep you alive and to allow the lifeboat crews to carry on their normal daily occupations without interruption. They cannot be wrong, even if you spend your day languishing on the beach, wishing that you had gone out after all.

INTUITION

There comes a time, after all the usual checks have been made with the weather centre, the coastguard and other forecasts, when the weather is still, and the clouds betray nothing. You look up, sniff, suck your teeth and gaze about. A deep feeling of apprehension slows you down while the rest are gleefully preparing for the trip.

Take careful note of the feeling: either cancel the trip or, if you do go ahead, be mentally alert to the possibility of the worst happening. If it doesn't, you'll be all right; but if it does you'll be prepared.

Plate 23 *The author filming near the Chenega Glacier in Alaska's Prince William Sound. Any change in the tide or wind direction can cause kayaks to be crushed by drifting ice coming together* (Photograph: Tom Caskey)

Tides and tidal streams

Paddle your kayak on the largest lake in the world, and if the wind doesn't blow the water will be calm. The big difference between the largest of great lakes and some small sea bay is this: the sea is a live, living thing; it does not need wind to make it violent, because its waters are continually in restless motion – in some places with quiet subtlety, in others with great speed and noise. Unlike the weather, however, the behaviour of water movements is much easier to predict. Any kayaker who has watched and studied water as it flows down a river, around rock and past obstructions on the bank should be able to apply his experience to the movements of the sea around our coastal areas. When a tidal stream surges around a headland or rushes between islands, its behaviour is almost the same, although on a larger scale, as that of water in a river.

Let us look at tides and their causes, at some of the sea conditions associated with them and at the resultant movements of the sea which are generally referred to as *tidal streams*. Very briefly, the moon acts like some huge magnet upon the earth. As the earth turns on its axis it draws the sea and gives the tides a rhythmic rise and fall. The moon pulls the water nearest it while the water on the opposite side of the earth also rises. Therefore *twice a day* every part of the world has a *high tide* and a *low tide*. When it is high tide on the eastern coast of North America it is low tide around the British Isles. When the tide is rising it is said to be *flooding* and when it goes down it is *ebbing*. There are approximately 6¼ hours between high and low water. If it is high tide at 07.00 hours one day, the following day it will be at 07.52, a difference of about 50 minutes each day.

Twice every month, when the moon has its greatest influence on the earth's waters, a little after new moon and full moon, *spring tides* occur (please note twice a *month*, not twice every spring). Tides will rise higher and fall lower then, and tide races and overfalls are more violent. Tidal streams run faster, thus giving more help or offering more resistance to paddlers. The water will uncover rocks and wrecks that are rarely seen, or flood the tiny area where you were going to stop for lunch.

Half-way between each spring tide, when the moon has the least effect on the oceans, we have what are called *neap tides.* Any epic crossings or expeditions are best planned to coincide with these.

Because the moon's track around the earth is elliptical, it is nearer the earth at certain times than at others. When nearest, it is said to be in *perigee*; when farthest away, in *apogee*. When it is in perigee at almost the same time as a spring tide, the highest and lowest tides and the fastest tidal streams will occur.

Because the coastline of the British Isles is so indented and broken, it is important to remember when planning expeditions that although the tide may be out where you are, it could well be that a few miles away the tide is still moving and has in fact some two or three hours to go before slack water occurs. There is also a lag between the time of high water at the mouth of an estuary and the time of high water 5 or 6 miles inland. Heavy rain and melting snows can also affect the time of the flood.

At high and low water the tide remains more or less still – that is, slack – for some little time, but in some places the water is never really slack. The rate falls off and the water then tends to flow at right angles to its original path. If the area is particularly bad, slack tides may create huge, uneasy upsurges and swirls as if the water is trying to decide what to do next. Anyone who has paddled over the position of the whirlpool in the Gulf of Corryvreckan at high tide will have been much aware of this.

It is not the movement of the tide up and down the beach that most affects us as kayakers during our paddling, but the tidal streams caused by the enormous amount of water which pours around the northern tip of Scotland and up the English Channel to fill the North Sea. As the tide floods and forces its way between islands it increases in speed, swirling round headlands and emptying bays and estuaries. The narrower the gap between the pieces of land, the faster the tidal stream flows (Figure 108). This is

H. W. Dover

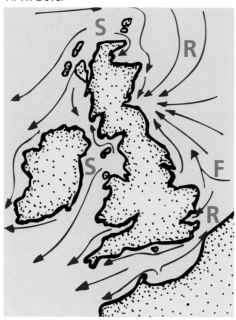

3 hours after H. W. Dover

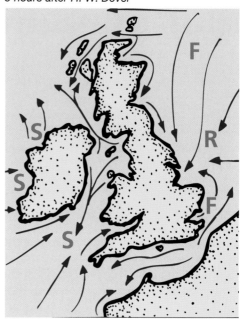

6 hours before H. W. Dover

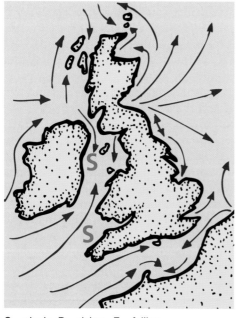

3 hours before H. W. Dover

Key: *S = slack   R = rising   F = falling*

Figure 106   *Tidal streams around the British Isles*

particularly forcibly illustrated in the tides around the west coast of Scotland, with its islands, sea lochs and narrows where the flood rushes up one side of an island only to overtake a slower-moving tidal stream or collide with another fast tidal stream going in the opposite direction. Such complex tidal streams, when coupled with bad visibility and unstable weather, make our coastal waters some of the most dangerous in the world to navigate.

A copy of the *Coastal Pilot* will give you all the information you need for specific pieces of water. For instance, if you wish to paddle across the Sound of Jura the *West Coast Pilot* will tell you the west-going stream begins +0410 HW Oban, which is some 28 miles to the north. You therefore add on 4 hr. 10 min. to Oban's HW time to find out when the west-going stream at the Sound of Jura begins, thus making the adjustment which is necessary to stop yourself being swept away in the wrong direction.

Let us suppose it is high slack and the tide is starting to ebb. At first the water moves slowly, then gathers speed until it is running at its fastest when it is half-way between high and low water, after which it gradually slows down again until it reaches low slack. The same speed change occurs when the tide starts to flood until it reaches high slack once more.

The speed of the tidal streams at any stage of the tide cycle can be estimated fairly accurately by the ratio 1:2:3:2:1. In rivers and estuaries the rate flow may not conform to the 1:2:3:2:1 rule and the water may be at its greatest speed soon after the tide has started to run. The rise and fall of the tide is sometimes worked out by applying the $1/12$, $2/12$, $3/12$, $3/12$, $2/12$, $1/12$ rule.

If a kayaker wishes to cross, for example, a mile-wide strait and the tide is running at more than 2 to 3 knots, he would do well to wait until the stream slackens off, thus saving himself a strenuous and prolonged ferry glide. It must be remembered that in any channel the water moves fastest at the centre. If the channel is several miles wide, as in Figure 108, it may be easier to leave point A while the tide is still running and arrive at the centre of the channel at slack water, and then to paddle on to B after the water has started to move again in the opposite direction. Because of the distance involved in long

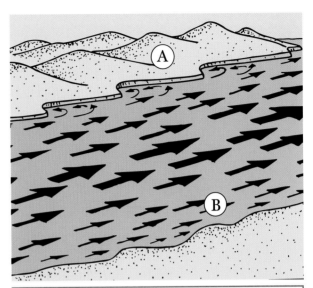

Figure 108 *Movement of water through a strait. The broad arrows indicate the fastest flowing water*

crossings such as the English Channel, it is difficult to work the tides successfully, so that any course line must be rather a dog-leg.

Along the south coast of England tides can be very complex, because when it is HW at one end of the Channel it is LW at the other. This can cause peculiar local conditions, such as the prolonged low-water condition at Portland that is known as the 'Gulder', or the one at Southampton where the first flood rises normally for about 2 hours after LW, then rises very slowly (almost slack) for about 2½ hours, after which the main flood tide runs for about 2´ hours until HW. Then to complicate matters it falls a little for about an hour until it rises again for over an hour, creating another HW. So if you are paddling in the Solent, get some local information from the Sea Kayaking Centre at Calshot or do your homework *well.*

If we know the time of high tide at a major port such as Dover, the time at which other parts of the coast will have high water in relation to it will always be the same, or remain constant. After reference to a table of tidal constants – a list of times which must be added to or subtracted from the high tide at Dover – it is easy to find out exactly what the tide is doing in a particular place at a particular time.

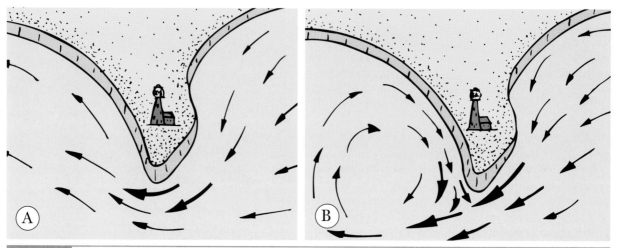

Figure 109 *Water behaviour off a headland.*
Although the tidal stream is running around the headland in A, it should be possible to negotiate the point. But if the opportunity is missed and the tidal stream runs at its maximum, it could produce a fast and dangerous back eddy as in B, which when it meets the tide race could produce large eddies and whirlpools

Figure 110 *Behaviour of water when passing between islands. Note the build-up of water at the upstream end of the islands accelerating into a race, where the fast water hits the slower tidal stream, which is itself starting to move faster because of the constrictive effect of the islands. The increased tidal speed will form an overfall as the flowing water reaches the point where the depth starts to fall away again after the shallows around the islands*

Tidal constants are marked on the maps in the AA *Members' Handbook*, and HW London Bridge and Dover are also given in *The Times* and *The Daily Telegraph*. If the homework is not done properly for your trip you might find yourself arriving at your lunch stop to be confronted with a sea of mud and slime, your only company rotting cycle and pram frames, old tyres and the pleasant tinkling sound of the local sewer discharging into the mud. The Wye, the Solway Firth, and various tidal stretches of our large industrial rivers, such as the Thames, Tees, Mersey, Tyne and many others, exhibit similar unpleasant characteristics at low tide. In such a situation you have few choices! Until the tide rises you can either read a book or you can set off dragging your kayak behind you, probing the mud in front with your paddle. If the mud gets too deep you would be well advised to sit on your boat grasping your paddle firmly and jerk and kick your way to the nearest solid landing. Setting off to 'squelch' and wade over a large expanse of mud, the depth of which varies from a few inches to an unknown number of feet, could at best be unpleasant and at worst prove fatal. So take care and work out your landing times correctly.

As the tidal streams travel around our coast, white-water conditions, sometimes of quite gigantic proportions, can be formed. A headland jutting out into a fast-moving tidal stream can cause the water to accelerate off its end, forming a *tide race* (Figure 109), which may extend for some considerable distance. Water rushing through narrows may produce roughly the same sort of water turbulence (Figure 110). Headlands usually have underwater shallows extending well out to sea. Water rushing over these underwater shelves produces what is called an *overfall* (Figure 110), the water falling and tumbling over itself and producing steep and sometimes breaking waves, very close together. In some places the same effect can be seen when fast tidal water passes over slower-moving deep water going in either the same direction or the opposite one, creating what might be called a false bottom and producing a large standing wave going nowhere like something out of a whitewater paddler's nightmare. One such wave seen off the west coast of Scotland by several independent, reliable witnesses has been estimated to be 8 to 12 ft. high. The chart marking in this area shows the water to be about 400 ft. deep.

Where two tidal streams or races move at different speeds, the meeting of these two bodies of water produces a *tide rip*. Off surfing beaches, rips are produced in a different manner (see Chapter 6).

Do not confuse tidal streams with currents which are in fact thermal changes in the water. A good example is the Gulf Stream, which is warm and travels to the British Isles from the Gulf of Mexico at about 3 m.p.h. If it wasn't for this warm current our waters would be frozen over every winter and we really would be emulating the Eskimos in more ways than one.

One final word! As a sea-going paddler you must make the tidal streams work for you and not against you. Always necessary in the days of sail,[1] this still applies to yachts, and how much more so must it be necessary for you, the kayaker, as you propel your kayak either with or against the wind and sea by the strength of your arm and nothing more. You are lucky in that your craft draws only a few inches of

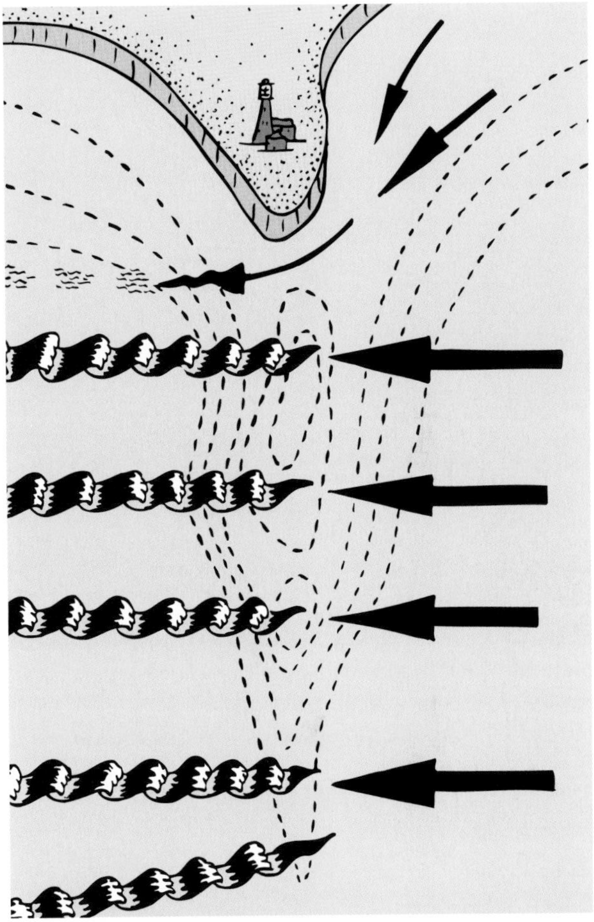

Figure 111 *A typical overfall. The rough water associated with this can extend 3 or 4 miles out to sea. The safe passage for a kayaker would be close to the headland unless there is heavy surf, in which case he must paddle just outside the surf line. However, the paddler must not forget the rough water caused by the race (Figure 106) off the headland, and unless he likes wild conditions, he may have to wait till the tide eases. Overfalls provide good training grounds for advanced sea work*

water and you can halt your progress towards rocks infinitely quicker than a yacht on the same path. A path extremely close inshore or around headlands is no problem to you, and using small back eddy streams in small bays means that you can, even at an adverse state of the tide, get from the water some help which is forever denied to larger craft.

[1]Old sailing ship maxim:
'Water goes off all promontories and into all bights.'

Plate 24 *A kayak paddler may be considered the master of a small powered craft able to go where others dare not venture. This is the view from the 'bridge'. Some effort was needed to paddle against the tide rushing between the rocks. The seal gave a good impression of a depth charge as we paddled through the gap* (Photograph: the Author)

Plate 25 *Crossing Scotland's the Firth of Forth near the Isle of May. The picture was taken in June 1975 during one of the training trips prior to my attempt to cross the North Sea six weeks later. It was at a time when I was experimenting with radar reflectors. I eventually came to the conclusion that loosely screwed up kitchen foil on the end of a piece of fishing rod was the simplest and best solution* (Photograph: Tom Caskey)

The term 'navigation' may sound rather grand when talking about kayaking, since the equipment on the deck of a sea kayaker's boat hardly turns the deck into a chart table. Yet quite advanced trips and expeditions are undertaken by paddlers.

As basic equipment for planning a trip, the sea kayaker needs charts of the area, Ordnance Survey maps, two rulers and a set of dividers or pencil compasses. Parallel rules are handy but not essential, as is a Sestral navigator. This is just a 360° protractor with a transparent plastic arm which swings round from the centre. It can be homemade quite cheaply and might prove a help in laying off a course. An orienteering compass is also handy. A chinagraph pencil is useful for writing on a waterproof-covered chart if the surface is glassy.

COMPASS

My first compass came out of a 3d lucky bag. It lay in the bottom, next to a whistle-whizzer and a 'Move-it-and-the-eyes-wink' coloured picture of Tom and Jerry. I set this tin and cardboard navigational wonder in clear moulding plastic to make it waterproof, then drilled a hole at one end for the string. Many a man has navigated further with much less. However, a compass is hardly the thing to economise on. I now use a K15 Suunto compass. It is luminous and the face is green, red and black. The course direction can be read off the part of the face closest to me.

CHARTS

Looking at a chart should open up a wonderland of information to you. What is the direction and speed of the tidal stream? What is on the sea bottom – sand or mud? If I make bivouac will there be a spring of fresh water? Will there be overfalls or races to fight against? All these questions should be answered when you look at your chart.

These charts, printed by HM Stationery Office, contain a wealth of information for those who know how to read them. Trying to remember the many abbreviations and symbols on them is an almost impossible job, so it is advisable to buy chart 5011 or to get a copy of *Reed's Nautical Almanac*.[1] Certain symbols should be memorised (Figure 112). After all, when out at sea the paddler cannot have a copy of Reed's readily to hand to thumb through at will. He has only his experience and memory to serve him. Most charts of the British Isles are now in metric, meaning that instead of the soundings being in fathoms and feet, they are now in metres.[2]

The new charts are easily recognisable due to the fact that they are coloured. All these soundings are taken from the chart Datum, a mark below which the tide seldom falls, which is below the level of Mean Low Water Springs.

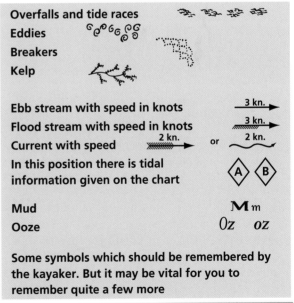

Some symbols which should be remembered by the kayaker. But it may be vital for you to remember quite a few more

Figure 112 *Important chart symbols*

[1] If you live in the United States you will need to buy chart No 1, Nautical Chart Symbols, Abbreviations and Terms.

[2] 1 fathom is 6ft. 1 knot is 1 sea mile per hour. 1 sea mile is approx. 2,020 yds.

There are a number of waterproof, self-adhesive, clear plastic coverings on the market. It is also possible to have small sections of the chart laminated. Once covered, the chart can be secured to the deck under the deck elastics or taped in place.

GLOBAL POSITIONING SYSTEM (G.P.S)

See Chapter 1.

OS MAPS

Kayak expeditions should always be carried out in conjunction with an Ordnance Survey Map. Camp sites have to be thought out and nearest roads for points of departure must be considered. If long trips along the coast are to be undertaken, careful thought has to be given to transport. When you finish your trip, a previously positioned mini-bus is a good way of getting back to the other vehicles left at the start. I remember one long crossing that meant somebody driving well over 100 miles to position the transport at the other side of the firth.

Weather conditions change for the worse very quickly and a landing spot which permitted a seal landing or a difficult one onto rocks may on the following day prove impossible. This will mean a long portage to find sheltered water again. The Ordnance Survey map will help you find the easiest route. While on the subject of escape routes on land, OS maps give Post Office telephones, AA and RAC boxes, youth hostels, public houses (the Englishman's escape for many years), railway stations and churches. After all, you never know just how bad your luck can turn out. I was once glad of a church to provide shelter for someone in an exposure bag while I waited for assistance from the mainland.

DEAD RECKONING

If a kayaker knows the course he paddles and the distance he has travelled, he can use this information to pinpoint his position by what is called *dead reckoning*.

Did I say pinpoint? If the sea were like a lake with no wind or currents, navigation at sea would be rather like fell walking. However, conditions are never quite like that. It is extremely difficult for a paddler to guess at his speed with tides running and winds blowing. His course, even with a compass, will hardly prove consistent because of the gyrations of his kayak. As in all things, however, practice makes perfect, or should I say *almost* perfect. After settling down to a steady speed over a fixed distance, using a good watch and with some trial and error, the kayaker can learn to work out his average speed under all sorts of varying conditions. He can then calculate the distance he should travel in a fixed time, and this will help him find his position.

CROSS BEARINGS

With your chart in front of you, it is easy to take a cross bearing from two fixed objects on the land. Choose two objects so that, after you have taken a bearing on them, the lines drawn from them on your chart are almost at right angles. The point of intersection should indicate your position on the chart.

If you are sitting in your kayak and about to set the course with your compass from a bearing taken from a chart previously, remember that the compass you carry points to magnetic north, *not* true north. If, therefore, your bearing was taken from grid – i.e. from an Ordnance Survey map or the outer ring of the chart compass rose – do not forget to *add* the magnetic variation. This varies between 15° and 9½° degrees, depending where you are in Britain, and is printed on the rose of a chart. Remember, in the British Isles:

> MAGNETIC TO GRID – **SUBTRACT**
> GRID TO MAGNETIC – **ADD**

If your front pocket is full of car keys, carabiners, a metal torch, a camera and exposure meter and a load of other ironmongery, don't wonder why your compass has taken you to Cap Gris Nez when in fact you set out for the end of Brighton Pier.[3]

[3]For a good laugh, place your transistor radio near your compass. Watch what happens and be warned.

TRANSIT BEARINGS

The system of transits is the oldest navigational aid in the world. Ever since men first ventured from land, sailors have set up two posts on a beach so that when they were kept in line the sea-going craft could keep clear of unknown dangers. Any chart or indeed OS map will provide an enormous number of ready-to-use transits, such as colliery tower in line with pier, a wireless mast in line with a buoy, one piece of land just jutting out in front of another, or two headlands kept in line. All examples provide either a leading line for the paddler to keep on, or a position line on a chart, more accurate than a bearing taken by a compass.

The sea kayaker will gain other benefits from the persistent use of transits. Once he is transit minded he will instinctively be aware of how the tidal stream or the wind is setting his craft, even when he is some distance offshore, without taking any bearing at all. Briefly, the paddler will develop 'feeling' for his position.

A bearing taken by transit is an ideal way of pinpointing (I mean it) wrecks for skin diving at a later date (if you are that way inclined). You will find the exact place every time by this method, something that cannot be said about taking cross bearings with a compass.

CORRECTING COURSE

It is very easy to be carried away at sea. You can be duped into thinking that the direction you aim for is the direction you go in: far from it.

Here is what happens. In figure 114 you set off from the coastguard C aiming for the lighthouse L. It is 4 miles away and you are paddling at a steady 4

Figure 113 *Transits. The paddler could look backwards and keep the pier lights in line, but will more likely line up the buoy and the headland and keep them in transit. He will see immediately any drift caused by an offshore wind. When he sees the church tower in line with the hill top, he knows it is time to change direction. Keeping them in transit his course will safely avoid the broken water over the reef at the entrance to the bay. The ship is using transit towers to guide it between the piers. When the transit beacons are lined up, this will tell the master to change direction towards them. He then uses these to keep him on course up the centre of the channel*

knots. Suddenly, a curtain of fog blots out the island. Your compass tells you to keep on aiming towards L. The fact you have overlooked is that tidal flow is from right to left at 3 knots. Result – at the end of the hour you will finish up 3 miles to the left of the island. Even if the fog providentially clears to let you see where you are, you will still have another 1½ hours' paddle to beat up against the tide to reach the island.

The solution is to correct your direction of travel, and here is how to do it.

1. You know how fast you can paddle (well, find out then) and in what direction you actually want to travel.
2. You can estimate how much tidal flow there is and in what direction.
3. From C mark off the tidal stream at 3 knots due west. Then, using compasses set at 4 nautical miles, draw an arch to cross the course line C–L at Y. Join XY, which represents your course to steer (approx. NE). CY represents the distance you will cover in 1 hour, 2¾ nautical miles.

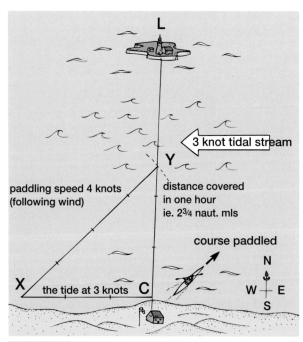

Figure 114 | *Hull shapes in cross-section*

The course bearings are best written next to your cockpit or on the chart where you can see them. Paddle on the course for an hour at a constant paddling speed and you should arrive at your pre-calculated position.

BUOYAGE AND ESTUARIES

Figure 115 shows a typical arrangement of buoys in an estuary, based on the I.A.L.A. Maritime Buoyage System 'A'. Those who kayak should familiarise themselves with the buoyage system that prevails in the area where they intend to paddle. Not every country has gone over to the I.A.L.A. system completely however, and in the United States, Central and South America, the Philippines and Japan, a certain amount of confusion is caused by the variety of traditional systems in use at present. In these areas, when entering a harbour from the seaward, the *port-hand* buoys are *black* (with a green or white light) while the *starboard-hand* buoys are *red* (with a red or white light). To anyone who is used to starboard Green and port Red, this can all be a little confusing.

It is forbidden to tie up to or climb on to any buoy used for navigation wherever you are in the world. When the first edition of this book was written, the fine for tying onto a buoy in the nearby Tyne Estuary was £5. Under the Merchant Shipping Act (1982) things have changed considerably and anyone who is now convicted of the offence can face a fine of up to £1,000.

Take great care in estuaries and tidal rivers. Large vessels have great difficulty in manoeuvring even if they do see you, which is most improbable. Beware of the upstream side of moored ships and barges. Once swept in between two moored ships you will find they tend to squeeze against buffers, closing from about 18 in. to 6 in. Your kayak won't stop them and neither will you (Figure 116). You can always tell which way the tide is setting by watching the behaviour of the water around the mooring buoys. It is unwise to practise rolling in estuaries and tidal rivers, but if you feel you must, wear a nose clip, keep your mouth shut and treat yourself afterwards to an antiseptic gargle. It is well to know the signals a ship will give when it alters course, so that you can take evasive action if necessary.

1 A short blast on the hooter means it is going to starboard.
2 Several short blasts on the hooter mean it is going to port.

If you are paddling round the stern of a boat and it gives three sharp blasts, get out of the way: it is going to go astern.

In fog, if a vessel is moving, it will give a long blast every 2 minutes, but if it has stopped and is going to sit it out, you will hear one blast, then a 1-second gap, another blast, then a space of 2 minutes, then a repetition of the signal again.

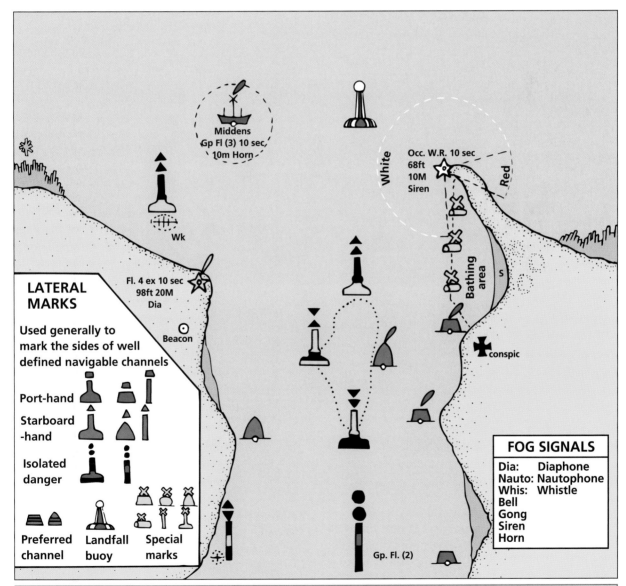

Figure 115.1 *Buoyage in an estuary (IALA System A – United Kingdom and Europe)*

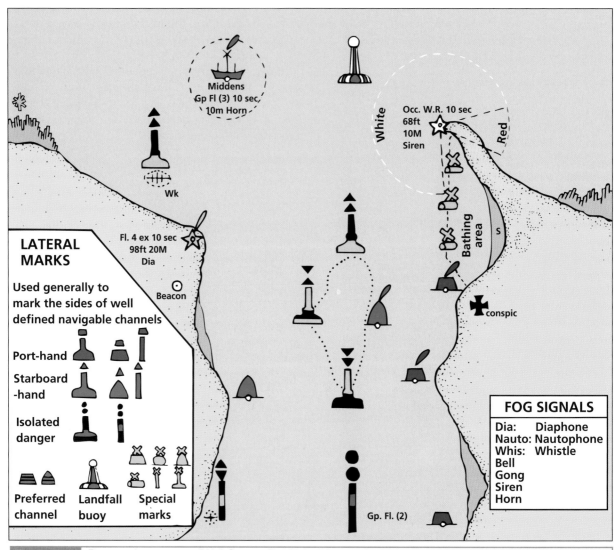

Figure 115.2 *Buoyage in an estuary (IALA System B – United States, Canada and Japan*

INTERNATIONAL COLLISION REGULATIONS

If you are paddling near busy shipping lanes, it will be easier to take evasive action if you know in advance what other larger vessels are going to do, especially if this entails a sudden alteration of course on their part. In all situations in which to remain on course would cause a collision, Master Mariners must abide by the International Collision Regulations. If you are not aware of what is happening, you may find that the captain's action is about to put 's craft exactly where you are sitting in your kayak!

1 **Meeting** Vessels that are meeting head-on alter course to starboard.
2 **Crossing** The vessel that has 'the other' crossing on its starboard bow alters course, usually to starboard, in order to pass round the stern of the other vessel.

Figure 116 *Black arrows indicate some danger spots:*

1 *Crew member finds convenient rubbish tip*

2 *Some of the water gushing from holes in the side of the ship may have ghastly origins*

3 *The upstream side of mooring buoys could cause a capsize*

4 & 5 *Two ships slowly squeezing together against buffers – a place of extreme danger*

6 *To capsize in here could be quite horrific*

7 *Beware of anglers and their lines*

3 Overtaking The vessel which is overtaking keeps clear of the vessel being overtaken.
4 Narrow channel Vessels keep to the starboard side.
5 Shipping separation lanes These should be crossed as nearly as possible at right angles.

As a kayak paddler you are master of a small 'powered vessel'. You should therefore make yourself aware of the problems facing other water craft and thus practice good seamanship.

ESCAPE ROUTES

These should be thought of well in advance so that if conditions become unfavourable and things in general get a little tense, the leader can take his group out of danger into safety. Figure 117 shows a typical expedition. Oban is the base, the camp site having been found by an OS map. The plan is to paddle down the western exposed sides of the islands of Kerrara, Luing, Scarba and part of Jura.

Any gale from the west will produce extreme paddling conditions but, as illustrated, there are ways back to base which will give reasonable shelter. The routes must be worked out from a chart. If your escape route lies between two islands and the tidal stream is against you, it may be impossible to get into the sheltered water. In such a case you land in the best place you can.

SPECIAL CHALLENGES

Fog

When I first started kayaking on the sea, very few people ventured out of sight of land. The outlook of most paddlers was very similar to that of sailors prior to the fifteenth century: it wasn't safe and if the fog was dense the last thing you wanted was to vanish seawards into it. If by some mischance one of those dense summer pea-soup fogs came down, it was out with the compass and grope your way back to the beach.

Be cautious by all means, but don't deprive yourself of some very interesting experiences by never attempting a trip in the fog.

Fog may be present before a trip starts or it can arrive like huge banks of moving steam whilst you are out at sea. It makes no noise as it creeps and envelopes everything in its path. Fog is caused when warm air blows off the land over a cool sea and cools the surface air down to its dew point. A clear sky will help the heat to radiate from the earth, and you will see that a slight breeze is needed to carry this warm air.

In really dense fog everything appears and sounds quite different from usual. Buoys and ships take on strange shapes. One minute dogs can be heard barking miles away and the next moment your companion's voice sounds muffled only a few yards away. You lose all sense of direction and after a while may even doubt your compass. Sometimes the sun seems to give a nice warm glow and the blue sky can be seen when you look up. The fog bank is not very high, and you may even paddle out of it. At other times it seems dark and black even at midday and there is no warm glow. This fog is high, cutting out the sun's bright glare.

If you would like to try a paddle in bad visibility, take your compass and go out a little way offshore into the fog. Don't try this in a harbour at first in case you wander into a shipping lane and get run down. Go off the beach, but not in big surf. Paddle about for 10 minutes or so and then find your way back to the beach. This will give you confidence in your compass. Then go out for about half an hour and wander around just for the thrill of it, knowing you can get back in again when you want to. Go out on a clear day and take some bearings off buoys and markers; then on the next foggy day paddle out and try to locate them. You will soon see how difficult this little exercise can be.

In fog, each member must carry a compass. The chances of getting separated from your group are very great, so you may find that you can actually use the whistle that has been bleached in the sun on its rotting cord on your lifejacket all these years. I often carry a trumpet type of fog horn manufactured by the Acme firm that makes the whistles. Some hand-held fog horns are driven by a can of compressed

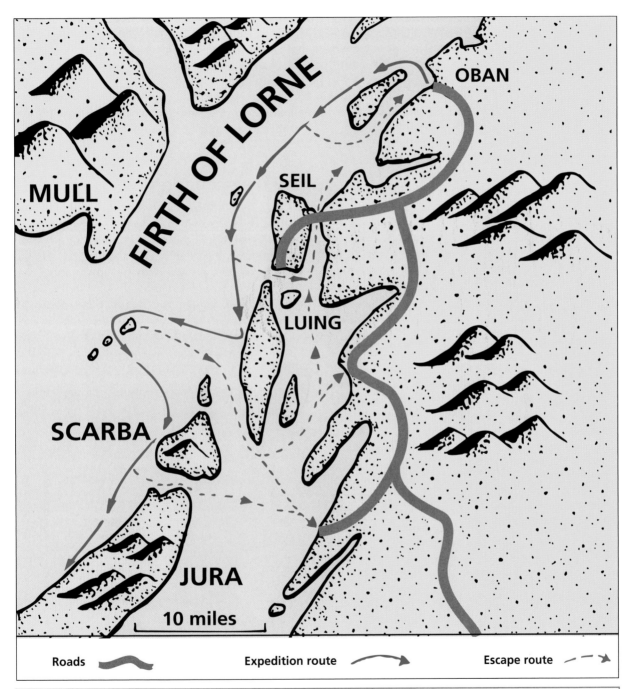

Roads ⌇⌇ **Expedition route** ➤ **Escape route** ⌁ ➤

Figure 117 *Escape routes. The sketch map shows the route of a typical sea expedition with Oban as the base for transport and main tents. All the escape routes therefore lead either back to base, via the shelter of the islands, or to the nearest road from where someone will have to walk or hitch-hike to base. Some expeditions offer a variety of escape routes by both land and sea. Some, however, offer none*

air. However, everybody will want to play with it so that, by the time you need it, instead of a strident hoot there will only be a prolonged and rather embarrassing hiss. In dense fog don't forget you cannot see anything and – what is probably more important – nobody can see you and you will not show up on a ship's radar. If you wish to make your own radar reflector, roll up some kitchen foil into a loose ball, 6-9 in. in diameter. Fix it to your hat or stick it on to 3ft. of old fishing rod and carry it upright on your rear deck. You will find it as good as anything you can buy.

Fog can make the surface of the sea very deceiving. I once set off for an island in fog with the sea like glass and no wind. I was familiar with the water and the distance involved was only a couple of miles, but after I had paddled the time it normally takes to get there, no island loomed up. It appeared it had either sunk or been towed away. I sat and wondered where I had gone wrong. Well, there is a good rule in fog: if you can't see, listen. So I strained my ears and could just hear something to the north, a rather peculiar sound I could not place. I headed towards it and soon the sky was filled with screaming, diving, swooping sea-birds around the cliffs of an island. I realised what I had done. Although the water was calm and smooth, the tidal stream was running very fast. This was obvious, however, only when I looked at the water in relation to the island it was rushing past. Out in the fog the water had appeared quite still, giving no hint that we were being swept further and further away from our destination. Remember then: land has a sound. It may be a train, dogs barking, the sound of birds or a combination of many things. So use your ears and listen carefully for, and be able to identify, the distinctive sounds of land.

The only way to locate something lost in fog – an island, a buoy, anything – is to use your compass and paddle a square. Paddle about 30 strokes for each side and then gradually increase the size of the box, sticking rigidly to compass bearings but of course remembering the drift.

Really thick fog does not usually arrive without warning. There are some ways of being able to predict it. First of all, was there fog yesterday or the day before? If the answer is yes and the general weather conditions have not changed, the chance is there may well be fog today.

Look at the surface of the sea. Is it hazy and is the horizon blurred and indistinct? Is the air blowing off the land and across the cool sea? All these are sure indications of fog, and it will be as well during the summer to pay attention to such tell-tale signs and to *carry a compass for even the shortest trip offshore.*

Kayaking at night

The first time most people find out what it is like to kayak at night is usually on a late return from a day's paddle. Whatever the reason, you now find yourself in a completely different situation, so you may as well enjoy it. Paddling at night is an exciting and interesting experience, and kayaking by the light of the moon can be almost like paddling on a moonbeam.

Lights may be confusing as to their number and location. It is quite easy to misinterpret the headlights of a car as it passes over the brow of a hill near the shore line. Don't forget that from seawards, flashing

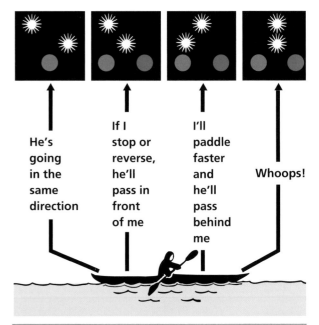

Figure 118.1 *When you paddle at night, it is the law that you are to show a white light to inform others of your position, especially if there is any fear of a collision*

buoys are seen against a backcloth of shimmering shore lights and can easily be missed. Lighthouses always seem to look nearer at night than they really are. Sometimes you may see as many as five or six all winking and flashing different colours. The most common type of light you will come across on your paddles is *group flashing* (Gp. Fl. on your chart) from a lighthouse, which is a set number of flashes repeated at a fixed interval. You can't get an accurate bearing by using these flashes, but lighthouses often have different coloured segments and in such cases you can get a bearing line as you pass from, say, the green segment to the red, since the division between the colours is shown on all admiralty charts. At night when vessels are stationary, their lights are usually very bright. Fishing boats may have their decks floodlit. I well remember coming upon a fishing boat at about 2 a.m. out of the blackness into the illuminated area surrounding the boat and being greeted with a certain amount of alarm by the white-faced man working on the deck.

All ships – all except you, that is – must show navigation lights: white masthead lights, with the one on the front mast lower than that on the rear mast; and a red light on the port side and a green light on the starboard side. Remember that from your low

position on the water the masthead lights may look almost level. Figure 118.1 shows some interesting combinations.

A man 40 ft. or more up on the bridge of a ship has a completely different view of lights and of traffic on the water from that of a kayaker. He cannot see you at all; you are completely invisible. By the time someone in the wheelhouse has made up his mind that he has actually seen your little new waterproof torch (by law you must be able to exhibit a white light to show your position if there is any danger of collision) and has then found some deck officer to make sure through his steamed-up glasses that it *was* a light, you are still in trouble, because he is travelling at 10 to 20 knots and is thus not likely to be able to slow down quickly. I know that when I must cross a shipping channel in the dark, I sit looking and listening for some time and then I cross at a speed that would do credit to a rather highly strung greyhound. If necessary, white or green hand flares can be fired to draw a boat's attention to your position. (Don't set off a blue one, or you will get the local pilot coming out to you, and will he be pleased!)

Probably the most important piece of equipment you will need and use, apart from what you normally carry, is a caver's headlamp or, failing this, a

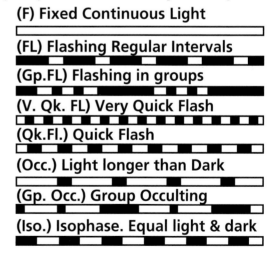

(F) Fixed Continuous Light

(FL) Flashing Regular Intervals

(Gp.FL) Flashing in groups

(V. Qk. FL) Very Quick Flash

(Qk.Fl.) Quick Flash

(Occ.) Light longer than Dark

(Gp. Occ.) Group Occulting

(Iso.) Isophase. Equal light & dark

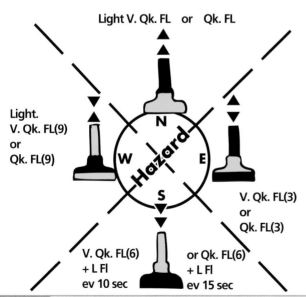

Light V. Qk. FL or Qk. FL

Light. V. Qk. FL(9) or Qk. FL(9)

V. Qk. FL(3) or Qk. FL(3)

V. Qk. FL(6) + L Fl ev 10 sec

or Qk. FL(6) + L Fl ev 15 sec

Figure 118.2 *Cardinal Marks*

flash light taped to your helmet. You will need this light for studying the chart and livening up the sometimes feeble glow of your luminous compass. However, bear in mind that some caver's lamps are not as waterproof as one would wish. You will also want another flash light handy on the foredeck (fastened to the kayak by a cord), which will have many uses, but not for warning ships of any size of your presence.

As a night navigator you will, of course, make a note of the specific lights you will encounter before setting out on a trip. For an example of what you might expect, see Figure 118.2.

Paddling at night should be tried only after you are a very competent daylight paddler. The leader must know his group and keep it small. Remember that it is one thing paddling through rough water when you can see what your paddle is going into or the speed at which the water is moving, and it is another thing entirely when you can hardly see anything.

LOCAL KNOWLEDGE

When you read the *Admiralty Pilot*, study a Tidal Stream Atlas, gaze long and hard at a chart or marvel at the accuracy of the symbols that inform you of the whereabouts of rips and races, you must bear in mind that this information is set out to inform the masters of deep-draughted vessels. Tiny craft like kayaks are not a priority. When you are planning your trip, therefore, remember that just because a rip or race is located at a certain position on a chart it does not mean that there are no other rips or races anywhere else on the same chart – or even in the same vicinity as those already marked. There are a couple of options open to you.

First, you can draw upon your experience. Using your knowledge of water behaviour, relate this to the speed of the tide, the depth of the water and the quality of the sea bottom. Link all this with any other factors that you think relevant and you should be able to build up a picture of what might happen at a certain location at a certain time in a particular area.

Your second alternative is to pick up the telephone or put pen to paper and contact someone who

knows all about the area. This goes under the heading of *local knowledge* and it takes a lot of beating.

Many years ago I had the salutary experience of learning just how valuable this type of information can be. A group of us had decided to make a first crossing of the Sound of Harris. This strait separates the islands of Harris and Uist in the Outer Hebrides. There were six of us earnestly studying the chart spread out on the oil-cloth-covered table of Leverbourgh's one and only café. We encouraged each other with the fact that the overall distance was only 20 miles, and that apart from a few rocky islets dotted about on our side of the sound it was obviously a very straightforward open crossing.

There was a ring of confidence in the remarks from around the table.

'It all looks reasonably uncomplicated.'

'The maximum speed is only 3 knots!'

'That shouldn't present any problem.'

We were all dedicated ocean paddlers of considerable experience. I felt that I had studied the chart until I could have drawn it in my sleep, and surely we knew by heart the 'Directions to Mariners' from the pages of the *Admiralty Pilot*. So, leaving the others to conclude their deliberations, I decided to get some fresh air.

Our brightly coloured kayaks, their charts and compasses affixed to the foredecks, were now all packed and ready. They lay resting on the weed-covered rocks at the base of a stone sea-wall, their bows already pointing eagerly towards the mist-shrouded outline of Uist way off to the south. I went out into the wind and wandered in the direction of the kayaks.

A very old man was leaning on the low stone wall. He held a blackened pipe in his gums and he gazed contentedly out across the white-tops and into the distance. I leaned sociably on the wall, next to him. We stood together for a while before he looked at the kayaks and found inspiration. He spoke very slowly, in the strong dialect of the islands, and he seemed to weigh every word. His head was nodding as he spoke.

'Och... aye... They're bonny wee boaties you've got there!'

I needed no other opening.

'These boats are called sea kayaks and they're built especially for use on the sea.'

I proceeded to expound the virtues of the sea kayak to his slowly nodding head. Eventually I paused for his reaction. His head was still nodding as he looked from me back out across the Sound again.

'Aye... aye... Mind, that's a dangerous bit of water out there.'

Once again my mouth went into operation ahead of my common sense.

'Oh, that's alright,' I said, 'we've all been paddling for a long time. We know what we're doing.' (Were they vultures or seagulls circling overhead?)

I reassured him that we had studied the charts, read the *Pilot* and had got a weather forecast. He nodded his head in silence for a time, then pointed with his pipe out towards a fishing vessel about a mile into the Sound.

'Ye see yon wee boaty out there?'

Yes, I could see it. He resumed his ponderous nodding, so I kept on watching the fishing boat. It appeared to be doing about 5 or 6 knots and was displaying quite a large bow wave. However, in spite of that I couldn't discern any forward movement. I made a derisory comment about what I considered was an underpowered engine.

'He's not going very fast, is he?' I said.

Plate 26 *Necessity is the mother of invention – or innovation. Fridtjof Nansen and Hjalmar Johansen sailing their united kayaks over the waters of the Arctic Ocean. 'There was nothing else to be done except lash the two kayaks together side by side. stiffen them with snowshoes under the straps and place the sledges athwart them, one before, one behind.'*

(Picture from an original watercolour by Otto Sinding from a sketch by Nansen, 1897. Courtesy of Alistair Wilson)

(Quotation from *Farthest North* Vol. II, by Fridtjof Nansen, Archibald Constable & Co. 1897)

He nodded in agreement as he gave his reply, which was as slow and gentle as it was horrific.

'Ahh,... no-o-o... he's going sideways!'

I ran back to the café and met the others emerging into the fresh air.

'Come and look at this,' I said pointing to the fishing boat. 'What do you think of that?'

There was a thoughtful silence as they studied the scene. I wondered who would say the magic words. Finally it was Chris who spoke.

'He's not going very fast, is he?'

I imitated the accent rather well.

'Ahh,... no-o-o... he's going *sideways*!'

Plate 27 *Killer Whales always make my heart pound. This large bull is off Robson Bight, Vancouver Island*

(Photograph: Will Nordby)

Some of the horrors that float about on our coastal waters under the name of sea kayaks bear little or no resemblance to the designs developed over many hundreds of years by the indigenous inhabitants of the Arctic. The genuine sea kayak of the Arctic was evolved by adapting a particular type of kayak to specific needs and conditions. Throughout its history it has been essentially a completely seaworthy boat in order to fulfil its primary function of being a hunter's boat.

The Eskimo has always had a constant fight for survival against what would seem to be overwhelming difficulties – the long dark winter, the eternal cold, and the never-ending search for food. The only element which can provide subsistence is the sea. It is from the sea that the Eskimo gets most of his food, from fish or from sea mammals such as the seal, walrus, sea otter and the whale. From these animals he also gets oil for his lamps and sinews and baleen for sewing skins and furs. The ivory and bones from these animals, as well as from his own dogs, can be made into weapons, tools, domestic implements and ornaments. The only other raw material available is driftwood, which floats in large quantities down rivers like the Yukon and Mackenzie and is then spread around the seas of the Arctic along the northern shores of Russia and the coasts of Greenland. But the right type of driftwood is rare and the scarcity of wood necessitates the retrieval of harpoon shafts while hunting and makes the kayak a highly prized piece of equipment, handed down from father to son.

The Eskimo used to hunt the whale in an open boat about 30 ft. long and 6ft. wide with a flat bottom. It was propelled by women and was named the *umiak* (the Russian word is 'baydara') or 'woman's boat'. Hunting the walrus and seal required a different type of boat altogether from the umiak, so the Eskimo developed what is probably the world's most famous single-handed craft. For elegance, grace and austere beauty, it has never been surpassed by any other type of solo craft. Since it also boasts speed, silence and seaworthiness, this is a true kayak or 'hunter's boat'.

When the Eskimo built a kayak, the frame was constructed first. Two long planks from 2 to 7 in. wide were used as gunwales, which were secured fore and aft in a position to take the bow and stern posts. The gunwales were supported by cross members or deck beams. Lashed on top of these with seal thong was a lath which ran down the centre of the deck. Rib frames of bent wood were mortised into the gunwale planks. The kayak was then turned on to its deck. A longitudinal lath was lashed to the bottom in the centre and an even number of laths, usually either four or six, secured at either side. Any slight gaps between the bent frames and the laths could be packed out by thick pieces of hide to stop the frames distorting (Figure 124). The frame was then covered tightly with seal-skin from which all the hair had been plucked. A small manhole was left in the deck. This was fitted with a wooden hoop coaming through which the skin was tightly stretched and tacked over with bone or ivory pins. As the skin shrank, it drew the coaming even tighter to the deck. When finished the kayak had to be light enough to be carried by the paddler either over his shoulder with his arm inside the manhole or, in the case of some Greenland kayaks, on his head with the cockpit coaming resting against his forehead. A walk from one bay to the next might save many miles of paddling, or make the difference between launching on a lee or weather shore.

In winter the man wore a hairless seal-skin jacket with a hood. This was the anorak or 'full smock'. The bottom hem of this could be pulled over the cockpit coaming and lashed tightly round the hoop with a long piece of thong. Two strips of narrow bone beading 6 or 7 in. long and about 1/4 in. wide were fixed by pins to the top edge of the coaming at the back. The two other pieces were fixed parallel to these but lower down (Figure 124). This arrangement formed a locating channel for the thong when it was wrapped around. Although the anorak was secured in this way only at the rear of the cockpit, it is doubtful whether the hunter would be able to wrench the jacket free in an emergency, so that a roll or an assisted rescue would be his only means of salvation.

Figure 119 *North Greenland/Hudson Bay kayak.*
This kayak is rather ugly when compared with other Greenland kayaks. The wide deck is flat except for the sheer up to the large round cockpit. Note the high wooden coaming. The man appears to sit quite loosely and slumped back. The paddle, drawn to scale, is long by Eskimo standards. In the photo which inspired this drawing, what appears to be a large full dustbin is stood on the deck just forward of the cockpit; this may give some indication of the stability of this particular kayak

In southern Alaska and the Aleutian Islands the hunter would wear a longer garment made from horizontal strips of seal-gut,[1] called the *kamleika* (originally this Russian word meant 'fur coat'). The 'half-frock', another garment worn by the hunter, was more like our spray cover. It was a short skirt of seal-skin tied round the cockpit rim to keep out the water and it could also tied under the armpits if necessary.

Kayaks from the far north of Greenland and certain parts of Hudson Bay have larger cockpits which are left unsealed[2] (Figure 119). Hunting the walrus can be very dangerous and if the prey turns and comes into the attack, the hunter can leave his kayak much more quickly if he is not fastened by thongs to the cockpit coaming. If the walrus slashes huge rents in the skin of his own boat, he can always seek safety on the deck of a companion's boat, thus saving himself from the wrath of the walrus, the bitter cold of the water, or death by drowning. It is almost unheard of for an Eskimo to swim.

Kayaks vary in pattern and shape, each having its own distinctive sea-going qualities and style. Each kayak is also tailored to the body measurements of the individual paddler and is worn like a garment rather than just 'sat in' like a rowing boat. To get into the boat the man first sits on the back deck, puts both feet up inside the kayak and wriggles until he is firmly in the manhole. His back is jammed against one of the cross beams protruding into the cockpit space. This means that any strain is taken on the wooden strut rather than by the wooden hoop. The hunter uses one of the curved hull frames as a footrest, and the kayak becomes rather like an extension of the man's body, responding to his every move.

Although methods of measuring may differ slightly, the system is basically the same. For instance the King Islander makes his kayak gunwales $2\frac{1}{2}$ arm spans long. The stem piece, which has a notch at the top to locate the gunwales, is the distance from the elbow to the finger tips (a cubit). The two middle thwarts are as long as the outstretched arm including the fingers. This makes the width about 25 in., but the flared sides bring the waterline beam down to about 18 in.

[1]Seal-gut was 3 in. in diameter, and when opened out it provided a strip 6 in. wide. Walrus-gut was even wider.

[2]R. Frank, *Frozen Frontier, The Story of the Arctic*, George G. Harrap, 1964.

Figure 120   *The death of a caribou – note the Inukshuks in the background.*
Killing caribou could be a very dangerous occupation. Note how the hunter keeps hold of his paddle rather than push it under the deck thongs, as he would if he were harpooning at sea

The King Islander had to face not only the very stormy waters of the Bering Sea but also a launching problem. His walrus-gut parka[3] was secured tightly round the cockpit coaming and he and his boat were then picked up by four men and thrown into the sea. His kayak therefore had to be very strong, so that just any wood was not good enough. The gunwales had to be straight-grained and matched. For the 10 thwarts, natural curved pieces of wood were used and the 25 to 30 rib frames were split from birch logs and bent by steaming. The willow cockpit hoop was an integral part of the framework. Compare this robust construction with that of the Nunamiut kayak.

The Nunamiuts, members of an inland tribe, lived by hunting the caribou in a kayak about 20 ft. long. The gunwales were two spruce strips bound together at the ends by rawhide thongs. The U-shaped ribs were green willow shoots the thickness of a man's thumb, bent and then mortised into the gunwales to form the hull. The five or seven longitudinal laths were strips of birch or spruce which did not extend completely to the stern or stem, where slender deck beams of willows were fixed, much less curved than the other beams. Even though this kayak was nowhere near so robust as its coastal cousin, it had violent usage.

The migrating herds of caribou were frightened into making river crossings at places chosen previously by the Eskimos. The women would creep up and frighten the herd towards the river. Piles of stones called inukshuks, which at a distance looked like groups of people (Figure 120), were used to divert the terrified animals to the chosen spot. Once in the water the herd was at the mercy of the kayak men who paddled amongst them, stabbing them

[3]From the Russian word for shirt. The Eskimo wood is ee-main-ee-tik

Figure 121 *Seal-hunting Eskimo*

with a spear high in the rib cage to one side of the backbone, piercing the heart or lungs. The thrust and withdrawal had to be quick, or the animal would thrash about and the man could be overturned and pitched in the icy water among the surging animals.

Some tribes such as the Aivilingmiuts used a heavy kayak for walrus and seal hunting and a lighter one for lake work and caribou hunting. But the Caribou Eskimos used a kayak similar to the one illustrated in Figure 123 for both purposes. If they were going to hunt sea mammals the kayak frame was covered with seal-skin, whereas if caribou were to be the victims then the same frame was covered with caribou skin. The Itiumiut Eskimos also had different kayaks for inland and sea work, and it is obvious that the Eskimo came to the same conclusion as that arrived at by so many modern paddlers – that there is no such thing as a general purpose boat for both river and sea.

A Greenland kayak equipped for hunting seals had a framework platform or tray called the *kayak stand* on the foredeck to carry a long coiled line (Figures 121 and 125). One end of the line was secured to the detachable head of the hunter's harpoon and the other end led under his arm to the back deck and was fixed to a large seal-skin float which itself was attached to the rear deck in a quick-release manner. Lying on the foredeck next to the harpoon might be a lance, while underneath the kayak stand, safe in its bag, would be a rifle.

Hidden behind a white camouflage shield mounted on the foredeck, the hunter would look for the seals. As soon as he saw his prey the hunter would paddle into range and, quickly shipping his paddle, withdraw the gun and fire. Then, gun away, he would paddle swiftly within harpoon range. The paddle would be pushed under the deck thong again and the harpoon hurled accurately and forcibly with the assistance of the throwing stick. During the time the kayak was running free with no paddle, it might have been held on course by means of a detachable skeg. As soon as the prey was harpooned, the flotation bag was released from the rear deck. Thus if the prey was

Figure 122 *North Baffinland kayak (length: 19' 3", width: 24"). The widest part is just rear of the cockpit (20" x 18")*

killed immediately it would not sink, or if it was only wounded and dived, it would then tire with the drag of the inflated bag.

The Baffinland kayak

This kayak from Baffin Bay (Figure 122) looks rather ungainly with its huge thick bow and flat squat stern. The cockpit slopes down towards the flat back deck and is horseshoe shaped. Apart from the forefoot at the bow, the boat is virtually flat bottomed. In spite of its rather unwieldy appearance, however, this kayak was reputedly easy to turn, presumably sliding round over the water on its flat bottom. However, its seaworthiness in extreme conditions must be suspect, because of this same flat bottom (see the section on hull shapes, Chapter 1).

The Caribou kayak

This kayak (Figure 123) came from the north-western shores of Hudson Bay. Although the caribou were hunted mainly at river crossings, they were also driven into small open-water lakes and were forced to cross narrow sea fjords.

When viewed in plan and elevation, the Caribou kayak could be compared quite closely with a modern competition slalom kayak, as it has a considerable rocker. The only real differences are the slender willowy bow and stern of the Caribou kayak

and its obviously seaworthy cockpit. A group of kayak hunters paddling in amongst a herd of frightened swimming caribou needed a kayak that would turn very quickly and had a strong covering, and a bow that could safely hook into the antlers of an escaping animal and divert it long enough for a companion to close in for the *coup de grâce*.

Greenland kayaks

Kayaks from this huge, sprawling landmass, specifically the designs from the west coast of Greenland, have influenced modern sporting sea kayaks more than any other type of Eskimo kayak. It was difficult to know which particular types would best illustrate the qualities of the West Greenland kayak. After a great deal of examining, measuring and sketching, I chose three which best illustrate not only the superb sea-going qualities but also the subtle local differences in design. I refer to all three kayaks by the names of the museums where they are to be found South Shields, Whitby and Newcastle (Figure 124–6).

It will be seen that the kayaks from South Shields and Whitby have extremely high sterns. There were very good reasons for this. When the hunter approached his quarry from down wind, the high stern would act as a kind of rudder. This meant that the kayak would continue to travel forwards, held straight and true, while the hunter, shipping his paddle, could fire his rifle or throw a harpoon. The

Figure 123 *Caribou kayak (West Hudson Bay). Length: 18' 6", width: 21", cockpit: 18" diameter*

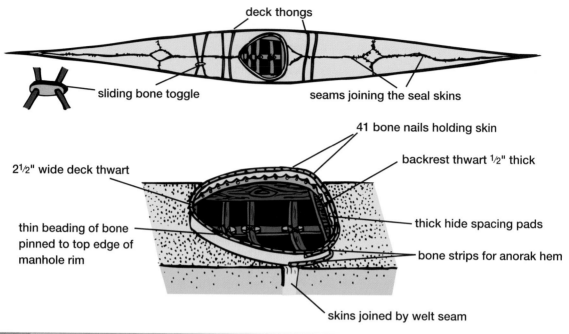

deck thongs

sliding bone toggle

seams joining the seal skins

41 bone nails holding skin

backrest thwart ½" thick

2½" wide deck thwart

thin beading of bone
pinned to top edge of
manhole rim

thick hide spacing pads

bone strips for anorak hem

skins joined by welt seam

Figure 124 *Whitby kayak. Plan view and detail of cockpit*

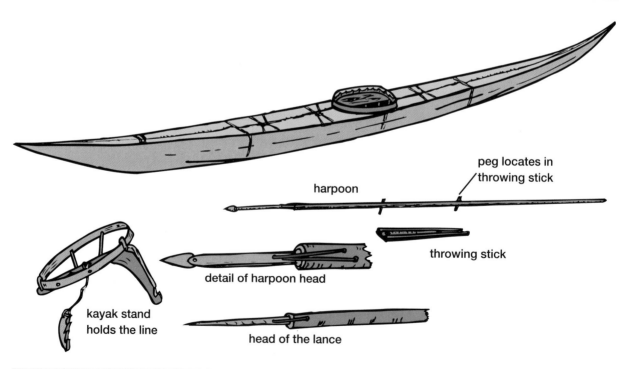

peg locates in
throwing stick

harpoon

throwing stick

kayak stand
holds the line

detail of harpoon head

head of the lance

Figure 125 *Newcastle-upon-Tyne kayak. Length: 17' 10". width 16"*

Figure 126.1 *Whitby kayak. Length: 18' 10", width: 16¾", internal cockpit sizes: 16" long by 15" wide*

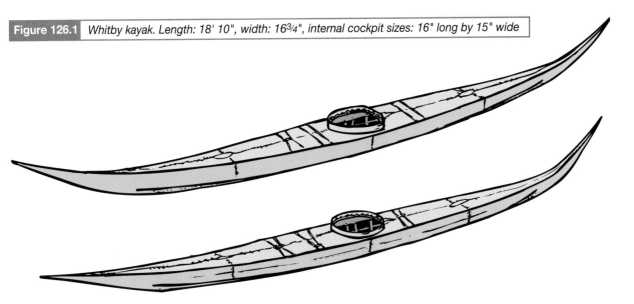

Figure 126.2 *South Shields kayak. Length: 17' 6", width: 16", round cockpit sizes: 16"*

bow and stern of the Newcastle kayak are less exaggerated and much lower than the other two, but the hull aft of the cockpit is very narrow, rising gently to a low, slim stern.

All three kayaks are rather straight sided and almost flat bottomed. It seems incredible that an adult male even of Eskimo proportions could get into any of the cockpits, since the width of all the hulls is only 16 in. at its widest part and the internal measurements at the cockpit can be as small as 15 in. Leg room is no less of a problem. The South Shields kayak has only 6 in. from the deck thwart in front of the cockpit to the bent frame at the bottom of the hull, into which a man must squeeze his feet, legs and thighs. It is hardly surprising that modern manufacturers when trying to imitate Eskimo designs have had to make considerable modifications to accommodate the European man.

East Greenland kayak

This differs in design from the other Greenland kayaks illustrated (Figure 128.2). Its length – usually 18 ft. but up to 20 ft. – and its long, low clipper bow and long, low stern make it a very fast hunting machine, with little for a beam wind to catch. As with all Greenland kayaks, the primary function was to carry a man while he hunted seal in sheltered waters amongst ice flows or fjords. In design it was not really meant for the use to which sporting paddlers now put it. Paddling into a steep head sea in any kind of wind would be a wet, chilling and dan-

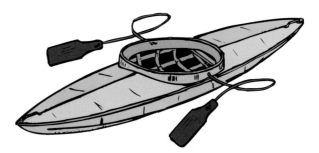

Figure 127 *Koryak kayak. Length: 9'*
The Koryaks were a gentle people. There was no comparison between them and the daring sea kayakers of the Aleutian Islands. However, this kayak was used on the sea but only on calm water. The small wooden hand paddles are fastened to the cockpit coaming by seal thongs. This kayak would probably manoeuvre rather like a modern swimming pool kayak. Note the thwart that acts as a back support

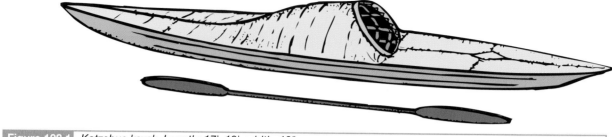

Figure 128.1 *Kotzebue kayak. Length: 17'–18', width: 18"*

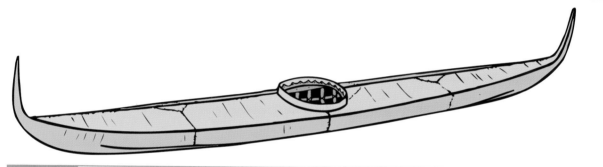

Figure 128.2 *East Greenland kayak. Length: 19' 6", width: 20"*

Figure 128.3 *Mackenzie Delta kayak. Length: 19' 6", width: 20"*

gerous business. Because its lines embody speed and slender grace, the design has been used as a basis for some modern kayaks of a similar type. The really roughwater kayaks, however, are those from the Aleutian and Alaskan areas.

The early King Island kayak and the Kotzebue Sound kayak

Both these kayaks are outlandish, perhaps even quaint in appearance, but no less seaworthy because of it. The bow of the early-type King Island kayak (Figure 128.4) would rise beautifully to short steep seas, while the steeply pitched deck would quickly shed heavy water breaking over it. Like the more modern King Island kayak it was paddled with a single-bladed paddle, except when the double-bladed paddle was used for speed during hunting.

The Kotzebue Sound kayak (Figure 128.1) with its low freeboard and flat deck would be constantly awash in anything but a reasonably calm sea, although I cannot imagine any water gaining access to the kayak via the manhole. With this tremendous amount of buoyancy amidships coupled with the flat deck, its rolling qualities can only be guessed at. Fast hunting-paddling was done with a double blade.

Kayak from the Aleutian Islands

Any account of Eskimo kayaks would be incomplete without a mention of the baidarkas (the Russian name for kayak) of the Aleutian Islands, which have some of the most dangerous waters in the world.

(See Figures 127.5 and 129). To hunt the whale

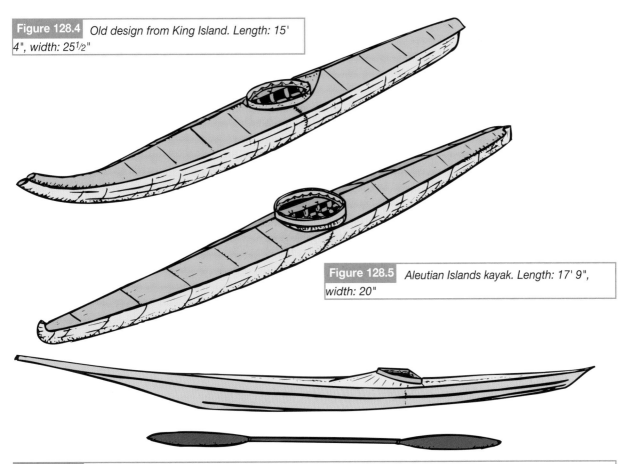

Figure 128.4 *Old design from King Island. Length: 15' 4", width: 25½"*

Figure 128.5 *Aleutian Islands kayak. Length: 17' 9", width: 20"*

Figure 128.6 *Labrador kayak (northern). Length: 24–26', width: 23"*
Like the Baffin Bay kayak this also has a flat bottom and is very stable. It is strongly built, heavy and very seaworthy. The cockpit is horseshoe shaped, flat along the back. The superb 'clipper bow' is five feet long. To assist in the turning of this very long kayak, the pautic or paddle is 10 ft. long

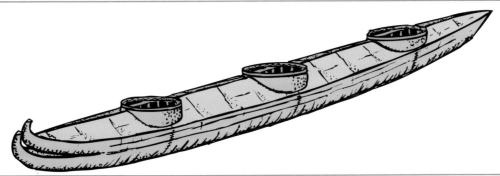

Figure 129 *Three-manhole Baidarka – Southern Alaska and Aleutian islands. Length: 25', width: 30"*
The Eskimos used a two manhole kayak (Baidarka) 21 ft. long by 23 in. wide. The three holes were a Russian idea; the middle one was used for transporting a passenger or carrying supplies

Figure 130 *Whale hunting from a baidarka*

and the sea-otter, the Aleuts used a narrow two-manhole baidarka 21 ft. long by 23 in. wide. It was very shallow, and in cross section the bottom was round and therefore very difficult to keep upright.

When hunting the sea-otter the Eskimos formed themselves into groups, from a few pairs to perhaps 100 on the water at one time. The front man in the kayak used a spear, while the man in the rear cockpit manoeuvred the kayak with a long double-bladed paddle. The flotilla would move quietly along in a line until someone saw an otter on the surface. He would raise a paddle in the air to warn the others and then paddle to the sea-otter's last position on the surface of the water before its dive,[4]

[4]Harold McCracken, *Hunters of the Stormy Sea*, Oldbourne, 1957.

where the rest of the group would form a large circle around him. As soon as the sea-otter resurfaced, the nearest hunter paddled towards it, giving the animal no time to fill its lungs. This happened time and time again until the duration of the dives got shorter and shorter. The hunters would then close in and the animal could be speared.

If the wind was violent and the air filled with rain and spray, a tired sleepy animal might lie on the top of the kelp beds, its head hidden under the floating seaweed. In such a case the hunters could stealthily approach close enough to strike out and kill the unsuspecting creature with a wooden club.

Perhaps the greatest conquest of all for the kayak hunter was the killing of a whale. Once these huge mammals were sighted, only the bravest and most experienced hunters with the strongest and heaviest and sharpest of harpoons would dare take to the water. Paddling out amongst the feeding school, the hunters would select the small calves for their attention. To force the harpoon – tipped with aconite poison – deep enough into a whale for a kill, the men would have to position themselves about 10 to 15 ft. away, and then throw the harpoon with the full force of the throwing stick, aiming for a point just below the huge dorsal fin.[5] On feeling the pain, the whale would explode into thrashing violence, its flukes waving high above the hunters before crashing down and churning up the water (Figure 130). It would not be unknown for the whale-hunting Eskimos to be killed by 'the hand of God', the name given in the Azores to these giant tails that would crash down onto the whaling 'canoas'.[6] With any luck, however, the baidarka would manoeuvre clear of the injured whale and also of any enraged bull or cow swimming near.

The Aleut might have been hunting the whale to this day had not greedy, vicious men thousands of miles away taken a hand in his destiny and altered his way of life forever. In 1725 Vitus Bering, a Dane, led a Russian expedition of geographic exploration to Siberia and the north Pacific coast. Survivors from this ill-fated venture took sea-otter pelts back to Russia, which excited the Russians so much that they sent other expeditions to obtain more furs. Many of the men who elected to go could see fortunes for themselves on the horizon. They were the human dregs of Siberia, pirates with no moral code or thought for human life. Their code of conduct was ruled by the knowledge that punishment for crimes was non-existent: 'God is high above, and the Czar is far away'.[7] These were the promyshleniki, the professional hunters. By murder and intimidation, the native Eskimos, the Aleuts, were taken hostage, enslaved and forced to hunt the sea-otter until it almost vanished from the area. The

Russians then had to turn their attentions farther afield, as far south as the coast of California. While the promyshleniki travelled in the comparative comfort of large boats called shitikas,[8] the Aleuts were forced to paddle their baidarkas over distances which can only be described as appaling. In the summer of 1783 a veritable armada of large boats with scores of accompanying Aleut hunters set off from Unalaska for Prince William Sound, a distance of over 1000 miles across storm-swept open sea. Fear of the knout and the knowledge that their wives and daughters were on board the shitikas kept the Aleuts paddling night and day at about 10 miles per hour, unable to stop, sleeping in the kayaks by turns, unable even to relieve themselves properly. Journeys such as these, with fear of stragglers or the sick being shot,[9] must have been a nightmare and reflect no credit on the colonising Russians of the eighteenth century. It is fortunate that the baidarka with its bifed stem was probably the finest sea kayak in an area of fine kayaks and that the Aleuts were brilliant sea kayakers.

The three-manhole baidarka (Figure 129) invented by the Russians to carry a passenger or goods was much larger than the two-hole hunter's boat. The single-manhole boat could also be used for seal hunting, while the clumsy family baidarkas could carry dogs, children, furs, wife, meat, nets and all the other luxuries of life. What faith in their husband's kayaking ability these women must have had in order to huddle happily inside the claustrophobic hull. The order of packing and distribution of the cargo (dogs with meat, wife or children?) can only be wondered at.

It is sad to think that many of the kayak and hunting skills described in this chapter are dying out or are already a thing of the past. The whaling

---

[5]*Ibid*

[6]Trevor Housby, *The Hand of God, Whaling in the Azores,* Abelard-Schuman, 1971

[7]McCracken, *op. cit.*

[8]Because of the shortage of materials and tools, the Russians built their boats from roughly shaped timbers fastened together by hide thongs in the absence of nuts, bolts and nails. Thus sewn together (shi-it) is Russian 'to sew', hence shitika). Some of the early models literally fell to pieces only a few miles from land, drowning the crew.

[9]McCracken, *op. cit.*

carried on by the Aleuts died forever during the 100-year Russian tyranny. The King Islanders no longer live on their rocky island but are now housed on the mainland and display their kayak skills mainly to impress the tourists. The Danish government is doing good work in encouraging the Greenland Eskimos to maintain and preserve their culture and way of life, but even many of their kayaks are now built with canvas and joined with nails. Fortunately, nails don't rust in the cold dry atmosphere.

The Eskimo is no longer dependent on his own skills for survival, and the kayak, the hunter's boat, sadly may soon be gone forever. However it is to be hoped that designers will preserve the tradition of the Eskimo kayak even if in glassfibre, and that people will be encouraged to learn to handle what must surely be the most demanding yet the most rewarding boat in the world.

ESKIMO PADDLES

At one time my idea of a typical Eskimo paddle was like the Newcastle paddle in Figure 131, which is from West Greenland. These paddles displayed a high degree of workmanship, with bone beading to stop the sides of the blade chafing and bone ends made from the shoulder-plate of a dog. Although some of the paddle looms from this area were rectangular in cross section, the majority I have seen have been oval, giving a firm, comfortable and positive hand grip. However, Eskimo paddle designs are almost as numerous as the kayak designs themselves.

Quite a number of paddles have some kind of anti-capillary groove or ring. Water constantly running down the loom on to the hands could be more than uncomfortable in freezing temperatures with a wind blowing, even if mittens were sometimes worn. The

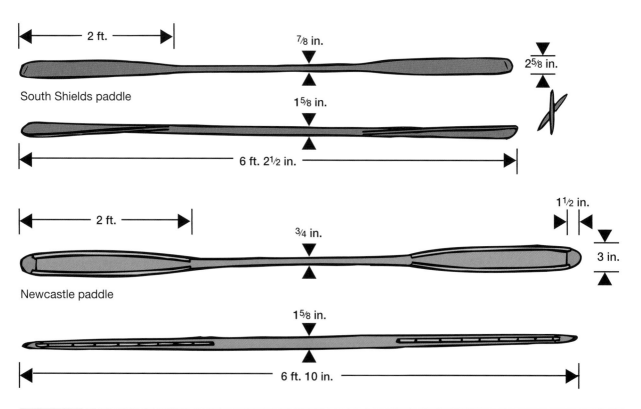

| **Figure 131** | *Comparative dimensions of West Greenland paddles. Not to scale* |

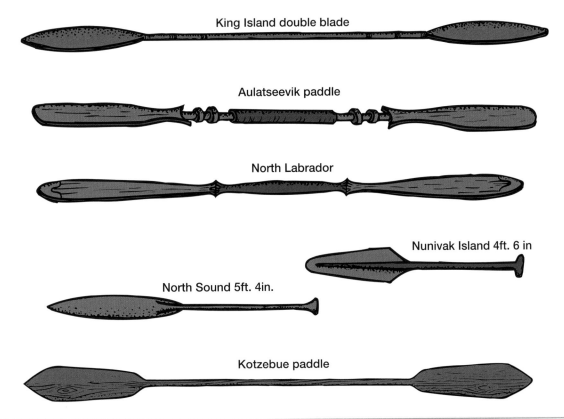

King Island double blade

Aulatseevik paddle

North Labrador

Nunivak Island 4ft. 6 in

North Sound 5ft. 4in.

Kotzebue paddle

Figure 132 *Eskimo paddles showing diversity of styles*

function of these anti-capillary devices is a little different from that of the one-time popular drip rings, which were used in the older European type of kayak before the adoption of spray covers. The idea behind these rings was to stop water running down the loom, down the arm and then dripping uncomfortably off the elbow, thus entering the large cockpit and then on to the knees and into the boat.

In Figure 132 the North Labrador paddle has shaped pieces to shed the water at the extremities of the loom. It was probably a very satisfactory arrangement. The Aulatseevik paddle seems to be the ultimate in Eskimo paddle comfort.[10] In a photograph I have seen of this, all the wide sections appeared to be bone sheathing an oval wooden interior. The hands were positioned in the space between the wide centre piece and the first bobbin; next came another drip ring to stop any stray drops of water which may have escaped the efficient

looking anti-capillary curve at the beginning of the blade. This Rolls-Royce of paddles was photographed lying across the cockpit of an Eskimo kayak, the interior of which was lined with what appeared to be white polar bear fur. The owner of this outfit was obviously a man who valued his creature comforts – I know the feeling well.

The most distinctive feature of the Labrador paddle is its length (Plates 32 and 33). It is hardly surprising, of course, that a boat of up to 26 ft. should need a large paddle 10 ft. long. An even longer paddle was used by the Nunamiut tribe, whose kayak has already been described. In front of the cockpit, a forked piece of willow or alder tree was used as a pivot for the almost 20-ft.-long paddle, which was hewn from spruce log.[11] Spare paddles

[11]Nicholas J. Gubsen, *The Nunamiut Eskimos, Hunters of the Caribou*, Yale University Press, 1965.

were sometimes carried by the hunters, especially those who used the single- and double-bladed paddles, such as the Eskimos of Alaska and some of the offshore islands, although I have never heard of Greenland Eskimos carrying spare paddles.

When the Eskimo gripped a double-bladed paddle, his hands were positioned about 4 hand-widths apart. This is quite close compared with modern practice, but anyone who tries to paddle in freezing conditions and wants to keep his hands dry without drip rings will find the Eskimo hand position practical. How the Koryaks (Figure 127) managed with their little hand paddles is not known to me. I've often wondered if through the years they developed extra long arms.

The Eskimo never used a feathered blade. Various theories have been put forward as to why this should be. Some say the blade is so narrow that the retardation caused by a head wind is hardly noticeable. The reason may, however, be much simpler: he may never have thought of it.

While investigating the various kayaks, I was surprised to see, laying in the cockpit of the South Shields kayak in storage at the local museum, a paddle which was feathered at 45° for a left-handed paddler (Figure 131). This may sound strange, considering the blades are of course flat, but it is extremely difficult to manipulate this paddle while trying to paddle right-handed. The loom is oval and has no twist along its entire length. Only the paddle blades themselves twist gently along their length, finally setting themselves at 45° to each other at the end.

Plate 28 *East Greenland kayaks ready for the hunt. These kayaks from Angmagssalik are fully equipped and ready to go for a seal hunt. With a width of only 20 in. and a length of 19½ ft. these kayaks were fast and sleek, but with their low freeboard they gave little protection and if the seas were rough, a paddle could expect water to break over the decks*
(Photograph by John Patersen, courtesy of the Danish National Museum,
Department of Ethnography, Copenhagen)

Plate 29 *'Eskimos in Kayaks – Mackenzie Delta'. In my eyes this is the most graceful of all the skin boats. Although this kayak formed the inspiration for one of my own early designs, I have never been able to discover why the bow and stern were so fine and yet turned up so acutely*
(Photograph: Ernest Brown – *The Search for the Western Sea* by Lawrence J. Burpee, Alston Rivers Ltd., 1908)

Plate 30 *Two people do not always need two cockpits – and is that a dog on the rear deck? In this picture by a unknown photographer a man and woman share a Nunivak Island kayak. Boats from this area were deep and buoyant. The remainder of the paddler's family might possibly be carried inside the hull. Care had to be taken that small children were not put at the same end as the dogs. In the event of a capsize it was possible for a single occupant to withdraw inside the body of the kayak*

(Smithsonian Institute Photo 34, 358-b)

Plate 31 *The non-stop distance you can paddle in a single kayak is limited to the number of hours you can stay awake. This is not the case with a double kayak, in which it is possible to sleep. This model of an Aleutian two-man-hole baidarka was made for me by Sergie Sovoroff of Nikolski. The rudder was a Russian innovation*

(Photograph: the Author)

Plate 32 *'Labrador Eskimo and Kayak.' Note the length of the paddle and the 'drip rings'. These huge kayaks were up to 24 ft. long and had a beam of 23 in. They were never rolled by their occupants, and in the event of a capsize the paddler would need assistance from a companion in order to get back into his boat*

(*Among the Eskimos of Labrador* by S. K. Hutton, MB, ChB Vict. Pub. Seeley & Co. Ltd. 1912.)

Plate 33 *'Labrador Eskimos ready for a seal hunt'*
(*Among the Eskimos of Labrador* by S. K. Hutton, MB, ChB Vict. Seeley, Service & Co. Ltd., 1912.)
(Photography: Moravian Missions)

Plate 34 *Aloysius Pikongonna at Nome, with the equipment used at King Island for hunting walrus or seals*
(Photograph: Bob and Ira Spring)

Plate 35 *Eskimo spearing a 'Sea Unicorn' (Narwhal), circa 1896. Note the feathered paddle*

Plate 36

Plate 37

Plate 38 *Modern custom-built replica of original one-hole baidarka taken from Atka on the Aleutian Islands. For those romantics who hanker after the 'old' days, there are now a growing number of craftsmen who will build for you an original design in the traditional manner. In this beautiful model by R. Bruce Lemon of Idaho, the frames are lashed together with waxed polyester instead of sinew. The skin is made from dead 14 oz. or 26 oz. nylon instead of the skin of a dead seal. This cover is then sewn together with braided nylon*   (Photograph: R. Bruce Lemon)

Plate 39 *This hunter from Nunivak Island is using a throwing stick and he is wearing the familiar wooden wedge shaped hat. When the need arises, he can bend his head forward and effectively shield his face from wind blown spray. In the event of a capsize he could either withdraw into the cockpit, breathe the air inside and wait for a companion to twist him upright or attempt to roll upright. Similar to the Toksook paddle mentioned earlier, the paddle is willow leaf in shape. The spine down the face of the blades is the key to its efficiency.*

(Photograph: Edward S. Curtis, courtesy of the University of Washington Libraries)

Conclusion

The whole coast of Britain, with its many islands, is suitable for sea kayaking expeditions which can open the door to adventure, thrills, discovery and to many strange and beautiful experiences.

It would take another book to recount the tales I have to tell. There is room here only to make passing reference to a few incidents – the pleasure of observing in all seasons the grey seals of the Farne Islands; the beautiful and eerie night trip around the Farnes when the phosphorescent plankton illuminated our wake with myriads of stars, and hundreds of birds flapped around our heads without uttering a single cry; the extreme tension during the paddle through fog across the Firth of Forth for the Isle of May and the tremendous feeling of elation when we realised our compass work had been accurate; the hilarity of finding that all discussion about pitching our tent to face the sunrise, the sunset or the prevailing wind had been an ironic waste of time, when we lay under the charred, flapping remnants after someone had set fire to it while making the coffee; the incredible satisfaction of overcoming everything the sea could throw at us, the freezing cold, the pounding waves breaking on reefs, the huge Atlantic swell, the lashing fury of a Force 8 gale, and, to add to the confusion, a 7 knot tidal stream cutting across our path as we slogged our way across the Sound of Harris to the coast of North Uist.

Plate 40 *A kayak is the ideal vehicle for carrying camping equipment. This campsite is on Heather Island, Alaska. Left to right: Chris Jowsey, the author and Tom Caskey. The columbian Glacier is in the background*

(Photograph: Alistair Wilson)

Plate 41 *Time for bed – pulling the boats up for the night... Herring Bay, Prince William Sound, Alaska*

Since the earlier editions of this book were written my kayaking has taken me to other countries and coastlines. I have looked into the eyes of a killer whale and felt the mist of its breath on my face. I have watched an iceberg leave the face of a glacier in silence and fall 300 feet to the sea and seen the approaching wave, only to hear the roar of the calving ice seconds later. I have enjoyed the antics of sea-otters and manatees and observed turtles and alligators at very close quarters.

And all from the seat of my kayak.

To those of you who are just starting to enjoy paddling on the sea, I say: take your kayak and first discover the world on your own doorstep. Remember that although the backdrop may be familiar, the sea itself is always changing and will never be the same.

To others I can now say, 20 years later, and with even more conviction, that kayaking on the sea is not just for the young; it is for the young in heart and the adventurous in spirit who want to fly with the wild swans.

Conversion table

Note: All units of measurements in the text are imperial. The following may be useful for conversion into metric.

10 millimetres	=	1 centimetre	=	0.395 inch (in.)
10 centimetres	=	[1 decimetre]	=	3.94 inches (in.)
[10 decimetres]	=	1 metre	=	1.094 yards (yd./yds.)
10 metres	=	[1 decametre]	=	10.94 yards (yd./yds.)
[10 decametres]	=	[1 hectometre]	=	109.36 yards (yd./yds.)
[10 hectometres]	=	1 kilometre	=	0.621 miles

A kilometre is approximately five-eighths of a mile

1 inch (in.)	=	2.54 centimetres		
1 foot (ft.)	=	30.48 centimetres		
1 yard (yd./yds.)	=	3 feet (ft.)	=	0.914 metre

1 square centimetre	=	0.155 square inch (sq.in.)
1 square kilometre	=	0.39 square mile

1 kilogram	=	2.205 pounds (lb.)

Bibliography

Abbot, R., *The Science of Surfing,* John Jones Cardiff Ltd., 1972.

American Red Coss, *Canoeing,* 1956.

Automobile Association, *Book of the Seaside,* Drive Publications, 1972.

Barret, John and Yonge, C. M., *Collins Pocket Guide to the Sea-Shore,* Collins, 1970.

Birket-Smith, Kaj, *The Eskimos,* Methuen, 1959.

Bowen, David, *Britain's Weather, Its Workings, Lore and Forecasting,* David and Charles, 1969.

British Canoe Union, *Canoeing in Britain,* Magazine back copies since 1963.

British Canoe Union, *Choosing a Canoe and Its Equipment.*

British Canoe Union, *Coaching Handbook.*

British Canoe Union, *The Eskimo Roll.*

Byde, Alan, *Beginner's Guide to Canoeing,* Pelham Books, 1973.

Byde, Alan, *Living Canoeing, A & C Black,* 1969.

Clark, Mike, *Canoeing,* Canoeing Press, Magazine Back copies since 1965.

Cock Oliver J., *A Short History of Canoeing in Britain,* BCU, 1974.

Cock, Oliver J., *You and Your Canoe,* Ernest Benn, 1956.

Dempsy, Michael, *The Skies and the Seas,* Ginn, 1966.

Frank, R., Frozen Frontier, *The story of the Arctic,* George G. Harrap, 1964.

Gubsen, Nicholas J., *The Nunamiut Eskimo, Hunters of the Caribou,* Yale University Press, 1965.

Harrington, *Richard, Face of the Arctic,* Hodder and Stoughton, 1954.

Housby, Trevor, T*he Hand of God, Whaling in the Azores,* Abelard-Schuman, 1971.

Houston, James, The White Dawn, Heinemann, 1971.

Ingstad, Helge, *Land Under the Pole Star,* Jonathan Cape, 1966.

Keatinge, W. R., *Survival in Cold Water,* Blackwell Scientific Publishers, 1969.

McCracken, *Harold, Hunters of the Stormy Sea,* Oldbourne, 1957.

McNaught, Noel, *The Canoeing Manual,* Nicholas Kaye, 1961.

Mawley, Robert and Seon, *Beaches, Their Life, Legends and Lore*, Chiltern, 1968.

Mowat, Farley, *The Desperate People*, Michael Joseph, 1960.

Mowat, Farley, *People of the Deer*, Michael Joseph, 1954.

Murray, W. H., *Islands of Western Scotland*, Methuen, 1973.

National Geographic Society, *The National Geographic Magazine*, June 1956, Vol. CIX No. 6.

Newing and Bowood, *The Weather* (A Ladybird Book), Wills and Hepworth, 1962.

Pemberton, John Lee, *Sea and Air Mammals* (A Ladybird Book), Wills and Hepworth, 1972.

Pilsbury, R. K., *Clouds and Weather*, Batsford, 1969.

Proctor, Ian, *Sailing Wind and Current*, Adlard Coles, 1964.

Pryde, Duncan, *Nunaga: Ten Years of Eskimo Life*, MacGibbon & Kee, 1972.

Reed, *Nautical Almanac*, Thos. Reed.

Robertson, Dougal, *Survive the Savage Sea*, Elek Books, 1973.

Rodahl, Koare, *Between Two Worlds*, Heinemann, 1965.

Ross, Frank Xavier, *Frozen Frontier, The Story of the Arctic*, 1964.

Ross, Dr. Helen, *Behaviour in Strange Environments*, 1974.

Sawyer, J. S., *The Ways of the Weather*, A & C Black, 1957.

Searl, F. H. L., *The Book of Sailing*, Arthur Barker Ltd., 1964.

Shenstone, D. A. and Beals, C. S. (Eds.), *Science, History and Hudson Bay*, Department of Energy, Mines & Resources, Ottawa, 1968.

Skilling and Sutcliffe, *Canoeing Complete*, Nicholas Kaye, 1966.

Spring, Norma, *Alaska, The Complete Travel Book*, Macmillan, 1970.

Staib, Bjorn, *Across Greenland in Nansens Track*, Allen and Unwin, 1963.

Sutherland, Charles, *Modern Canoeing*, Faber and Faber, 1964.

Tegner, Henry, *The Long Bay of Druridge*, Frank Graham, 1968.

United States National Museum Bulletin No. 230, *The Bark Canoes and Skin Boats of North America*, Adney and Chapelle, 1964.

Watts, Alan, *Wind and Sailing Boats*, Adlard Coles, 1965.

Whitney, Peter Dwight, *White Water Sport*, The Ronald Press Co., New York, 1960.

Zim, Herbert S., *Waves*, World Work, 1968.

Index

Let this happen to you.

Expectations

It must be beautiful.	Naturally.
It must be swift.	In rough seas, the flex of skin kayaks gives you a remarkable advantage: smooth passage over waves with less effort. The secret of Inuit inspired kayaks.
It must be strong.	6061 T6 aluminum alloy frame. Reinforced urethane fabric skin.
It must be dry.	Deck and hull seams are now welded. Shut. We call it Feathercraft Sealskin Technology. You call it DRY.
It must fly.	Folded Feathercrafts travel at 550mph.

Feathercraft is folding.

Feathercraft
FOLDING KAYAKS AND ACCESSORIES

4-1244 Cartwright Street
Vancouver BC
Canada V6H 3R8
tel 604 681-8437
www.feathercraft.com
info@feathercraft.com

USK Web Site

On Line Sea Kayaking Education Resource

Welcome to the University of Sea Kayaking

- Skill of the Month
- Quick Tips
- Yakisms
- Manufacturer Links

- Club Links
- USK Store
- USK Library

"The inexperienced become courageous and the experienced learn finesse."

Derek shares his years of experience with skills & techniques to help the paddler gain confidence leaning, edging & bracing.

Don't just read about it, see Derek C. Hutchinson in action in Beyond the Cockpit. USK Video Volume 3.

University of Sea Kayaking

USK "In Depth" Instructional Video Series

Volumes 1 & 2 - Capsize Recoveries & Rescue Procedures

Volume 3 - Beyond the Cockpit featuring Derek Hutchinson

Volume 4 - The ABC'S of the Surf Zone

Professional educator Wayne Horodowich shares his 20+ years of teaching experience in these comprehensive videos.

Available in: DVD, VHS & PAL

When you have a question about sea kayaking education your first stop should be the

USK Web Site.

"Your Sea Kayaking Education Resource"

www.useakayak.org

Stunning coastline and cultural splendour.

Explore the author's home town.

With breathtaking scenery, beautiful beaches, rugged cliffs, a wealth of attractions and fine sports facilities, South Tyneside has it all. For a visitor guide introducing you to timeless history and cultural splendour contact:

Tourism Officer, South Tyneside Council,
Lifelong Learning and Leisure,
Central Library, Prince Georg Square,
South Shields NE33 2PE.
Telephone: 0191 424 7982.
email: michele.maving@s-tyneside-mbc.gov.uk
www.visitsouthtyneside.co.uk

 South Tyneside Council

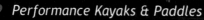

Simon River Sports
Performance Kayaks & Paddles

Take Your
Adventure
to the Next Lev

www.simonriversports.com

Expertly Designed Racing Wings, Performance Touring Paddles & Kayaks

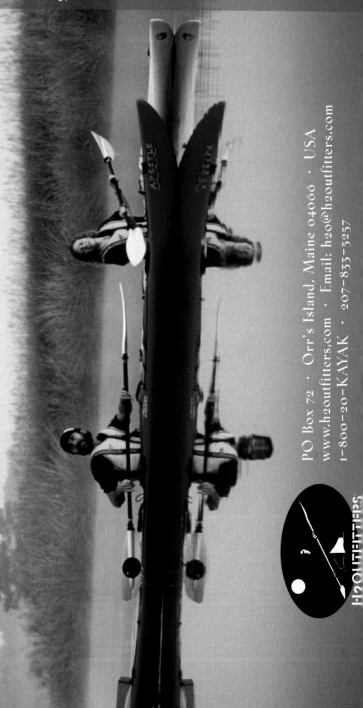